*The Good Lives Model for Adolescents
Who Sexually Harm*

The Good Lives Model for Adolescents Who Sexually Harm

Edited by Bobbie Print, CQSW

Foreword by Tony Ward, PhD

The SaferSociety PRESS

Brandon, Vermont

Printed in the United States of America
10 9 8 7 6 5 4 3 2 1

Library of Congress Cataloging-in-Publication Data

The good lives model for adolescents who sexually harm / edited by Bobbie Print, CQSW ; foreword by Tony Ward, PhD. -- First edition.
     pages cm
 Includes index.
 ISBN 978-1-884444-94-4
1. Teenage sex offenders--Rehabilitation. 2. Adolescent psychotherapy. I. Print, Bobbie, editor of compilation.
 RJ506.S48G66 2013
 618.92'8914--dc23
                    2013031772

P.O. Box 340
Brandon, Vermont 05733
www.safersociety.org
(802) 247-3132

Safer Society Press is a program of the Safer Society Foundation, a 501(c)3 nonprofit dedicated to the prevention and treatment of sexual abuse. For more information, visit our website at www.safersociety.org

The Good Lives Model for Adolescents Who Sexually Harm
$40 plus shipping and handling
Order # WP158

Contents

Foreword

I have been familiar with the work of Bobbie Print and the G-map team for many years now and have been lucky enough to visit their center on a number of occasions to share research and therapy ideas. On every occasion I was struck by the tremendous enthusiasm of the staff for their work with adolescents who harm sexually and their total commitment to clinical excellence. Bobbie and her team are pioneers as well as talented practitioners, always seeking to develop more effective ways of treating young people.

I was delighted when Bobbie and the G-map staff decided to adopt the Good Lives model (GLM) as a practice framework to structure their therapeutic work with adolescents who sexually harm; however, I was curious about just how they would achieve this. Clearly, adolescents are very different from adults who sexually harm, and changes would be necessary if the GLM was going to prove useful with this population. After reading the manuscript I have to say, I think it is superb! I am extremely impressed by their painstaking analysis of the GLM and the systematic way they made changes to the model to better fit their practice with adolescents. For example, the way the primary human goods are grouped and the new labels for GLM concepts make perfect sense for this population.

In my view, their grasp of the GLM is profound. They have worked with the model from the inside out, making sensible practice adjustments but preserving its core ideas and ethical heart. This is a terrific book that documents G-map's journey with the GLM and demonstrates clearly their clinically creative and skillful translation of it into extremely useful therapeutic guidelines for work with adolescents who display harmful sexual behaviors.

In the hands of Bobbie Print and the G-map staff, the GLM has been transformed into a flexible and clinically sophisticated practice framework capable of integrating cutting-edge and effective techniques within a strengths-based framework. The writing is clear and the analysis is sure-footed. There is considerable detail on how to go about assessing and treating adolescent sex offenders from a GLM perspective, all of which is beautifully illustrated with ongoing case examples. In my opinion, this book is likely to prove a landmark publication in the field of sexual offending and is sure to attract clinicians and researchers alike. It is simply brilliant!

Tony Ward, PhD, DipClinPsyc
Professor of Psychology
Victoria University of Wellington, New Zealand

Acknowledgments

The G-map staff group owes enormous gratitude to the inspiration, endless enthusiasm, and support that we received from Dave O'Callaghan and Tony Morrison. Their influence permeates all that we do, and we miss them.

We thank Helen Bradshaw, Dr. James Bickley, and Nigel Print for their support and guidance in producing this book. Additional thanks to Sarah Pearson and Cath Heap for their patience and skills in typing and retyping the manuscripts for this book.

Finally, we thank all of the young people with whom we have worked, many of whom contributed to our development of the Good Lives model. Most of these young people have inspired us with their courage, humor, determination, resilience, and hard work. We hope that they are all out there enjoying good lives.

About the Authors

Mark Adshead, DipSW, PQCSW, PGD Forensic Mental Health, PCEP (Youth Justice)
Mark started working in residential care in 1995 with young people with emotional and behavioral problems who were remanded to local authority accommodation, and moved to Social Services Department Adolescent Support Team in 1999. In 2001 he moved to youth offending services and became operational manager in 2005. Mark joined G-map in 2008 as a senior practitioner.

Anthony Beech, DPhil (Oxon), BSc, FBsPS, CPsychol (Forensic)
Professor Anthony Beech is head of the Centre for Forensic and Criminological Psychology at the University of Birmingham, United Kingdom, and a Fellow of the British Psychological Society. He has authored over 150 peer-reviewed articles, 40 book chapters, and six books in the area of forensic science/criminal justice. In 2009 he received the Significant Achievement Award from the Association for the Treatment of Sexual Abusers in Dallas, and the Senior Award from the Division of Forensic Psychology, British Psychological Society. His particular areas of research interest are risk assessment; the neurobiological bases of offending; reducing online exploitation of children; and increasing psychotherapeutic effectiveness of the intervention with offenders. His recent research has examined Internet offending; new approaches to treatment of offenders; and the neurobiological basis of offending. Anthony is research consultant to G-map.

Dr. Dawn Fisher, BA Hons., MClinPsych, PhD
Dawn is the lead consultant psychologist at St. Andrew's Healthcare, Birmingham, and an Honorary Senior Research Fellow at the University of Birmingham. Dr. Fisher provides consultancy to G-map. She has worked with those who sexually harm throughout her career and has published widely on the topic and spoken regularly at conferences.

She has been involved in research evaluating the effectiveness of intervention programs for those who sexually harm, co-authored an accredited sex offender treatment program, and was a member of the Correctional Services Panel for several years. She was a founder member of National Association for the Treatment of Abusers (NOTA).

Dr. Helen Griffin, BA (Hons), PA Dip, NVQ4, ForenPsyD, CPsychol
Prior to joining G-map in January 2006, Helen worked with socially excluded young people. She has a background in research and has completed work for the Youth Justice Board, Youth Justice Trust, and G-map. Helen is a senior practitioner and head of research with G-map.

Sharon Leeson, RNMH, Dip HE (Community Nursing)
Sharon has been a senior practitioner with G-map since 2002. Her background is in learning disability nursing in hospitals and in community residential settings, as well as community nursing, where she worked with adults with challenging behavior. While working with G-map, Sharon has trained nationally on assessment and intervention with adolescents with learning disabilities who display sexually harmful behavior. Sharon is one of the facilitators of G-map's group-work program for young people with learning disabilities.

Julie Morgan, BSC (Hons), MA
Julie trained as a probation officer and worked in a health service developing a new community service that worked with young people with learning disabilities who have sexually harmful behavior. She was seconded part-time to G-map in 1997 and became a full-time member of staff in 1998. Julie became a clinical manager at G-map in 2003 and service manager in 2005.

Elleen Okotie, BA (Hons), DipSW, MA, PQ1
Elleen is a senior practitioner with G-map. Her work experience includes local authority social work with children and families, and specialist work with young people who sexually harm and victims of abuse. Elleen is co-author of research on "Study of the Experiences of Black and Asian Young People Whose Behaviour is Sexually Harmful to Others," which was published in 2002 by the Assessment, Intervention, and Moving On (AIM) Project. Prior to joining G-map in January 2006 she was employed by the National Society for the Prevention of Cruelty to Children (NSPCC) for seven years.

Bobbie Print, CQSW

Bobbie Print is director of G-map Services. She is an honorary lecturer at the University of Birmingham's Department of Forensic and Family Psychology. Bobbie has worked with young people who sexually harm for 25 years. She was a founding member of National Association for the Treatment of Abusers (NOTA) and has published and trained widely on working with young people who sexually harm.

Paul Quest, BA (Hons), Dip SW, PQ1

Paul has worked with adults with learning disabilities and as the manager of a forensic residential unit for adults who had been resettled into the community from long-stay hospitals. He has also worked in children's residential care and youth offending services before joining G-map in 2010. Paul is a senior practitioner at G-map.

Laura Wylie, BA (Hons), Psychology, MSc Forensic Psychology

Prior to joining G-map in January 2009, Laura spent 10 years working and conducting research across a range of forensic settings. This included providing psychological services to adolescents with emotional and behavioral difficulties within a secure care setting, and to adult sex offenders within the Scottish Prison Service. Laura has also worked with victims of sexualized violence, as well as conducting a process evaluation of a community-based treatment program for adolescents with sexually harmful behavior.

Introduction

JULIE MORGAN

G-map is a small independent service that specializes in working with young people who display harmful sexual behavior. We provide therapeutic intervention with young people, their families, and their caregivers, as well as training, supervision, and consultancy to a variety of professional agencies.

G-map was formed in 1988 and is based in Greater Manchester, United Kingdom. We have a multi-disciplinary staff team comprised of professionals with backgrounds in social work, health, youth services, criminal justice, and psychology. We work with children and young people aged 6 to 18 years, with the scope for services to be extended to those over 18 years in circumstances where individual needs or complexities dictate. The children and young people who are involved in our program are referred by statutory agencies that include children's services, health services, and youth justice services; they can be living at home or in foster care, specialist residential care, or secure accommodations.

Most of the young people we work with present with complex needs and high levels of trauma. We have found individual work to be the most suitable mode of intervention, although some will also join our group-work program and most will be involved in family work.

In the early years of our practice we struggled to find frameworks and models that we considered appropriate and useful in working with adolescents. Almost everything that was published was based on work with adults who sexually harmed, and the general approach was confrontational, controlling, and deficit-oriented. While we attempted to draw on such models we quickly recognized that not only was the approach counter-therapeutic, but it proved extremely difficult to motivate young people and their families to engage in our program. We therefore began to adapt existing models and focused increasingly on developing a strengths-based approach that promoted a positive psychology philosophy and a more holistic response to the young people we worked with. We first encountered the Good Lives model in 2004, and its appeal was immediate. Not only was the model strengths-based but it involved individuals working toward achieving goals rather than the focus being on diminishing deficits, it accommodated multi-agency working, and it considered the individual as a whole and not just a collection of potential risk factors.

The incorporation of the Good Lives model into our practice with adolescents has taken some time and has required a certain amount of adaptation to the model. In addition to the G-map staffs' involvement in developing a Good Lives approach we have consulted with other professionals, the young people involved in our program, and their families and caregivers. The result is that we now provide a program of work with adolescents (those aged 13 to 18) that is fully underpinned by a Good Lives approach so that our assessments, therapeutic interventions, and multi-agency workings involve Good Lives assessments, Good Lives plans (GLPs), and Good Lives evaluations (GLATs).

The purpose of this book is to share our experience of adapting the Good Lives model for use with the adolescents with whom we work. In our view, the model has proved to be an exciting, positive, and helpful framework that we have enjoyed exploring, experimenting with, and employing. We hope that readers find the following pages informative, helpful, and useful in applying the model to their work with adolescents who display harmful sexual behaviors.

All members of the G-map team have been involved in the production of this book in the hope that we can present to readers the reasons for using the GLM, the adaptations we have made to the model to enhance its use with adolescents, how our intervention is guided by the model, and the benefits we have enjoyed from incorporating the model into our practice. We have used case illustrations in order to clearly demonstrate the practical application of the model and have tracked three particular case examples through several chapters to show how Good Lives is developed at different stages of intervention.

Readers may note that some of the terminology used throughout the text varies from that often used in the literature. For example, we avoid labeling young people with the term *sex offender* as this implies a description of who or what they are. Instead we refer to them as young people "who have displayed harmful sexual behavior" or "who have sexually harmed" to ensure that they are considered primarily as young people although they have exhibited problematic behaviors. Additionally, we do not use the term *treatment*, as it is generally a medical term that implies the recipient has an illness that professionals try to "cure" by the administration of therapy. Instead we use the more generic term *intervention*, which is more suggestive of involvement to effect change.

CHAPTER 1

Background to the Good Lives Approach to Intervention

ANTHONY BEECH

INTRODUCTION

Successful intervention with those who sexually harm is incredibly important due to its implications for society in general, and for the individuals who commit the harm (Harkins et al. 2012). Therefore it is essential that professional intervention is the most effective possible. Mounting evidence suggests that intervention that adheres to the Risk–Need–Responsivity (RNR) approach (developed by Andrews and Bonta 2010) is an effective approach. In fact, RNR is seen as the premier correctional rehabilitative theory in that it provides a clear direction for intervention and has a strong empirical base for reducing re-offending in those who sexually harm (Hanson et al. 2009), as well as general offenders (Andrews and Bonta 2010). Intervention following this approach adheres to three overarching principles: (1) The highest-intensity intervention should be offered to the highest-risk offenders—the *risk* principle (i.e., targeting intervention at those who most need it); (2) intervention should target the factors that lead the individual to commit crimes—the *need* principle (i.e., targeting intervention at individuals' specific problems—their criminogenic needs); and (3) it is offered in a manner that maximizes the likelihood that the individual benefits from it—the *responsivity* principle (i.e., matching intervention to the individual's abilities and motivation).

However, there is increasing recognition that intervention utilizing the RNR approach can only go so far. In fact, it is of note that between 12 percent and 50 percent of adults who sexually harmed and completed a program of intervention, and 46 percent of general offenders, go on to re-offend (Ward, Rose, and Willis 2012). It is also of note that in the RNR approach there is an over-reliance on avoidance goals (e.g., recognizing where not to go, what not to do, etc.), while placing less focus on the overall well-being of the individual, or the inherent value and rights of the individual involved in intervention (Ward, Gannon, and Birgden 2007; Ward and Stewart 2003a, b, c). Therefore, the RNR approach can be viewed as less motivating than intervention adhering to approach goals (i.e., pursuing a better life that is incompatible with offending).

Probably the primary critics of the RNR approach, as it stands, are Tony Ward and colleagues (e.g., Ward, Mann, and Gannon 2007), who note that the RNR approach focuses on the identification of risk factors, and intervention targeted at the reduction in the level of these risk factors. They argue that this is akin to a pincushion approach, where each risk factor constitutes a pin, and intervention focuses on the removal of each risk factor (Ward, Gannon, and Birgden 2007, 88). Ward et al. (2007) further note that the current RNR model lacks the "conceptual resources" to adequately guide therapists and engage offenders in an integrated holistic approach.

Hence, there has been a move toward a more positively oriented intervention approach. This approach also holds a number of other benefits (Marshall et al. 2005), in that intervention should be about instilling knowledge, skills, and competence to lead to fulfilling lives, which should be incompatible with offending. This approach, to date, has been most fully realized in the Good Lives model (GLM) rehabilitation framework (Ward, Mann, and Gannon 2007; Ward and Stewart 2003a, b, c), which acts as an overarching rehabilitative framework, with the ability to incorporate the RNR approach. Therefore, the aim of this chapter is to examine such strengths-based approaches to interventions with those who commit harmful sexual acts, and positive psychology more generally, before describing the Good Lives model in more detail.

STRENGTHS-BASED APPROACHES
AND POSITIVE PSYCHOLOGY

There have been people from a number of disciplines who have described the value of individuals leading fulfilling and positive lives. Philosophers such as Kekes (1997), describe the value of focusing on the human effort to create many different forms of "good lives," particularly noting that a moral stance on the part of individuals and society is needed to achieve this. Rorty (1989), on the other hand, argues that it is authors (e.g., George Orwell, Vladimir Nabokov), rather than philosophers, who have been instrumental in shaping ideas about what is fair and just in society, as opposed to cruel and inhumane, and describing what can be regarded as a fulfilling, just, and positive life. As for psychological ideas, it can be said that the suggestion of focusing on the positives is something that William James was writing about as "healthy mindedness" more than a century ago (i.e., James 1902). Those who can be broadly described as having a humanistic approach in psychology have advocated a positive approach to mental health, for example Rogers's (1961) "fully functioning person" approach and Maslow's (1968) "self-realizing person" approach.

RESILIENCE IN YOUNG PEOPLE

In the last 10 years, the idea of focusing on the positive attributes of individuals has become a major part of assessment and intervention in a number of the caring disciplines. In the social work field Benard (2006), for example, notes that a number of studies indicate that positive protective factors or "resilience" are at least as important as, if not more important than, risk factors in the lives of children and families. It is reported that about 75 percent of children and young people, even from the most deprived, stressed, dysfunctional families, can somehow manage to overcome these obstacles in later life (Rhodes and Brown 1991), whereas children who experience multiple and persistent risks, around half still achieve good developmental outcomes (Rutter 1987; 1989). Here resilience is seen as a "self-righting capacity" for healthy growth and development. Bremer (2006, 87) notes that "resilience is a concept that goes hand in hand with risk, for without present risk, or adverse circumstances, there cannot be resilient action or reaction."

Bremer (2006) also notes that resilience is a concept that refers to the ability of a child to maintain positive growth and socially appropriate behavior in the face of adverse circumstances. Bremer further indicates that resilience is often viewed as a mediator when risks, such as those within the individual (*developmental problems*), within the family (*abuse*), or in the community (*anti-social peers*), are present and that building blocks of resiliency are protective factors (*strengths*), which are those elements of personality, family function, and community environment that mediate adverse circumstances.

The incorporation of strengths and resilience factors in clinical assessments of young people is supported by research that has shown they can have a significant impact on the likelihood of general recidivism (Hoge, Andrews, and Leschied 1996) but are only now starting to be examined in work with those who harm sexually. The Department of Health (2000) identified the importance of the inclusion of resilience in assessments of young people and their families and recognized the following as significant positive factors for adolescents:

- Supportive relationships with at least one parent
- Supportive relationships with siblings and grandparents
- A committed non-parental adult who takes a strong interest in the young person and serves as an ongoing mentor and role model
- A capacity to develop and reflect on a coherent story about what has happened and is happening to them
- Talents and interests
- Positive experiences in school
- Positive friendships
- The capacity to think ahead and plan their lives

Gilgun (1999) has developed a Clinical Assessment Package for Risks and Strengths (CASPARS) that provides equal weighting to child and family strengths and risks rather than focusing solely on deficits in the general assessment of young people. In her research, Gilgun (1990) identified that having a confidant was a significant factor in reducing recidivism and that the presence of healthy peer, family, and community relationships was also positively significant. Since then Gilgun (2003) has gone on to look at how factors and qualities associated with resilience can be used when individuals are at risk of committing sexually harmful behaviors.

Bremer (2001) has developed the Protective Factors Scale (PFS), which can be employed to assess the level of intervention required by young people who sexually harm. Here she argues that accessing positive factors that promote resiliency is important in attempting to engage young people in intervention. The PFS consists of 10 items covering personal development (general behavior, school attendance, social and emotional adjustment); sexuality (harmful sexual behavior, personal boundaries, sexual preferences); and environmental support (caregiver stability, family style, and cooperation).

In the United Kingdom, the AIM2 model (Print, Morrison, and Henniker 2001) examines strengths and concerns in young people and is widely employed by practitioners. The original AIM model was introduced in 2001 across Greater Manchester. Four domains were considered in relation to the young person: (1) *harmful behavior specific*; (2) *development*; (3) *family/caregivers*; and (4) *environmental*. The assessment information is organized around two continua: strengths and concerns. The framework has been modified (based on work by Griffin and Beech 2004) to link and expand, the approach to the risk-etiology model developed by Beech and Ward (Beech and Ward 2004; Ward and Beech 2004). Griffin et al. (2008) looking at 70 young people found that AIM2 items linked to recidivism suggested that two fairly robust measures of strengths and concerns could be identified. The *Concerns* scale consists of eight items: (1) known previous sexually harmful behaviors; (2) sexually harmed a stranger; (3) threatened or used violence during sexually harmful behavior; (4) any general convictions; (5) cold callous attitude toward sexually harmful behaviors; (6) impulsive behaviors; (7) emotional regulation problems; (8) maintains contact with pro-criminal peers. The *Strengths* scale also consists of eight items: (1) healthy physical development; (2) above-average intelligence; (3) positive talents/interests; (4) positive attitude from significant adults in the young person's life; (5) positive emotional coping displayed by significant adults in the young person's life; (6) at least one emotional confidant; (7) positive evaluations from work/education staff; (8) positive relationships with professionals. This work is of course of a preliminary nature but suggests that for young people the importance of strengths cannot be underestimated.

The question that remains unanswered at the present is the extent to which strengths factors are important in adults. This is an area of research that has only just begun to be explored, particularly in the Structured Assessment of Protective Factors (SAPROF; see www.saprof.com/content/2012/11/SAROF-2nd-Edition), which has recently been developed as an instrument for the structured assessment of protective factors for violence risk. The SAPROF aims to contribute to an increasingly accurate and well-rounded assessment of risk for future violent behavior. Retrospective results at the Van der Hoeven Kliniek in the Netherlands show good inter-rater reliability and good predictive validity for violent recidivism. Moreover, the changeability of the protective factors in the SAPROF during intervention provides an indication for the usability of the SAPROF as a guideline for positive intervention planning and risk management (Robbé, de Vogel, and Stam 2012). Frequent users of the SAPROF in forensic psychiatry state that the instrument can be helpful in formulating intervention goals, justifying stages of intervention, atoning intervention phasing, and facilitating risk communication.

In adult work, criminologists have also been keen to understand the processes by which individuals desist from risky criminal behavior in order to lead more fulfilling lives. The background to this is that it has been noted for a number of years that many individuals drift in and out of criminal activity during their lives, rather than crime being a stable lifelong trait (Glaser 1964; Matza 1964), and that for some, clear voluntary termination of serious criminal participation can be observed (Shover 1996). As for explanations as to how individuals stop committing offenses, criminologists have started to use the term *desistance*, which refers to the moment that a criminal career terminates (Farrall and Bowling 1999).

DESISTANCE

Maruna (2001) suggests that desistance from crime is all about individuals carrying out a fundamental and intentional shift in their sense of self and their place in society. The idea here is that the individual "quits crime in the same way as one resigns from a legitimate occupation." As for explanations as to why individuals desist, Maruna (2001) suggests that some individuals stop committing crimes or start "making good" through the process of using "redemptive scripts." A redemptive script, according to Maruna, is a process by which a person "rewrite(s) a shameful past into a necessary prelude to a worthy productive life" (87). The process of making good involves: (1) establishing the "real me"; (2) having an optimistic perception of self-control over one's destiny; and (3) the desire to be productive and give something back to society.

These ideas seem to suggest the importance of an individual's strengths in terms of positive psychological characteristics, such as self-efficacy and an internal locus of control. Bandura (1994, 71) notes that "self-efficacy beliefs" are said to "determine how people think, feel, and motivate themselves and behave." Bandura further notes that these play a key role in motivating people. As motivation is cognitively generated, they form ideas about what they are capable of, they generally make plans to achieve these, and they anticipate the possible outcomes of these actions and behaviors. People's beliefs about self-efficacy can be developed through four main sources: (1) *mastery experiences*—being successful at something builds robust beliefs in one's own abilities, therefore difficult problems/tasks are there to be accomplished, rather than to be avoided; (2) *vicarious experiences* provided by social models—seeing other people similar to oneself succeed acts as a positive model for one's own possibilities to achieve; (3) *social persuasion*, which is seen by Bandura as another avenue to strengthen an individual's resolve to succeed; and (4) a *reduction of stress reactions*, therefore altering "negative emotional proclivities and interpretations of physical states" (Bandura 1994).

As for a psychological approach to the idea of experiencing a positive and fulfilling life, Seligman and Csikszentmihaly (2000), in a special issue of *American Psychologist* on positive psychology, argue that the seemingly exclusive focus on pathology in psychology has resulted in a model of the human being that lacks the positive features, which for most make life worth living. They further go on to note that social and behavioral sciences can play an important role in the identification of positive family environments where children can grow up in a nurturing environment, and which factors are important in an individual's life to lead to a sense of well-being.

POSITIVE PSYCHOLOGY

The positive psychology approach attempts to promote human welfare by concentrating on strengths in an individual rather than focusing on deficits (Ward, Polaschek, and Beech 2006); to put it more succinctly, the application of positive psychology is the optimization of human functioning (Linley and Joseph 2004). The positive psychology approach suggests that there are a number of basic tenets in regard to human functioning—in particular that human beings are naturally predisposed to seek out things that make them feel good; that it is the expression of essential human qualities such as love, work, interpersonal skills, aesthetic sensibilities, perseverance, courage, forgiveness, originality, spirituality, talents, and wisdom that yields happiness, psychological well-being, and fulfillment; and that these should be the focus of work with individuals. A numbers of authors have focused on different aspect of positive psychology, such as: strengths-based approaches (e.g., human and environmental); emotion-focused work (e.g., resilience, happiness, self-esteem within individuals); cognitive-focused work (e.g., creativity, well-being, self-efficacy); self-based (e.g., the pursuit of authenticity, uniqueness-seeking, and humility); interpersonal (e.g., compassion, empathy, and altruism); biological (e.g., toughness); and specific adaptive coping approaches (e.g., the search for meaning, humor, and spirituality in life) (see Snyder and Lopez 2006 for a thorough description of these approaches). Therefore, even though positive psychology is a fairly new discipline, a number of books have already been written on the subject (see Aspinall and Staudinger 2003; Jospeh and Linley 2006; Linley and Joseph 2004).

An early description of the application of a positive psychology approach to intervention with those who sexually harm can be found in James Haaven's work with intellectually disabled sexual offenders (Haaven and Coleman 2000). Here the distinction is made between the [bad] "old me" and the [better] "new me." The "old me" is the type of person who committed harmful sexual acts when his or her life goals for well-being and fulfillment were pursued in an inappropriate way. The "new me" involves a new sets of plans and goals around the positive approach to the acquisition of an individual's life goals, taking account of an individual's preferences and relative strengths. (See chapter 5 for a description of how this model is used in assessment of adolescents who sexually harm.) Applying a more positive approach to intervention with mainstream individuals who have sexually harmed has been most eloquently, and rigorously, described by Ward and colleagues (e.g., Ward and Fisher 2006; Ward and Gannon 2006; Ward and Mann 2004; Ward and Stewart 2003a, b, c).

THE "GOOD LIVES" APPROACH TO SEX OFFENDER TREATMENT

To examine the Good Lives[1] approach in detail, Ward, Polaschek, and Beech (2006) note that human beings are naturally inclined to seek certain types of experiences or "human goods" and experience high levels of well-being if these goods are obtained. Ward, Mann, and Gannon (2007) note that *primary goods* are defined as "states of affairs, states of mind, personal characteristics, activities, or experiences that are sought for their own sake and are likely to achieve psychological well-being if achieved" (4). Ward and others suggest that harmful sexual behavior arises as a result of an attempt to obtain these goods in an inappropriate manner, out of frustration at being unable to achieve these goods in a "normal" manner, or out of an imbalance in goods acquisition, so that some goods are prioritized over others (e.g., sexual gratification taking precedence over emotional intimacy). Therefore, harmful sexual behaviors are seen as ways of achieving goods through either: (1) a *direct route* where an individual does not have the skills or competencies to achieve these in an appropriate manner; or (2) an *indirect route* where the behavior takes place to relieve the negative thoughts and feelings individuals have about their inabilities of achieving the goods they are striving for. The list of 11 primary goods that all individuals strive toward is detailed in chapter 3.

An important thing to note here is that these goods that individuals aspire to do not necessarily have any particular moral values; they are experiences and/or activities that produce a sense of well-being and will enable individuals to function better if some or all can be achieved. According to Ward, Rose, and Willis (2012), criminal behavior results when individuals lack the internal and external resources to satisfy their needs in pro-social ways. It has been observed in a number of studies that many of those who sexually harm have not had the opportunity and support to achieve a positive "Good Lives plan" in life, and fulfill the identified goods, due to adverse experiences such as abuse, neglect, and poor attachment as children (Beech and Mitchell 2005). All kinds of problems (psychological, social, and lifestyle) can emerge when these primary goods are pursued in inappropriate ways. Therefore, such experiences can lead individuals who harm others to have a view of the world that is threatening—one in which their level of interpersonal functioning is low, they feel that they have little control over events, and they have distorted views about sexuality leading to inappropriate sexual urges toward children or non-consenting adults. Because of these problems, many of those who sexually harm lack the skills and capabilities to lead a fulfilling life as adults (Ward and Stewart 2003a, b, c; Wilson and Yates 2009).

---

1. This approach, although having a lot in common with the positive psychological approach, was developed separately (Ward et al. 2006).

Ward and Mann (2004) note that the absence of certain goods such as *agency* (i.e., a low level of interpersonal functioning), *inner peace* (a high level of stress and tension), and *relatedness* (a low level of intimate or romantic involvement with others) have been strongly related to inappropriate, dysfunctional behaviors in adults. Table 1.1 shows the routes that Ward, Rose, and Willis (2012) suggest can lead to sexually harmful behaviors under the GLM formulation of offending.

Table 1.1 Routes to Offending in the GLM

1. An individual might use inappropriate strategies (secondary goods) to achieve primary goods.
2. An individual's Good Lives plan might suffer from a lack of scope, in that a number of goods are omitted from his/her life plan.
3. There may be conflict in the pursuit of goods that might result in acute psychological stress and unhappiness.
4. An individual might lack internal and external capabilities to satisfy primary goods in the environment he or she lives. *Internal capabilities* include relevant knowledge and skill sets, while *external capabilities* include environmental opportunities, resources, and supports.

Source: Ward, Rose, and Willis 2012.

Willis, Yates, Gannon, and Ward (2013) suggest that the GLM approach can accommodate the major RNR principles, within a broader strengths-based framework. Therefore, obtaining a good life and achieving a sense of well-being should be key determinants in how intervention with those who sexually harm is conducted. The Good Lives approach can hopefully promote strengths such as self-efficacy, encourage responsibility and ownership for an individual's behavior, and build motivation.[2] These will now be examined.

PROMOTING SELF-EFFICACY

An individual's beliefs about self-efficacy can be developed through four main sources: (1) *mastery experiences*; (2) *vicarious experiences*; (3) *social persuasion*; and (4) reductions in *stress levels*. Here Ward, Gannon, and Birgden (2007, 6) suggest that the major aim of interventions with those who sexually harm should be to "equip the offenders with the skills, values, attitudes, and resources necessary to lead a different kind of life,

---

2. These can all be broadly seen as being related to *excellence in agency* (being in control and getting things accomplished), as well as promoting *inner peace* (reductions in emotional stress and turmoil).

one that is personally meaningful and satisfying and does not involve inflicting harm on children or adults." Therefore, the aim of interventions with those who sexually harm is to get them to lead meaningful, non-offending lives. Ward et al. (2007) also note that such an approach should both be about promoting goods as well as reducing risk; therapy should therefore accentuate the positives rather than getting individuals to focus on the negatives in their lives. Part of this ethos would be an avoidance of terms like *dynamic-risk-factors-risk* and *relapse prevention*, these perhaps being replaced with terms such as *intervention need* and *self-management*.

Ward et al. (2007) also suggest a major part of getting intervention right would be to achieve the correct mix of promoting positive goods in individuals' future lives (*approach goals*), while also still working with them to recognize and deal with future risk situations, behaviors, and thoughts and feelings (*avoidance goals*). As Ward et al. (2007) note, this may be a delicate balancing act in that just promoting well-being may produce a more socially skilled and happy offender; on the other hand, just managing risk without promoting the individual's well-being could lead to aversive management of risk factors (i.e., telling people that this is what they cannot do anymore), leading to individuals feeling unmotivated, disengaged, and hostile regarding the therapeutic process.[3] Hence, Ward et al. (2007) suggest that taking a Good Lives approach here can be helpful to practitioners in that those who sexually harm can be clearly seen as "human agents," and their harmful behavior is understandable in the light of the pursuit of human goods.

ENCOURAGING RESPONSIBILITY AND OWNERSHIP FOR AN INDIVIDUAL'S BEHAVIOR

The concept of *locus of control* can be broadly seen as relating to agency. This concept is described by Colman (2001) as a cognitive style or personality trait characterized by a generalized expectancy about the relationship between behavior and the subsequent occurrence of punishment or reward. Thus, those with an internal locus of control tend to expect positive reinforcements as a consequence of their own efforts, while people with an external locus of control view rewards or punishments as being due to chance, luck, fate, or the actions of powerful others. Therefore, it can be seen that those with an external locus of control are less likely to be successful in undertaking plans and actions leading to positive mastery experiences, leading to reductions in negative affective states and levels of stress *(inner peace)*.

---

3. See Mann (2000) for suggestions about managing resistance and rebellion in relapse prevention work. In this approach there is also a strong emphasis on motivating offenders, creating a sound therapeutic alliance, and establishing positive group norms in therapy.

Individuals who have sexually harmed and not received therapeutic intervention tend to have an external locus of control (e.g., Fisher, Beech, and Browne 1998), and therefore regard things that happen as being due to others. Such individuals are less likely to benefit from intervention unless they can be encouraged to take responsibility for their behavior and become more internally controlled (Fisher et al. 1998). Individuals can be encouraged to take responsibility and develop a more internal locus of control in the GLM approach, as it is a model that builds and/or inculcates strengths in the individual, promoting *excellence in agency.*

RESEARCH ON THE GOOD LIVES MODEL

There has not been a huge amount of research thus far on the Good Lives approach to intervention. However, to give some examples from the United Kingdom, Harkins et al. (2012) compared the GLM approach to intervention with those who sexually harm with a standard relapse prevention program (based on RNR principles). The comparisons examined attrition rates, change in areas targeted in intervention and achievement of a post-intervention profile, and views of therapists and participants. There were no differences in attrition rates or the rates of achieved change between the two programs, indicating that they were equally effective at retaining participants and accomplishing change on areas targeted within program. However, both practitioners and participants reported the experience of the GLM approach module in a much more positive, future-focused manner, in comparison with those who attended the relapse prevention module. In a bigger study of 601 adults who had been convicted of sexually harmful acts, Barnett, Mandeville-Norden, and Rakestrow (2013) compared changes in psychometric scores over intervention for those who had attended the relapse prevention (RP) program in the community with the rates among those who had attended a revised version of the program based on the GLM of rehabilitation. Again the groups were compared on a number of outcomes. No differences were found in attrition rates, or the amount of change over intervention for the majority of the measures examined. However, analysis suggested that those attending the GLM were more able to sustain a functional score across a number of measures of criminogenic needs (i.e., pro-offending attitudes and socio-affective functioning) post-intervention.

The GLM approach, as Willis, Ward, and Levenson (2011) note, is linked to the notions of human dignity and rights, and takes a positive psychological approach to intervention with those who sexually harm. Research is only just beginning, but preliminary results would suggest that both practitioners and participants in therapeutic work regard intervention as a more positive experience than standard RNR approaches to therapy. The GLM also provides an overarching model in which intervention is undertaken. As Willis, Ward, and Levenson (2011) state, this approach can include the following in intervention terms: individual focus, holistic focus, positive and respectful forms of program delivery, a strengths-based approach, emphasis on the social environment, focus on skills development, and therapeutic orientation. Taking such an approach into account can hopefully increase the efficacy of intervention for this often "hard to treat" group. This motivating aspect may ultimately be a key factor in desistance for the individual who has sexually harmed. That is not to say that adopting such an approach is not without its problems. Willis, Ward, and Levenson (2011) note that these can relate to policy and law, lack of resources, punitive attitudes toward this group, community barriers, program administration, and knowledge of the GLM approach, some or all of which would apply to attempts to rehabilitate those who sexually harm.

REFERENCES

Andrews, D., and J. Bonta. 2010. *The psychology of criminal conduct*, 5th ed. New Providence, NJ: LexisNexis.

Aspinall, L. G., and U. M. Staudinger. 2003. *A psychology of human strengths: Fundamental questions and future directions for positive psychology*. Washington, DC: American Psychological Association.

Bandura, A. 1994. Self-efficacy. In V. S. Ramachaudran (ed.), *Encyclopaedia of human behaviour*, vol. 4, 71–81. New York: Academic Press.

Barnett, G., R. Mandeville-Norden, and J. Rakestrow. 2013. The Good Lives model or relapse prevention: What works better in facilitating change? *Sexual Abuse: A Journal of Research and Treatment*.

Beech, A. R., and I. J. Mitchell. 2005. A neurobiological perspective on attachment problems in sexual offenders and the role of selective serotonin re-uptake inhibitors in treatment of such problems. *Clinical Psychology Review* 25:153–182.

Beech, A. R., and T. Ward. 2004. The integration of etiology and risk in sex offenders: A theoretical model. *Aggression and Violent Behavior* 10:31–63.

Benard, B. 2006. Using strengths-based practice to tap resilience to families. In D. Saleeby, *Strengths perspective in social work practice*, 197–220. Boston: Allyn and Bacon.

Bremer, J. F. 2001. The Protective Factors Scale: Assessing youth with sexual concerns. Plenary address at the 16th Annual Conference of the National Adolescent Perpetration Network, Kansas City, MO, May 2001.

Bremer, J. F. 2006. Building resilience: An ally in assessment and treatment. In D. S. Prescott (ed.), *Risk assessment of youth who have sexually abused: Theory, controversy, and emerging issues*, 222–38. Oklahoma City: Wood N Barnes.

Colman, A. M. 2001. *A dictionary of psychology*. Oxford, UK: OUP.

Department of Health. 2000. *Studies which inform the development of the Framework for the Assessment of Children in Need and Their Families*. London: The Stationery Office.

Farrall, S., and B. Bowling. 1999. Structuration, human development and desistance from crime. *British Journal of Criminology* 39:253–68.

Fisher, D., A. R. Beech, and K. D. Browne. 1998. Locus of control and its relationship to treatment change in child molesters. *Legal and Criminological Psychology* 3:1–12.

Gilgun, J. F. 1990. Resilience and the intergenerational transmission of child sexual abuse. In M. Q. Patten (ed.), *Family sexual abuse: Frontline research and evaluation*, 93–105. Newbury Park, CA: Sage Publications.

Gilgun, J. F. 1999. CASPARS: Clinical assessment instruments that measure strengths and risks in children and families. In M. C. Calder (ed.), *Working with young people who sexually abuse: New pieces of the jigsaw puzzle*, 48–58. Lyme Regis, UK: Russell House Publishing.

Gilgun, J. F. 2003. Working with young people who have sexual behaviour problems: Lessons from risk and resilience. Presented at G-map conference, Working Holistically with Young People Who Sexually Harm. Bolton, UK, June 2003.

Glaser, D. 1964. *Effectiveness of a prison and parole system*. Indianapolis, IN: Bobbs-Merrill.

Griffin, H., and A. R. Beech. 2004. An evaluation of the AIM framework for the assessment of adolescents who display sexually harmful behaviour. Available from www.youth-justice-board.gov.uk.

Griffin, H., A. R. Beech, B. Print, J. Quayle, and H. Bradshaw. 2008. The development and initial testing of the AIM2 model to assess risk and strengths in young people who sexually offend. *Journal of Sexual Aggression* 14:211–25.

Haaven, J. L., and E. M. Coleman. 2000. Treatment of the developmentally disabled sex offender. In D. R. Laws, S. M. Hudson, and T. Ward (eds.), *Remaking relapse prevention with sex offenders: A sourcebook*, 369–88. Thousand Oaks, CA: Sage Publications.

Hanson, R. K., G. Bourgon, L. Helmus, and S. Hodgson. 2009. The principles of effective correctional treatment also apply to sexual offenders: A meta-analysis. *Criminal Justice and Behavior* 36:865–91.

Harkins, L., V. Flak, A. R. Beech, and J. Woodhams. 2012. Evaluation of a community-based sex offender treatment program using a Good Lives model approach. *Sexual Abuse: A Journal of Research and Treatment* 24:519–43.

Hoge, R. D., D. A. Andrews, and A. W. Leshied. 1996. An investigation of risk and protective factors in a sample of youthful offenders. *Journal of Child Psychology and Psychiatry* 37:419–24.

James, W. 1902. *Varieties of religious experience*. Available from www.pinkmonkey.com/dl/library1/book1126.pdf.

Joseph, S., and P. A. Linley. 2006. *Positive therapy: A meta-theory for positive psychological practice*. London: Routledge.

Kekes, J. 1997. *Moral wisdom and good lives.* Ithaca, NY: Cornell University Press.

Linley, P. A., and S. Joseph. 2004. *Positive psychology in practice.* Chichester, UK: John Wiley and Sons.

Marshall, W. L., T. Ward, R. E. Mann, H. Moulden, Y. M. Fernandez, G. Serran, and L. E. Marshall. 2005. Working positively with sexual offenders: Maximising the effectiveness of treatment. *Journal of Interpersonal Violence* 20:1096–114.

Maruna, S. 2001. *Making good: How ex-offenders reform and rebuild their lives.* Washington, DC: American Psychological Association.

Maslow, A. H. 1968. *Towards a psychology of being.* New York: Van Nostrand.

Matza, D. 1964. *Delinquency and drift.* New York: Wiley.

Miller, W. R., and S. Rollnick. 2002. *Motivational interviewing: Preparing people for change*, 2nd ed. New York: Guilford Press.

Print, B., M. Morrison, and J. Henniker. 2001. An inter-agency assessment and framework for young people who sexually abuse: Principles, processes and practicalities. In M. C. Calder (ed.), *Juveniles and children who sexually abuse: Frameworks for assessment*, 271–81. Lyme Regis, UK: Russell House Publishing.

Rhodes, W., and W. Brown. 1991. *Why some children succeed despite the odds.* New York: Praeger.

Robbé, M., V. de Vogel, and J. Stam. 2012. Protective factors for violence risk: The value for clinical practice. *Psychology* 3:1259–63.

Rogers, C. R. 1961. *On becoming a person.* Boston: Houghton-Miffin.

Rorty, R. 1989. *Contingency, irony and solidarity.* Cambridge, UK: Cambridge University Press.

Rutter, M. 1987. Psychosocial resilience and protective mechanisms. *American Journal of Orthopsychiatry* 57:316–33.

Rutter, M. 1989. Pathways from child to adult life. *Journal of Child Psychology and Psychiatry* 30:23–54.

Seligman, M. E. P., and M. Csikszentmihalyi. 2000. Positive psychology: An introduction. *American Psychologist* 55:5–114.

Shover, N. 1996. *Great pretenders: Pursuits and careers of persistent thieves.* Boulder, CO: Westview Press.

Snyder, C. R., and J. S. Lopez. 2006. *The handbook of positive psychology.* Oxford, UK: Oxford University Press.

Tierney, D. W., and M. P. McCabe. 2002. Motivation for behaviour change among sex offenders: A review of the literature. *Clinical Psychology Review* 22:113–29.

Ward, T., and A. R. Beech. 2004. The etiology of risk: A preliminary model. *Sexual Abuse: A Journal of Research and Treatment* 16:271–84.

Ward, T., and D. Fisher. 2006. New ideas in the treatment of sexual offenders. In W. L. Marshall, Y. M. Fernandez, L. E. Marshall, and G. A. Serran (eds.), *Sexual offender treatment: Controversial issues.* Chichester, UK: John Wiley and Sons.

Ward, T., and T. A. Gannon. 2006. Rehabilitation, etiology, and self-regulation: The comprehensive Good Lives model of treatment for sexual offenders. *Aggression and Violent Behavior* 11:77–94.

Ward, T., and R. Mann. 2004. Good lives and the rehabilitation of offenders: A positive approach to treatment. In A. Linley and S. Joseph (eds.), *Positive psychology in practice*, 598–616. New York: John Wiley.

Ward, T., T. A. Gannon, and A. Birgden. 2007. Human rights and the treatment of sex offenders. *Sexual Abuse: A Journal of Research and Treatment* 19:195–216.

Ward, T., K. Louden, S. M. Hudson, and W. L. Marshall. 1995. A descriptive model of the offence chain for child molesters. *Journal of Interpersonal Violence* 10:452–72.

Ward, T., R. Mann, and T. A. Gannon. 2007. The Good Lives model of rehabilitation: Clinical implications. *Aggression and Violent Behavior* 12:87–107.

Ward, T., D. Polaschek, and A. R. Beech. 2006. *Theories of sexual offending.* Chichester, UK: John Wiley and Sons.

Ward, T., C. Rose, and G. Willis. 2012. The rehabilitation of offenders: Good lives, desistance, and risk reduction. In G. Davis and A. Beech (eds.), *Forensic Psychology,* 2nd ed. Oxford, UK: Wiley Blackwell.

Ward, T., and C. A. Stewart. 2003a. The treatment of sex offenders: Risk management and good lives. *Professional Psychology: Research and Practice* 34:353–60.

Ward, T., and C. A. Stewart. 2003b. Criminogenic needs and human needs: A theoretical model. *Psychology, Crime, and Law* 9:125–143.

Ward, T., and C. A. Stewart. 2003c. The relationship between human needs and crimogenic needs. *Psychology, Crime, and Law* 9:219–24.

Willis, G. M., T. Ward, and J. S. Levenson. 2011. The Good Lives model (GLM): An evaluation of GLM operationalization in North American treatment programs. *Sexual Abuse: A Journal of Research and Treatment.*

Willis, G. M., P. M. Yates, T. A. Gannon, and T. Ward. 2013. How to integrate the Good Lives model into treatment programs for sexual offending: An introduction and overview. *Sexual Abuse: A Journal of Research and Treatment* 25:123–42.

Wilson, R. J., and P. M. Yates. 2009. Effective interventions and the Good Lives model: Maximizing treatment gains for sexual offenders. *Aggression and Violent Behavior* 14:157–61.

CHAPTER 2

The Development of Practice with Adolescents Who Sexually Harm

BOBBIE PRINT, DAWN FISHER, AND ANTHONY BEECH

For many years little attention was paid to young people who harmed sexually; such behavior was frequently dismissed as "experimentation" or "boys being boys." It was only as a result of the development of a systematic response to sexual harm by adults in the 1980s that sexually abusive behaviors by adolescents began to receive attention (Naylor 1989).

It is now widely recognized that adolescents who harm sexually are responsible for a significant proportion of all reported sexual offenses. For example, in England and Wales, HM Ministry of Justice statistics (2013) indicate that 12.4 percent of all those cautioned or convicted for a sexual offense were aged between 10 and 17 years, although the British Crime Survey (2009–2012) indicates that 30 percent of the most serious sexual offenses against females were reported to have been committed by males under the age of 20 (HM Ministry of Justice, Home Office, and the Office for National Statistics 2013). In the United States, 17.5 percent of reported sexual offenses (not including forcible rapes or prostitution) and 9 percent of forcible rapes were committed by young people under the age of 18 (FBI 2010).

As a consequence of this increased awareness the professional response to this group of young people has developed significantly over the past 30 years so that there is currently an array of legislation, assessment models, and intervention programs designed specifically for adolescents who sexually harm. The aim of this chapter is to outline the course of some of these developments and to discuss various advances and difficulties that have emerged along the way.

DEFINING THE PROBLEM

Sexual activity in adolescents is recognized as part of "normal" sexual development (Gil and Cavanagh-Johnson 1993; Ryan and Lane 1997); most is not considered harmful but an important and essential part of the developmental process. A central difficulty when discussing adolescent sexual behaviors, however, is the dearth of evidence regarding what constitutes "normal" sexual behavior in this age group. A small number of national and international studies have been undertaken. For example, in a worldwide study, Patton et al. (2012) identified that most Western countries have a significant numbers of boys and girls under 15 who have engaged in sexual activity. Similarly, Martinez, Copen, and Abma (2011) reported that in the United States 43 percent of teenage girls and 42 percent of teenage boys had experienced sexual intercourse, while in the United Kingdom a comparable survey reported that approximately a quarter of young people engaged in sexual intercourse before the age of 16 years (NHS Infomation Centre 2011). Such studies suggest that a significant proportion of teenagers engage in sexual activity, including sexual intercourse, and yet many countries would deem such behaviors criminal as those involved are below the legal age of consent.

Some definitions have suggested that rather than relying entirely on the legal age of consent, focus should be more on the age difference between young people involved in sexual behaviors. For example, the Committee of Enquiry into sexual harm by children and young people in the United Kingdom (NCH 1992) recommended that there should be cause for concern when there was more than a two-year age difference between participants, or when one of those involved was pre-pubertal and the other post-pubertal. However, such a definition does not cover all the circumstances where harmful behaviors can occur—for example, where those involved are of a similar age, or where an adolescent sexually harms an adult. Most definitions, therefore, also include consideration as to whether a power imbalance, lack of informed consent, or use of coercion was involved (Lovell 2002). While such contributions have helped build definitions of harmful sexual behavior in adolescence, there remain inconsistencies between many legal and welfare definitions, and questions still arise as to what constitutes power, coercion, and consent. This lack of clarity can result in inconsistencies in response from one area to another so that a young person in one district may be drawn into the professional system or even criminalized, while in a neighboring authority they would receive little or no response. There remains, therefore, a need for further discussion and consideration in order to reach a greater consensus on defining harmful sexual behavior in adolescents.

THE LEGAL RESPONSE

Since the 1990s there has been a proliferation of criminal law regarding those who commit illegal sexual behaviors. For example, in 1994 the United States introduced the Jacob Wetterling Act, and in 1997 the Sex Offender Act was introduced in the United Kingdom. Both laws introduced national registries of those convicted of sexual offenses. Since that time Australia, Canada, France, Ireland, South Korea, and Japan have introduced similar legislation. Initially these acts were intended to address the growing public outcry regarding adults who committed horrendous violent sexual offenses. However, much of the introduced legislation covered adolescents who sexually harmed. In the United Kingdom, for example, children over the age of criminal responsibility (10 years) can be placed on the sex offender register, while in the United States the introduction of the Adam Walsh Act in 2006 requires young people, aged 14 and over, who are convicted of certain offenses to be included on registers, and for their details to be made publicly available.

The intention of much of the introduced legislation is to track and manage those who sexually harm in order to prevent further offending. The implied idea is, "Once a sex offender, always a sex offender." Evidence regarding adolescents, however, shows that this assumption is not valid. A number of studies have shown that recidivism rates for adolescents who sexually harm are actually quite low—that is, between 5 and 14 percent (Caldwell 2007; Day et al. 2008; Schram, Milloy, and Rowe 1992; Vandiver 2006; Worling and Curwin 2000; Zimring et al. 2009)—although violent and other non-sexual re-offending rates are considerably higher (16 to 54 percent) (Caldwell 2009; Nisbet, Wilson, and Smallbone 2004; Waite et al. 2005; Worling and Curwen 2001). These findings seem to fly in the face of the argument for sexual offender registration for young people, and studies have demonstrated that notification and registration when applied to young people have had little, or no, deterrent effect (Letourneau et al. 2010; Letourneau and Miner 2005). Thus Meiners-Levy (2006) notes that the laws governing adolescents who sexually harm contradict the developmental research about children and adolescents.

The consequences of such legal responses are, however, that adolescents can face restrictions in social acceptance, employment, education, and where and with whom they live and associate (Harris, Lobanov-Rostovsky, and Levenson 2010) and thus create a negative impact on peer relationships, social isolation, and sense of identity

(CSOM 2007). The resultant stigma, isolation, and lack of opportunities may only act to aggravate known risk factors regarding low self-esteem, social isolation, and hopeless views of the future (Lobanov-Rostovsky 2010; Miner 2007).

THEORETICAL MODELS OF ETIOLOGY

One of the early, most influential emerging theories shaping work with adults and young people who sexually harmed was the Sexual Assault Cycle (Ryan et al. 1987; Wolf 1984). This model described harmful sexual behavior as a self-reinforcing process, involving an individual moving through a predictable progression from having poor social skills and a negative self-image, to expecting rejection and feeling angry, leading to using harmful sexual thoughts as a soothing technique, followed by planning to act on thoughts, and eventually committing sexually harmful behaviors. The resultant feelings of fear about getting caught, and further negative impact on esteem, resulted in a pattern of action that was primed to be repeated. Another early model was Finkelhor's (1984) Four Preconditions model, which suggested a linear progression to sexually harmful behavior, from having the motivation to sexually abuse to overcoming internal inhibitions, overcoming external inhibitors (i.e., creating the opportunity), and overcoming the resistance of the victim. At the time that these models emerged differences between adults and adolescents who sexually harmed were not fully understood, and it was generally assumed that they were alike in most ways (see, for example, Bumby and Talbot 2007; Chaffin, Letourneau, and Silovsky 2002; Longo and Prescott 2006). Both of these models, therefore, were used to guide practice with adolescents as well as adults. As knowledge in the field expanded, however, both models have been criticized as not fully explaining the breadth and types of offending (Ward, Polaschek, and Beech 2006), and there has been a significant development in theoretical models since the 1980s—for example, the Self Regulation model (Ward and Hudson 1998, 2000; Ward, Hudson, and Keenan 1998), and the Integrated and Pathways models (Ward and Beech 2005; Ward and Seigert 2002). However, most have focused on adults; very little systematic research has been conducted on whether such adult models have validity with adolescents. Given our current understanding about adolescents who sexually harm there is reason to question the immediate applicability of such adult models. They originate from studies of adults and pay sparse, if any, attention to factors that we recognize as significant for adolescents, such as developmental factors, learning styles, family and environmental factors, or the impact of trauma. Evidence shows that adolescents who are more likely to commit further sexually harmful acts are those who have histories of significant abuse, trauma, and family dysfunction (Caldwell 2002; Rich 2011).

Some attention to the development of harmful sexual behaviors in adolescents has looked to elements of social learning theory that link behavior to personal and environmental factors; for example, a child who has been sexually harmed may regard the behavior as normal and experience harmful sexual behaviors to others as psychologically, physically, or socially rewarding (Burton, Nesmith, and Badten 1997). A study by Hunter and Figueredo (2000) added support for social learning theory in that it found that adolescents who harmed sexually often lacked self-confidence, social competence, and family support.

More recently attachment and trauma theories have begun to influence understanding of harmful sexual behavior in young people (Creedon 2004; Rich 2006; Smallbone 2006; Burton 2013). These authors suggest that early insecure attachment or experiences of trauma in childhood can negatively impact an individual's cognitive, emotional, and social development and create lifelong problems in a range of abilities such as emotional regulation, capacity for empathy, and formation of close, meaningful, and intimate relationships. These difficulties can then result in young people resorting to harmful sexual behaviors, as they cannot fulfill their sexual and emotional needs in age-appropriate and consensual ways. The advancement of neurobiology in recent years has further supported the importance of attention to attachment difficulties and trauma experiences in young people who sexually harm (Longo et al. 2013). Neuroscience has shown that such early negative experiences can interfere with brain development (Schore 2002; Teicher et al. 2002). Attention to such developmental issues is essential to promote the best outcomes for young people who display sexually harmful behaviors.

INTERVENTION MODELS AND METHODS

Early programs designed for adolescents who harmed sexually were largely psycho-educationally based (Knopp and Stevenson 1989) and relied on providing young people with information as to why the behavior was unacceptable, explaining the need for change, and helping them to make better choices in the future. As the number of intervention programs and research expanded rapidly during the late 1980s and early 1990s, cognitive behavioral therapy (CBT) emerged as the most commonly used method (Freeman-Longo et al. 1995), reflecting a professional shift in viewing intervention more as "treatment" than "education." The CBT approach, as its name implies, has been developed from combining cognitive and behavioral techniques into a comprehensive treatment program. The *behavioral* component of treatment is aimed at helping individuals to develop appropriate behaviors and skills while the *cognitive* component tackles an individual's distorted pattern of thinking. A relapse prevention (RP) approach (Marlatt 1982), a widely employed approach used in the field of addictions, has often been used with CBT and in the early 1980s was adapted for use with those who sexually harmed (Pithers et al. 1983). For a number of years RP has been a commonly used model with both adults and adolescents who sexually harmed (McGrath et al. 2010). RP employs a range of techniques to help individuals identify patterns of "high risk" behaviors and to learn and rehearse techniques to reduce or avoid such risks. RP is commonly carried out in group-work settings, as it is regarded as being more cost-effective to treat a number of individuals at one time, and there are benefits from peer group influences. The types of work that would be covered typically include work on denial and minimization, distorted thinking about harmful sexual behavior, modifying or controlling problematic arousal, lifestyle and personality problems, risk management, and sex education. In practice, RP is very avoidance-focused and often relies on the assumption that individuals are highly motivated to change. It has been criticized for suggesting that all individuals follow the same pathway to their harmful behavior (Cumming and McGrath 2005; Ellerby, Bedard, and Chartrand 2000; Ward and Hudson 1998), and it is often de-motivating for participants given its avoidance-focused approach.

In early CBT-RP approaches, it was common practice to use a challenging, confrontational style in the belief that individuals had to overcome denial and take full responsibility for their behaviors before therapeutic work could be meaningful (Abracen and Looman 2001; Salter 1988). Techniques such as "hot seating" were frequently used with adults and young people (Carich, Newbauer, and Stone 2001; Burton et al. 1998), whereby an individual in the group was required to provide a detailed account of his or her harmful behaviors while other group members were encouraged to challenge any signs of denial, minimization, or justification. However, confrontational styles were increasingly criticized as likely to increase symptoms associated with trauma (Jenkins 1990) and according to Prescott and Longo (2006) could lead to increased shame, replicate abusive environments, and inhibit healthy sexual development in adolescents.

Further doubts about the CBT-RP approach were raised in the following years (Hanson 2000; Laws, Hudson, and Ward 2000; Ward, Polaschek, and Beech 2006; Yates and Ward 2007). In response to the uncertainties raised, the Risk–Need–Responsivity (RNR) model (Andrews, Bonta, and Hoge 1990) became increasingly popular. The model comprises a set of three principles for effective intervention. While it is not a intervention approach in itself, it provides a format in which intervention should be delivered to maximize effectiveness. The principles of the RNR are: (1) The risk principle asserts that the intensity of intervention should be matched to the level of risk; (2) the need principle states that intervention should target the needs of the individual that trigger the harmful sexual behaviors (criminogenic needs); and (3) the responsivity principle describes how treatment approach and presentation should be tailored to the abilities and learning style of the participating individual (Andrews, Bonta, and Wormith 2011). Several meta-analytic studies examining the outcomes of programs employing CBT embedded with RNR principles have shown strong empirical support (Andrews and Dowden 2005; Dowden and Andrews 2004; Hanson et al. 2009), and it has become the basis of national intervention programs for adults who sexually harm in several countries including Canada, England, Scotland, and Hong Kong.

Intervention programs for adolescents who harm sexually have typically followed the pattern described above. Less than 10 years ago, Letourneau and Miner (2005) found that the majority of programs for adolescents who had sexually harmed in North America continued to follow adult-oriented models; a Safer Society Foundation report (McGrath et al. 2010) found similar results. However, research support for the relevance and appropriateness of adult models adapted for adolescents who sexually harm has not been demonstrated (Hunter and Longo 2004). Indeed research has increasingly identified several features and characteristics that differentiate adolescents from adults who sexually harm including: experiencing more difficulties with families; more exposure to violence, trauma, and abuse; fewer social skills; and lower rates of recidivism (Barbaree and Marshall 2006; Caldwell 2002; Fanniff and Becker 2006; Miranda and Corcoran 2000; Worling and Långström 2006). Adolescents are less socially mature in that their cognitive and emotional capacities are not fully developed, and their harmful behaviors are generally less violent (Righthand and Welch 2001). There is also evidence that sexual arousal is fluid and dynamic across adolescence (Hunter and Becker 1994), and there is a lack of research to support the idea that they are troubled by problematic sexual thoughts and arousal to the same extent as adults who sexually harm (Johnson 2005; Smallbone 2006; Zimring 2004). The National Centre on Sexual Behavior of Youth (2003) produced a fact sheet that proposed that as the needs of adolescents who harm sexually are significantly different from those of adults in a number of ways, they often posed a manageable risk to the community that could be maintained under supervision, or in outpatient programs.

These observations suggest that there are clear differences in the neurological, cognitive, and social development of adolescents compared with adults (Letourneau et al. 2009; Medoff 2004). On the basis of such findings many have argued that intervention models for adolescents who sexually harm should not mirror those designed for adults but instead should be modified to ensure that they meet the developmentally specific needs of young people (Bumby and Talbot 2007; Longo 2003; Rich 2003; Righthand and Welch 2001: Ryan and Lane 1997).

Caldwell (2009) suggested it is important to treat adolescents who harm sexually in "developmentally sensitive ways" that should include the building of pro-social bonds in the home and at school, as well as the inculcation of positive responses to social stressors. Others have identified that building self-esteem, motivation, and confidence to make positive life changes, improving family functioning, and increasing the adolescents' associations with peers are additional significant targets for intervention (Bumby and Talbot 2007; Righthand and Welch 2001). Many programs for young people who sexually harm have increasingly incorporated these ideas over the years. In Vermont, for example, David Prescott (2002) coordinated a program that directed intervention toward developing relationships within a collaborative context. Direct communication regarding intervention progress was instantiated; activities and family contact became fundamental components of the program, rather than privileges.

Additionally, there is growing evidence to show that adolescents who harm sexually may have more in common with their peers who commit non-sexual offenses than with adults who sexually harm (Caldwell 2007; Fanniff and Becker 2006; Letourneau and Miner 2005; Nisbet, Wilson, and Smallbone 2004; Seto and Lalumière 2006; Smallbone 2006). Consequently, some propose that emphasis should be given to socio-ecological theories that have been employed with delinquent youth and focus on the significance of family, peer group, school, and community (Borduin and Schaeffer 2002; Longo and Prescott 2006; Letourneau and Miner 2005; Saldana, Swenson, and Letourneau 2006). Programs that encourage and facilitate involvement of a young person's natural support systems generally appear to be most effective with many adolescents and children (Hanson et al. 2009; Reitzel and Carbonell 2006; St. Amand, Bard, and Silovsky 2008). Indeed some of the most promising outcomes with adolescents who sexually harm have been found in programs using multisystemic therapy (MST) (Borduin, Schaeffer, and Heiblum 2009; Letourneau et al. 2009). MST is an intensive family and community-based intervention that uses the strengths in a young person's natural environment, such as family, school, and peer group, to promote positive change.

As outlined in chapter 1, an approach that is strengths-based and not exclusively focused on criminogenic needs and deficits has been recognized as effective in reducing recidivism (Hoge, Andrews, and Leschied 1996; Page and Schaefer 2011). A strengths-based approach involves a collaborative style that encourages young people's engagement and motivation by inviting them to identify goals and then to enhance or develop the skills and strengths to attain them. Marshall and his colleagues (2005) assert that working collaboratively with individuals toward these goals will enhance compliance and maximize intervention effects.

Such an approach is probably most fully encapsulated in the Good Lives model (GLM). It is a strengths-based model that can incorporate relevant theories, models, and methods—for example, elements of the RNR, trauma, and socio-ecological theory (see chapter 3). The GLM has proven useful in that it invites participants to draw on and develop strengths and skills to help them to achieve satisfying lives in healthy and adaptive ways so that they do not resort to harmful behavior to meet their needs. The approach offers individuals the opportunity to identify and gain meaningful personal benefits rather than purely focusing on diminishing negative thoughts, feelings, and behaviors. This has proven extremely helpful in motivating and engaging individuals and has provided professionals with an umbrella framework that can assist in assessment of needs and therapeutic planning. The GLM is rapidly increasing in usage with both adults and adolescents who sexually harm. In a survey of US and Canadian treatment programs, McGrath et al. (2010) found that 35 percent reported using the GLM.

As our knowledge and understanding of young people who harm sexually increases it is becoming increasingly clear that interventions should be tailored to their specific characteristics, needs, and circumstances. Theories, research, and intervention programs developed for adults who harm sexually should be questioned and tested, their relevance carefully considered, before they are used with adolescents. Evidence and practice in allied fields such as attachment, trauma, and adolescent non-sexual offending should be further explored and utilized. The GLM offers a strengths-based framework that can be used in conjunction with other relevant models and theories and as such has the potential to support an approach to working with adolescents that can incorporate focus on the specific needs of adolescents. While, to date, the model has been largely discussed and demonstrated with adults who sexually harm, the remaining chapters of this book show that it is has eminent suitability and applicability for use with adolescents.

REFERENCES

Abracen, J., and J. Looman. 2001. Issues in the treatment of sexual offenders: Recent developments and directions for future research. *Aggression and Violent Behavior* 1:1–19.

Andrews, D. A., J. Bonta, and R. D. Hoge. 1990. Classification for effective rehabilitation: Rediscovering psychology. *Criminal Justice and Behaviour* 17(1):19–52.

Andrews, D., J. Bonta, and J. Wormith. 2011. The Risk–Need–Responsivity model: Does the Good Lives model contribute to effective crime prevention? *Criminal Justice and Behavior* 38:735–55.

Andrews, D. A., and C. Dowden. 2005. Managing correctional treatment for reduced recidivism: A meta-analytic review of programme integrity. *Legal and Criminological Psychology* 10:173–87.

Barbaree, H. E., and W. L. Marshall. 2006. *The juvenile sex offender*, 2nd ed. New York: Guilford Press.

Borduin, C. M., and C. M. Schaeffer. 2002. Multisystemic treatment of juvenile sexual offenders: A progress report. *Journal of Psychology and Human Sexuality* 13:25–42.

Borduin, C. M., C. M. Schaeffer, and N. Heiblum. 2009. A randomized clinical trial of multisystemic therapy with juvenile sexual offenders: Effects on youth social ecology and criminal activity. *Journal of Consulting and Clinical Psychology* 77:26–37.

Bumby, K. M., and T. B. Talbot. 2007. Treating juveniles who commit sex offenses: Historical approaches, contemporary practices, and future directions. In M. C. Calder (ed.), *Working with children and youth who sexually abuse: Taking the field forward*, 245–61. Lyme Regis, UK: Russell House Publishing.

Burton, D. L. 2013. Adolescents who have sexually abused: Trauma and executive functioning. In R. E. Longo, D. S. Prescott, J. Bergman, and K. Creeden, *Current perspectives and applications in neurobiology: Working with young persons who are victims and perpetrators of sexual abuse*, 87–98. Holyoke, MA: NEARI Press.

Burton, D. L., A. A. Nesmith, and L. Badten. 1997. Clinician's views on sexually aggressive children and their families: A theoretical exploration. *Child Abuse and Neglect* 21(2):157–70.

Burton, J., L. A. Rasmussen, J. Bradshaw, B. J. Christopherson, and S. C. Huke. 1998. *Treating children with sexually abusive behavior problems: Guidelines for child and parent intervention*. Binghamton, NY: Haworth Press.

Burton, D., and J. Smith-Darden. 2001. *North American survey of sexual abuser treatment and models summary data*. Brandon, VT: Safer Society Foundation, Inc.

Caldwell, M. F. 2002. What we do not know about juvenile sexual reoffense risk. *Child Maltreatment* 7:291–302.

Caldwell, M. F. 2007. Sexual offense adjudication and recidivism among juvenile offenders. *Sexual Abuse: A Journal of Research and Treatment* 19:107–13.

Caldwell, M. F. 2009. Sex offender registration and recidivism risk in juvenile sexual offenders. *Behavioural Sciences and the Law* 27(6):941–56.

Carich, M. S., J. F. Newbauer, and M. H. Stone. 2001. Sexual offenders and contemporary treatments. *Journal of Individual Psychology* 57(1):4–17.

Chaffin, M., E. Letourneau, and J. Silovsky. 2002. Adults, adolescents, and children who sexually abuse children. In J. E. Meyers, L. Berliner, J. Briere, C. T. Hendrix, C. Jenny, and T. A. Reid (eds.), *The APSAC handbook on child maltreatment*, 2nd ed., 205–32. Thousand Oaks, CA: Sage Publications.

Creeden, K. 2004. The neuro-developmental impact of early trauma and insecure attachment: Re-thinking our understanding and treatment of sexual behavior problems. *Sexual Addiction and Compulsivity* 11:223–47.

CSOM (Center for Sex Offender Management). 2007. *The effective management of juvenile sex offenders in the community.* Retrieved January 15, 2013, from http://www.csom.org/train/juvenile/index.html.

Cumming, G., and R. J. McGrath. 2005. *Supervision of the sex offender: Community management, risk assessment, and treatment.* Brandon, VT: Safer Society Press.

Day, D. M., I. Bevc, F. Theodor, J. S. Rosenthal, and T. Duchesne. 2008. *Change and continuity in criminal offending: The criminal careers of the Toronto sample.* Toronto, Canada: Ministry of Children and Youth Services.

Dowden, C., and D. A. Andrews. 2004. The importance of staff practice in delivering effective correctional treatment: A meta-analytic review of core correctional practice. *International Journal of Offender Therapy and Comparative Criminology* 48:203–14.

Ellerby, L., J. Bedard, and S. Chartrand. 2000. Holism, wellness, and spirituality: Moving from relapse prevention to healing. In D. R. Laws, S. M. Hudson, and T. Ward (eds.), *Remaking Relapse Prevention with Sex Offenders: A Sourcebook,* 427–52. Thousand Oaks, CA: Sage Publications.

Fanniff, A., and J. Becker. 2006. Developmental considerations in working with juvenile sexual offenders. In R. E. Longo and D. S. Prescott (eds.), *Current perspectives: Working with sexually aggressive youth and youth with sexual behavior problems,* 119–41. Holyoke, MA: NEARI Press.

FBI. 2010. *Uniform crime reports.* Retrieved January 18, 2013, from Crime in the U.S.: http://www.fbi.gov/about-us/cjis/ucr/crime-in-the-u.s/2010/crime-in-the-u.s.-2010/tables/10tbl32.xls.

Finkelhor, D. 1984. *Child sexual abuse: New theory and research.* New York: Free Press.

Freeman-Longo, R. E., S. Bird, W. F. Stevenson, and J. A. Fiske. 1995. *1994 nationwide survey of treatment programs and models: Serving abuse reactive children and adolescent and adult sexual offenders.* Brandon, VT: Safer Society Press.

Gil, E., and T. Cavanagh-Johnson. 1993. *Sexualized children: Assessment and treatment of sexualized children and children who molest.* Rockville, MD: Launch Press.

Hanson, R. K. 2000. What is so special about relapse prevention? In D. R. Laws, S. M. Hudson, and T. Ward (eds.), *Remaking relapse prevention with sex offenders: A sourcebook,* 27–38. Thousand Oaks, CA: Sage Publications.

Hanson, R. K., G. Bourgon, L. Helmus, and S. Hodgson. 2009. The principles of effective correctional treatment also apply to sexual offenders: A meta-analysis. *Criminal Justice and Behavior* 36:865–91.

Harris, A. J., C. Lobanov-Rostovsky, and J. S. Levenson. 2010. Widening the net: The effects of transitioning to the Adam Walsh Act's federally mandated sex offender classification system. *Criminal Justice and Behavior* 37(5):503–19.

HM Ministry of Justice. 2013. *Ministry of Justice adult re-convictions: Results from the 2009 cohort, England and Wales.* Statistics bulletin. London: Department of Justice.

HM Ministry of Justice, Home Office, and the Office for National Statistics. 2013. *An overview of sexual offending in England and Wales.* Statistics bulletin. London: Department of Justice.

Hoge, R. D., D. A. Andrews, and A. W. Leschied. 1996. An investigation of risk and protective factors in a sample of youthful offenders. *Journal of Child Psychology and Psychiatry* 37:419–24.

Hunter, J. A., and J. V. Becker. 1994. The role of deviant sexual arousal in juvenile sexual offending. *Criminal Justice and Behavior* 21:132–49.

Hunter, J. A., and A. J. Figueredo. 2000. The influence of personality and history of sexual victimization in the prediction of juvenile perpetrated child molestation. *Behavior Modification* 29(2):259–81.

Hunter, J., and R. E. Longo. 2004. Relapse prevention with juvenile sexual abusers: A holistic/integrated approach. In G. O'Reilly, W. Marshall, A. Carr, and R. Beckett (eds.), *Handbook of clinical intervention with young people who sexually abuse.* Sussex, UK: Brunner-Routledge.

Jenkins, A. 1990. *Invitations to responsibility: The therapeutic engagement of men who are violent and abusive.* Adelaide, Australia: Dulwich Centre Publications.

Johnson, B. R. 2005. Comorbid diagnosis of sexually abusive youth. In R. E. Longo and D. S. Prescott (eds.), *Current perspectives: Working with sexually aggressive youth and youth with sexual behavior problems.* Holyoke, MA: NEARI Press.

Knopp, F. H., and W. F. Stevenson. 1989. *Nationwide survey of juvenile and adult sex-offender treatment programs and models.* Brandon, VT: Safer Society Press.

Laws, D. R., S. Hudson, and T. Ward. 2000. *Remaking relapse prevention with sex offenders: A sourcebook.* Thousand Oaks, CA: Sage Publications.

Letourneau, E. J., D. Bandyopadhyay, K. S. Armstrong, and D. Sinha. 2010. Do sex offender registration and notification requirements deter juvenile sex crimes? *Criminal Justice and Behavior* 37(5):537–52.

Letourneau, E., and M. Miner. 2005. Juvenile sex offenders: A case against the status quo. *Sexual Abuse: A Journal of Research and Treatment* 17:293–312.

Letourneau, E. J., S. W. Henggeler, C. M. Borduin, P. A. Schewe, M. R. McCart, J. E. Chapman, and L. Saldana. 2009. Multisystemic therapy for juvenile sexual offenders: 1 year results from a randomized effectiveness trial. *Journal of Family Psychology* 23(1):89–102.

Lobanov-Rostovsky, C. 2010. Juvenile justice, legislative and policy responses to juvenile sexual offences. In G. Ryan, T. F. Leversee, and S. Lane (eds.), *Juvenile sexual offending: Causes, consequences, and correction*, 3rd ed., 183–200. Hoboken, NJ: John Wiley and Sons.

Longo, R. E. 2003. Emerging issues, policy changes, and the future of treating children with sexual behavior problems. In R. A. Prentky, E. S. Janus, and M. C. Seto (eds.), Sexually coercive behavior: Understanding and management. *Annals of the New York Academy of Sciences* 989:502–14.

Longo, R. E., and D. S. Prescott. 2006. *Current perspectives in working with sexually aggressive youth and youth with sexual behavior problems.* Holyoke, MA: NEARI Press.

Longo, R. E., D. S. Prescott, J. Bergman, and K. Creeden, eds. 2013. *Current perspectives and applications in neurobiology: Working with young persons who are victims and perpetrators of sexual abuse.* Holyoke, MA: NEARI Press.

Lovell, E. 2002. *Children and young people who display sexually harmful behaviour.* London: NSPCC.

Marlatt, G. A. 1982. Relapse prevention: A self-control program for the treatment of addictive behaviors. In R. B. Stuart (ed.), *Adherence, compliance, and generalization in behavioral medicine*, 329–78, New York: Brunner/Mazel.

Marshall, W. L., T. Ward, R. E. Mann, H. Moulden, Y. M. Fernandez, G. Serran, and L. E. Marshall. 2005. Working positively with sexual offenders: Maximising the effectiveness of treatment. *Journal of Interpersonal Violence* 20:1096–114.

Martinez, G., C. E. Copen, and J. Abma. 2011. *Teenagers in the United States: Sexual activity, contraceptive use, and childbearing, 2006–2010.* Hyattsville, MD: US Department of Health and Human Services.

Medoff, D. 2004. Developmental considerations in the forensic assessment of adolescent sexual offenders: Victim selection, intervention, and offender recidivism rates. *Forensic Examiner,* 26–30.

McGrath, R. J., G. F. Cumming, B. L. Burchard, S. Zeoli, and L. Ellerby. 2010. *Current practices and emerging trends in sexual abuser management: The Safer Society 2009 North American Survey.* Brandon, VT: Safer Society Press.

Meiners-Levy, S. 2006. Challenging the prosecution of young sex offenders: How developmental psychology and the lessons of Roper should inform daily practice. *Temple Law Review* 79(499):504–05.

Miner, M. H. 2007. Reaction essay: The fallacy of juvenile sex offender risk. *Criminology and Public Policy* 6(3):565–72.

Miranda, A. O., and C. L. Corcoran. 2000. Comparison of perpetration characteristics between male juvenile and adult sexual offenders: Preliminary results. *Sexual Abuse: A Journal of Research and Treatment* 12:179–88.

National Center on Sexual Behavior of Youth. 2003. *What research shows about adolescent sex offenders.* NCSBY Factsheet no. 1 (July).

Naylor, B. 1989. Dealing with child sexual assault. *British Journal of Criminology* 29(4):395–407.

NCH (National Children's Homes). 1992. *The report of the committee and the Enquiry into Children and Young People.* London: NCH.

NHS Infomation Centre. 2011. *Health survey for England.* London: NHS Information Centre.

Nisbet, I. A., P. H. Wilson, and S. W. Smallbone. 2004. A prospective longitudinal study of sexual recidivism among adolescent sex offenders. *Sexual Abuse: A Journal of Research and Treatment* 16:223–34.

Page, J., and S. Schaefer. 2011. *From risks to assets: Toward a strengths-based approach to juvenile justice reentry into the community.* Minneapolis: Center for Urban and Regional Affairs.

Patton, G. C., C. Coffey, C. Cappa, D. Currie, L. Riley, F. Gore, L. Degenhardt, D. Richardson, N. Astone, A. O. Sangowawa, A. Mokdad, and J. Ferguson. 2012. Health of the world's adolescents: A synthesis of internationally comparable data. *The Lancet* 379(9826):1665–75.

Pithers, W. D., J. K. Marques, C. C. Gibat, and G. A. Marlatt. 1983. Relapse prevention: A self-control model of treatment and maintenance of change for sexual aggressives. In J. Greer and I. R. Stuart (eds.), *The sexual aggressor: Current perspective on treatment,* 214–39. New York: Van Nostrand Reinhold.

Prescott, D. S. 2001. *Emerging strategies in juvenile risk assessment: Controversies, developments, possibilities.* At 2nd Annual Reunion Conference on Collaborating in Treatment with Sexually Aggressive Youth and Their Families, Biddeford, ME, October 26.

Prescott, D. S. 2002. Collaborative treatment for sexual behavior problems in an adolescent residential center. *Journal of Psychology and Human Sexuality* 13(3–4):43–58.

Prescott, D. S. and R. E. Longo. 2006. Current perspectives: Working with young people who sexually abuse. In R. E. Longo and D. S. Prescott (eds.), *Current perspectives: Working with sexually aggressive youth and youth with sexual behavior problems*, 45–62. Holyoke, MA: NEARI Press.

Reitzel, L. R., and J. L. Carbonell. 2006. The effectiveness of sexual offender treatment for juveniles as measured by recidivism: A metaanalysis. *Sexual Abuse: A Journal of Research and Treatment* 18:401–21.

Rich, P. 2003. *Understanding, assessing, and rehabilitating juvenile sexual offenders*. Hoboken, NJ: John Wiley and Sons.

Rich, P. 2006. *Attachment and sexual offending: Understanding and applying attachment theory to the treatment of juvenile sexual offenders*. Hoboken, NJ: John Wiley and Sons.

Rich, P. 2011. *Understanding, assessing, and rehabilitating juvenile sexual offenders*, 2nd ed. Hoboken, NJ: John Wiley and Sons.

Righthand, S., and C. Welch, 2001. Juveniles who have sexually offended: A review of the literature. *Office of Juvenile Justice and Delinquency Prevention Report*. Washington, DC: Office of Juvenile Justice and Delinquency Prevention.

Ryan, G., and S. Lane. 1997. *Juvenile sexual offending: Cause, consequences and correction*. San Francisco: Jossey-Bass.

Ryan, G., S. Lane, J. Davis, and C. Isaacs. 1987. Juvenile sex offenders: Development and correction. *Child Abuse and Neglect* 11:385–95.

Saldana, L., C. C. Swenson, and E. Letourneau. 2006. Multisystemic therapy with juveniles who sexually abuse. In R. E. Longo and D. S. Prescott (eds.), *Current perspectives: Working with sexually aggressive youth and youth with sexual behavior problems*, 563–77. Holyoke, MA: NEARI Press.

Salter, A. C. 1988. *Treating child sex offenders and victims: A practical guide*. Thousand Oaks, CA: Sage Publications.

Schore, A. N. 2002. Dysregulation of the right brain: A fundamental mechanism of traumatic attachment and the psychopathogenesis of posttraumatic stress disorder. *Australian and New Zealand Journal of Psychiatry* 36:9–30.

Schram, D. D., C. C. Milloy, and W. E.Rowe. 1991. *Juvenile Sex Offenders: A Follow Up Study of Reoffense Behavior*. Olympia, WA: Washington State Institute for Public Policy, Urban Policy Research and Cambie Group International.

Seto, M. C., and M. L. Lalumière. 2006. Conduct problems and juvenile sexual offending. In H. E. Barbaree and W. L. Marshall (eds.), *The juvenile sex offender*, 2nd ed., 166–88. New York: Guilford Press.

Smallbone, S. W. 2006. Social and psychological factors in the development of delinquency and sexual deviance. In H. E. Barbaree and W. L. Marshall (eds.), *The juvenile sex offender*, 2nd ed., 105–27. New York: Guilford Press.

St. Amand, A., D. E. Bard, and J. F. Silovsky. 2008. Meta-analysis of treatment for child sexual behavior problems: Practice elements and outcomes. *Child Maltreatment* 13:145–66.

Teicher, M. H., S. L. Andersen, A. Polcari, C. M. Anderson, and C. P. Navalta. 2002. Developmental neurobiology of childhood stress and trauma. *Psychiatric Clinics of North America* 25(2):397–426.

Vandiver, D. 2006. A prospective analysis of juvenile male sex offenders: Characteristics and recidivism rates as adults. *Journal of Interpersonal Violence* 21(5):673–88.

Waite, D., A. Keller, E. McGarvey, E. Wieckowski, R. Pinkerton, and L. Brown. 2005. Juvenile sex offender re-arrest rates for sexual, violent non-sexual and property crimes: A ten-year follow-up. *Sexual Abuse: A Journal of Research and Treatment* 17(3):313–31.

Ward, T., and A. R. Beech. 2005. An integrated theory of sexual offending. *Aggression and Violent Behavior* 11:44–63.

Ward, T., and S. M. Hudson. 1998. The construction and development of theory in the sexual offending area: A meta-theoretical framework. *Sexual Abuse: A Journal of Research and Treatment* 10(1):47–63.

Ward, T., and S. M. Hudson. 2000. A Self Regulation model of relapse prevention. In D. R. Laws, S. M. Hudson, and T. Ward (eds.), *Remaking relapse prevention with sex offenders: A sourcebook*, 79–101. Thousand Oaks, CA: Sage Publications.

Ward, T., S. M. Hudson, and T. Keenan. 1998. A Self Regulation model of the sexual offence process. *Sexual Abuse: A Journal of Research and Treatment* 10:141–57.

Ward, T., D. Polaschek, and A. R. Beech. 2006. *Theories of sexual offending*. Chichester, UK: John Wiley and Sons.

Ward, T., and R. J. Siegert. 2002. Toward a comprehensive theory of child sexual abuse: A theory knitting perspective. *Psychology, Crime, and Law* 9:319–51.

Wolf, S. 1984. A multi-factor model of deviant sexuality. Paper presented at the International Conference on Victimology, Lisbon.

Worling, J. R., and T. Curwen. 2000. Adolescent sexual offender recidivism: Success of specialized treatment and implications for risk prediction. *Child Abuse and Neglect* 24:965–82.

Worling, J. R., and T. Curwen. 2001. Estimate of Risk of Adolescent Sexual Offense Recidivism (the ERASOR—Version 2.0). In M. Calder (ed.), *Juveniles and children who sexually abuse: Frameworks for assessment*, 372–97. Lyme Regis, UK: Russell House Publishing.

Worling, J. R., and N. Långström. 2006. Risk of sexual recidivism in adolescents who offend sexually: Correlates and assessment. In H. E. Barbaree and W. L. Marshall (eds.), *The juvenile sex offender*, 2nd ed., 219–47. New York: Guilford Press.

Yates, P. M., and T. Ward. 2007. Treatment of sexual offenders: Relapse prevention and beyond. In K. Witkiewitz and G. A. Marlatt (eds.), *Therapists' guide to evidence-based relapse prevention*, 215–34. Burlington, MA: Elsevier Press.

Zimring, F. E. 2004. *An American travesty: Legal responses to adolescent sexual offending*. Chicago: University of Chicago Press.

Zimring, F., W. G. Jennings, A. Piquero, and S. Hays. 2009. Investigating the continuity of sex offending: Evidence from the second Philadelphia birth cohort. *Justice Quarterly* 26:58–76.

CHAPTER 3

The Journey:
G-map's Adaptation of
the Good Lives Model

HELEN GRIFFIN AND LAURA WYLIE

As a model of rehabilitation the Good Lives model (GLM) appears to have applicability to a diverse range of populations (Laws and Ward 2011; Sorbello et al. 2002). In the context of working with those who sexually harm, the GLM has been more commonly applied to adults in the United Kingdom. In its original form, the language and terminology of the GLM lends itself more easily to adult usage, yet the principles and ethos that underpin the model have wider relevance. It was this potential that inspired and captured the imagination of a group of practitioners at G-map, who were led to embrace the model and adapt it for use with young people. As proponents of strengths-based practice initiatives, the G-map staff was naturally receptive to the ideology of the GLM. This chapter will detail the journey we have undertaken toward a model that has clinical utility specific to the needs of adolescents who display harmful sexual behaviors. It will include descriptions of the adaptations made and the rationale behind them, as well as considering wider implications of the GLM and their significance to the G-map program.

As with many other specialist programs (Hanson 2000), G-map historically placed emphasis on the use of the Risk–Need–Responsivity (RNR) model (Andrews and Bonta 2010; Andrews, Bonta, and Hoge 1990; Bonta and Andrews 2007), and the relapse prevention model (Marlatt and Gordon 1980; Pithers 1990). The models were tailored to the specific needs and strengths of each adolescent with an emphasis on individualism, creativity, and flexibility. This resulted in an array of theoretical models and methods being used and consequently a lack of an overall coherent framework. Moreover, while having an awareness of the importance of adopting a systemic approach with young people (Borduin et al. 1990) and already engaging families and professionals within its work, G-map lacked a consistent model to support the various processes.

The GLM proposed by Ward and colleagues provides a framework that offers flexibility in guiding practice and has the potential to facilitate the involvement of a young person's systems in a more consistent way. By looking at young people more holistically and considering how they might best meet their needs, the focus extends beyond their criminogenic needs, personal skills, and cognitions to encompass and harness the resources that exist externally within their networks and communities. This process means that not only are young persons responsible for change, but the systems around those individuals also hold some accountability for intervention progress.

Thus, the GLM provided a conceptual and practical framework that was compatible with G-map's organizational aspirations. However, the program's extensive experience of working with young people who display harmful sexual behavior suggested that aspects of the model would benefit from revision in order to be more applicable to that population. Being a small organization meant that G-map had the advantage of being able to adopt a collaborative approach to the exploration and eventual adaptation of the GLM. Consequently practitioners felt empowered and were able to embrace the adapted model as a core framework of their practice.

ADAPTING WARD'S LIST OF PRIMARY GOODS

The first component of the process was considering the utility of Ward's list of primary goods for use with young people. It is valuable to reflect on the journey undertaken by Ward and colleagues in arriving at a list of needs. In its earliest stages of development there appeared to have been less emphasis on the definitive categorization of goods (Ward and Stewart 2003). Initially Ward (2002) envisaged three classes of primary goods that corresponded to the body, self, and social life. These three classes were influenced by Deci and Ryan's (2000) Self-Determination Theory of Needs that depicted the pursuit of autonomy, relatedness, and competence as inherent to all individuals. After reviewing the literature across a number of disciplines, including psychology, social science, practical ethics, evolutionary theory, and philosophical anthropology, Ward and colleagues reached the consensus that nine distinct primary goods could be identified, each representing a cluster of related components (Ward and Brown 2004; Ward and Marshall 2004). While these primary goods (Ward and Marshall 2004; Yates, Kingston, and Ward 2008) have been detailed in chapter 1, it is useful to revisit them here for the purpose of comparison with G-map's adapted model. They were as follows:

- *Life* (including physical functioning, healthy living, and sexual satisfaction)
- *Knowledge* (including insight and information)
- *Excellence in play and work* (including hobbies, leisure, and mastery)
- *Excellence in agency* (including making autonomous decisions and being self-directed)
- *Inner peace* (including emotional self-regulation and emotional safety)
- *Relatedness and community* (including having close and intimate relationships with others, and feeling connected to social groups)
- *Spirituality* (including finding a sense of purpose and meaning)
- *Happiness* (including pleasure and satisfaction, such as that derived from sport, food, and sex)
- *Creativity* (including artistic pursuits and seeking novel experiences)

The conceptualization of goods within the GLM has continued to evolve, with recent adaptations informed by empirical research. For example, Purvis (2010) sought to examine the etiological assumptions underpinning the classification of goods and proposed that *relatedness* and *community*, as well as *excellence in play* and *excellence in work*, were separate, resulting in the current classification of 11 primary goods (e.g., Ward and Gannon 2006; Ward, Yates, and Willis 2011).

While adopting the primary goods proposed by Ward and colleagues in principle, G-map sought to explore an alternative interpretation and classification of these goods that would be more meaningful to and have greater resonance with its service users. This began with the provisional establishment of eight primary goods or "needs," as they were to become known within G-map's adaptation, which had a high correlation with Ward and Marshall's (2004) nine primary goods. These were as follows:

- *Healthy living* (including physical health, mental health, and sexual satisfaction)
- *Safety* (including having rules and boundaries, stability, self-regulation, and safety for self and others)
- *Knowledge* (including creativity and curiosity)
- *Status* (including mastery, achievement, competency, reputation, recognition, and power)
- *Independence and self-management* (including control, autonomy, self-directedness, and self-care)

- *Emotional satisfaction* (including freedom from emotional turmoil and stress, self-respect, self-esteem, self-confidence, and self-actualization)

- *Relationships* (including intimate relationships, sexual relationships, romantic relationships, family relationships, social and community relationships, and sense of acceptance)

- *Meaning and purpose* (including spirituality, fulfillment, hope, generosity, honesty, and fairness)

PILOTING OUR GLM ADAPTATION

Following this preliminary step, a process of consultation was initiated, including the establishment of a focus group comprising professionals within and external to G-map, and gathering feedback from young people accessing G-map services. Young people were approached both individually and within a group-work setting, and feedback was also obtained from their support networks. On the basis of the feedback, the list of needs cited above was reviewed and a set of categorical descriptors was defined and described. These adaptations reflected the needs of the service user, accessibility in terms of the language employed, practical use in terms of the judgment of clinicians, and the views of service users as to how the composite parts clustered within each need.

At this stage of development, consideration was also given to how this adaptation of the GLM might acknowledge or reflect existing theories and frameworks. For example, these needs had transferability to Maslow's Hierarchy of Needs (1969), as well as consistency with the broader literature on child and adolescent development such as attachment theory and the Search Institute's developmental assets framework (Benson 1997; Scales and Leffert 2004). Furthermore, within the United Kingdom, Children's Services were being reformed in light of the Every Child Matters agenda (HM Government 2004).

Every Child Matters was a government initiative launched in 2003 that aimed to ensure that services for children and young people achieved five main outcomes. These were to: (1) *be healthy* (including physical, mental, emotional, and sexual health); (2) *stay safe* (including freedom from abuse, and safety from crime, injury, death, bullying, and discrimination); (3) *enjoy and achieve* (including being empowered to participate and achieve in school and recreation); (4) *make a positive contribution* (including following rules, developing positive and respectful relationships, and supporting the community and environment); and (5) *achieve economic well-being* (including being empowered to participate in further education and/or employment, and enjoying an acceptable standard of accommodation and community resources).

In view of the importance of multi-disciplinary work with young people who present with harmful sexual behavior (Erooga and Masson 2006; Lobanov-Rostovsky 2010), particularly encompassing Child and Adolescent Mental Health, Youth Offending Services, and Social Care Teams, it was beneficial in the United Kingdom that the descriptors for the Good Lives needs complemented the ethos and language of the Every Child Matters agenda.

Six primary needs were established during the subsequent phase of development. These were as follows:

- *Being healthy* (including physical health, emotional health, mental well-being, self-esteem, sexual satisfaction, and sexual confidence)
- *Having fun and achieving* (including status, knowledge, reputation, competence, thrill and excitement, play, creativity, learning new skills, and fulfillment)
- *Being my own person* (including self-directedness, life skills, autonomy, self-control, self-actualization, and empowerment)
- *Having a purpose and making a difference* (including charitable acts, generosity, conforming to societal rules/norms, respect for others, and spirituality)
- *Having people in my life* (including intimacy, relationships with family, peers, community, and boy/girlfriends, and having an emotional confidant)
- *Staying safe* (including safety to self, safety to others, and encompassing risk management)

The model was implemented by G-map and piloted over a six-year period before undergoing further revision in 2012.

The revision process involved consulting with external professionals and young people involved in the program, using clinical experience and service-user feedback obtained from semi-structured interviews. A pilot study was undertaken with these groups using evaluation tools designed to capture information related to the GLM more broadly, and more specifically the adapted primary needs. The tools employed by G-map to evaluate its Good Lives approach are discussed in chapter 10. Key changes related to the needs of *staying safe, being healthy,* and *having fun and achieving* resulting in a model comprising eight needs (see table 3.1).

Table 3.1 G-map's Current Classification of Primary Needs

PRIMARY NEEDS	DEFINITIONS
Having Fun	This need relates to the human drive to engage in recreation and play. It encompasses any activity or pursuit that young people might engage in to have fun, or where they experience fun as an indirect result. It incorporates the following: • Play • Thrill • Amusement • Enjoyment • Entertainment • Excitement Examples of how this need could be attained include the following: • Going to a theme park • Playing a sport • Going to the theater • Reading a book (where a sense of fun is inherent to the young person's pursuit or experience of these)
Achieving	This need relates to the human desire to attain a sense of mastery and accomplishment. It involves any activity or pursuit through which the young person gains a sense of achievement. It includes the following: • Knowledge • Learning • Talents • Fulfillment • Competence • Status Examples of how this need could be attained include the following: • Passing an exam • Learning to ride a bike • Painting a picture • Being accepted as a member of a sports team • Being popular amongst friends (where a sense of achievement is inherent to the young person's pursuit or experience of these)

PRIMARY NEEDS	DEFINITIONS
Being My Own Person	This need relates to the human desire to be autonomous and to be an effective agent of personal change. It refers to any circumstance in which the young person expresses his or her sense of self, functions independently, or influences outcomes. It comprises the following: • Independence • Self-motivation • Making decisions • Self-reliance • Expressing self-identity • Empowerment • Life skills • Internal locus of control • Self-actualization Examples of how this need could be attained might include the following: • Choosing to dress in a particular style • Self-care skills • Setting future goals • Financial independence
Having People in My Life	This need relates to the human desire to relate to others, to belong, and to forge close and affectionate attachments to others. It encompasses all relationships in which a young person attains a sense of affiliation, social acceptance, and closeness. These can include the following: • Family • Peers • Community • Romantic and intimate relationships It can also refer to the young person availing of an emotional confidante. Examples of how this need could be met include the following: • Making friends • Attending a youth club • Having a boyfriend/girlfriend • Spending time with family • Having a trusted person to talk to It refers more to close relationships where the young person spends time with others and can feel supported by them, rather than superficial relationships.

continues on the next page

Table 3.1, continued

PRIMARY NEEDS	DEFINITIONS
Having a Purpose and Making a Difference	This need relates to the human desire to attain a sense of meaning and significance that extends beyond the individual self. It involves seeking to transcend the limitations of being a separate entity and feeling part of a larger whole. Ways in which this need can be realized include the following: • Ascribing to positive social values and codes of behavior • Conforming to societal norms • Spirituality • Making a positive contribution Specific examples could include the following: • Donating money to charity • Doing things for others without expecting reward • Respecting others • Lawful behavior • Having a belief or faith in something outside of oneself
Emotional Health	This need relates to the human drive to attain a sense of inner calm, emotional equilibrium, safety, and competence. It involves the young person having the resources to self-soothe, being emotionally literate and being emotionally resilient. It can comprise the following: • Emotional safety • Emotional regulation • Mental health • Well-being Examples of how this can be achieved include the following: • Using calming self-talk • Empathizing with another person • Living in an environment that is free from conflict • Seeking support to manage difficult feelings • Restoring a sense of emotional well-being through exercise or other activities

PRIMARY NEEDS	DEFINITIONS
Sexual Health	This need relates to the biological drive to achieve sexual gratification and pleasure. It involves sexual competency and satisfaction and may include the following: • Sexual knowledge • Sexuality • Sexual development • Sexual confidence • Sexual pleasure and fulfillment This need might be attained through the following more specific examples: • Sexual education classes at school • Having a positive sexual identity • Having a positive experience of puberty • Speaking to supportive others about sexual anxieties • Use of masturbation • Sexual experiences
Physical Health	This need relates to the human propensity to achieve physical well-being and is largely derived from taking care of the body. This may include the following: • Sleep • Diet • Exercise • Hygiene • Physical safety • Physical functioning Examples of how a young person might meet this need include the following examples: • Getting sufficient rest • Eating well • Regular exercise • Bathing regularly • Being free from physical harm

ANALYZING THE FEEDBACK

One of the things we learned from the piloting process was that professionals external to G-map were confused about the meaning of the *staying safe* need (i.e., does it mean safety to self or safety to others?). Some of our external professionals understood it to refer to the young person having pro-social attitudes or victim empathy as opposed to its intended meaning of having achieved a sense of emotional or physical safety, or not engaging in harmful behaviors. Moreover, there was a consensus among the professionals involved in the pilot that the essence of staying safe, with regard to the young person's safety of self, could be usefully captured under the need of *being healthy* since this incorporates the notions of being free from neglect and abuse as well as emotional safety. The other aspect of staying safe, that is, the young person's safety in respect to behavior toward others, was originally incorporated into the adapted GLM to ensure that risk management was explicitly captured within the primary needs. This was symptomatic of wider political and societal expectations that encouraged an overt emphasis on risk. However, over time it became apparent that this aspect was somewhat disparate with the other needs in that it did not embody the sense of human drive and aspiration associated with other needs. For example, while needs such as *relatedness, competence,* and *autonomy* are perceived as intrinsically motivating (Deci and Ryan 2000), the self-management of risk or safety to others is not necessarily so intuitive. Furthermore, the practical application of this adapted GLM indicated that risk management and safety to others functioned more usefully as a lens through which all needs and means (i.e., how individuals meet their needs) are considered, consistent with the overarching rationale of the original GLM, as opposed to constituting a discrete entity. As a result, *staying safe* was removed from the list of primary needs and in the context of risk management was instead reflected more holistically throughout the model, while safety to self was subsumed within the need of *being healthy*.

The single category of *being healthy* became redundant over time, as G-map practitioners increasingly began to differentiate between emotional, physical, and sexual health when understanding the function of harmful sexual behaviors and approaches to rehabilitation. The validity of viewing these pathways as distinct was borne out by observations that the young people involved often had difficulties with both emotional and sexual health that separately contributed toward their harmful behaviors and required different interventions. Furthermore, the evaluation tools used to pilot the adapted GLM supported the rationale for splitting *being healthy* into separate components (see Griffin et al. 2012). For example, the umbrella need of *being healthy* precluded insight into whether emotional, sexual, or physical health, or a combination of these, was related to the origins or maintenance of the young person's harmful sexual behavior and how related needs should be emphasized for the attainment of a fulfilling and safe life. Consequently *being healthy* was separated into the three primary needs: *physical health, emotional health,* and *sexual health.*

In relation to *having fun* and *achieving,* it became increasingly apparent that while there are commonalities between these two concepts, such as creativity that can be experienced through creative play as well as within formal educational settings, there are also significant differences. In practice, displaying harmful sexual behavior in order to obtain thrill and excitement *(having fun)* is different from harmful sexual behavior aimed at gaining status or knowledge *(achieving),* and they therefore have different implications for intervention. Furthermore, by focusing on these needs simultaneously, in circumstances where the young person was adequately achieving—for example, through being successful in college—his or her need to have fun might be overlooked or vice versa. As these issues were not adequately reflected within the adapted model, the category was split, allowing for separate focus on the components of fun and achieving. It is notable that Ward and colleagues reached a similar conclusion when they separated the goods of *excellence in play* and *excellence in work* (Purvis 2010).

While implementing the Good Lives approach in practice, some subtle changes were made to the way needs were conceptualized. For example, originally when a young person appeared to exert significant control over his or her environment, it was typically interpreted within the need of *being my own person.* However, it soon became apparent that control was often being exerted as a means of attaining a sense of emotional safety at times of threat and was instead defined as integral to the need of *emotional health.* To illustrate this point, the following is an example of a partial problem formulation that was written in the early stages of implementing G-map's adapted GLM:

> Peter's experience of a positive sense of belonging has been adversely affected by his poor attachments and his sexual and physical victimization. As a result, we have hypothesized that Peter experiences his world as dangerous, leading to him to feel powerless and weak. Thus, he has developed a core belief that if he were stronger he would avoid being abused, creating his desire for control. By exerting control over others, we believe Peter gains a sense of emotional safety otherwise unavailable to him. Peter's primary needs have therefore been identified as *having people in my life, emotional health,* and *independence.*

In this example Peter was exerting control as a means of making himself feel safe *(emotional health)* rather than as a means of exploring his autonomy and sense of self *(independence).*

A further conceptual issue related to the need of *having people in my life* was that it could refer to a young person explicitly seeking a sense of intimacy through his or her peer relationships, as well as seeking proximity to a primary figure as part of his or her attachment behavior, in order to use the primary figure as a secure base. While the former relates to social relationship, the latter is inextricably linked to *emotional health,* as proximity-seeking can be a means of emotionally regulating when feeling distressed and under threat. The interplay between *emotional health* and *having people in my life* is reflected in Peter's problem formulation. Within its Good Lives adaptation, G-map decided to include both elements within the need of *having people in my life* (i.e., belonging through affiliation with others and through proximity-seeking to a primary figure).

The extensive discussions practitioners had in the course of reaching a consensus about how needs are construed and operationalized is testament to the fact that the GLM is not an exact science. Indeed, therein lies a key strength of the GLM: namely that it is not overly prescriptive. From this point of view the adapted needs presented in table 3.1 have been derived through a process of evolution and could continue to evolve in line with developments in knowledge and practice. The utility of the model is dependent on its ability to translate to everyday practice and its flexibility to accommodate change as new ideas and information become available. The GLM has proven invaluable as a framework to help understand the needs that drive a young person's behavior, and thus inform what interventions should be implemented and prioritized to help the individual meet those needs more appropriately (Wylie and Griffin 2012). It can accommodate complementary theories and models to further explain why a young person could not adequately meet his or her needs in pro-social ways and so help to identify treatment needs. For example, the GLM, while being part of case formulation, does not provide the finer details of how and why the problematic behavior emerged, and why needs were not met through more appropriate means; nor does it inform the sequencing of work or determine when intervention should end. Instead it acts as an overarching framework to guide treatment with individual models pertaining to issues such as attachment and trauma acting as key components integral to driving and directing treatment.

Pivotal to ensuring that the GLM translated effectively into everyday practice was that the language and terminology employed were accessible to both professionals and service users. G-map's consultation process, involving both team members and external practitioners, indicated that the terms *primary goods* and *secondary goods* were not particularly meaningful to most and thus did not readily translate into everyday professional practice. Professionals also anticipated that young people would more readily associate the term *goods* with merchandise, leading to potential confusion. Resultantly, the term *primary goods* was changed to *primary needs* (or simply *needs*); *secondary goods* became *means*. Furthermore, with regard to internal and external conditions or capabilities, the terms *internal* and *external resources* were employed within the adaptation. Otherwise, the language used within the original model had resonance with the professional group. With regard to service users, the consensus was that there would be benefit in revising the terminology more comprehensively. These adaptations were undertaken collaboratively with service users through a series of focus groups. The adapted terminology for use with young people is presented in table 3.2. The list relates to the GLM generally, rather than being specific to harmful sexual behavior needs. However, given that much of professional intervention is required to focus on the needs young people were meeting through their harmful sexual behavior, significant consideration needed to be given to establishing a shared language that could facilitate discussions relating to this. While this was critical to the adaptation process overall, it will be explored in detail in chapter 6, where it can be best exemplified within the context of a Good Lives plan.

Table 3.2 G-map's Adapted Terminology for Use with Young People

LANGUAGE USED IN ORIGINAL GLM	LANGUAGE USED IN ADAPTED MODEL
Primary goods	My needs
Secondary goods	How I meet my needs
Overarching need	My most important need
Internal conditions (capabilities)	The strengths and skills I have to help me meet my needs
External conditions (capabilities)	How others can help me meet my needs
Internal obstacles	The things about me that get in the way of meeting my needs
External obstacles	The things around me that get in the way of meeting my needs
Conflict	Which of my needs fight against each other?
Scope	Which needs do I neglect?

It is important to note that G-map made a conscious decision to maintain the term *Good Lives* within its adapted model, reflecting an ethos of inclusiveness and belief in the possibility of change, and the language and ideology inherent to Every Child Matters (HM Government 2004). However, this ideology is not always shared by wider society, since it can be controversial to suggest that those who harm sexually are deserving of "good lives." It would appear that there has been some reticence about using this term in the context of both adolescent and adult rehabilitation. Traditionally, those who harm sexually have been viewed by society as "bearers of risk," with "no acknowledgment of their status as fellow human beings or particular interest in promoting their well-being" (Ward 2007, 189). Ward (2007) and Ward and Connolly (2008) make the argument that violating others' human rights—for example, through offending—and having human rights are not mutually exclusive, in that all individuals automatically hold human rights as members of the human race. Moreover, they assert that a society that isolates the offender and denies him or her the opportunity to attain human needs, such as establishing relationships and emotional well-being, may impede the offender's ability to effectively pursue pro-social goals, resulting in an increased risk of further offending. Acknowledging the human rights of offenders is not to detract from the overall priority of upholding the public's rights to live in a safe society (Erooga 2008). The tenet of Ward's argument is that advocating a "good life" for offenders, with the aim of promoting desistance, is most likely to achieve this objective. While UK legislation has given consideration to the human rights of those who perpetrate harmful sexual behavior, Erooga (2008) cautions that society remains vulnerable to the influence of media-driven responses to high-profile crimes, likely to cause swings in public and political opinion toward more punitive approaches to offender processing and treatment. Part of the professional role in this field of work is to inform and educate the political and public arenas about the rehabilitation of those who sexually harm, in order to achieve a consensus about what is both ethical and most effective, with the objective of making society safer. The GLM offers a strengths-based approach to rehabilitation, and importantly its language, which embodies the notion that offenders have a right to a "good life," may help in the pursuit of these goals, thereby protecting the public.

CONSIDERING AGE AND CULTURE

The primary needs used within both the GLM and G-map's adapted model could, on first impression, appear quite abstract. However, it is important to understand that these models are not intended to act as a one-size-fits-all solution, but to guide interventions based on the characteristics and circumstances of the particular individual. Young people will place a different emphasis on each of the needs according to their individual personalities, characteristics, and priorities. Furthermore, their diverse life experiences will mean that they differ in relation to their access to internal and external resources, as well as the obstacles they encounter. Moreover, they will have individual preferences for meeting needs through certain means, based on their strengths, interests, roles, and personal identities. As a result, it is not possible to have one generic plan that would be meaningful or motivational to all young people. For example, reading a book could for one young person meet the need of *achieving* through being a source of knowledge; for another young person it could meet the need of *emotional health* through providing a relaxing diversion from his or her problems; and for yet another, it could meet the need of belonging through representing a way of participating in a peer group discussion. Since the practicality of meeting specific needs can vary considerably among individuals, it is important that practitioners are careful not to imbue the young person's intervention plan with their own interpretations, perceptions, and values.

A further consideration when working with young people is that they are less inclined to plan for the future and have a more limited capacity to delay gratification in comparison with adults (Reyna and Farley 2006). Additionally, they are often subject to more restricted choices by virtue of the rules and boundaries that govern their social world and reflect their age and developmental stage. These necessitate that the means they use to meet their Good Life needs are age-appropriate, realistic, and incorporate small and measurable steps through which they can quickly attain a sense of achievement and positive feedback, the latter being motivational in their pursuit of longer-term goals. Developing an approach to assessment and treatment that is sensitive to and reflective of the needs of its client group was a key motivation for G-map when embarking on its journey of adaptation. In respect to the ways in which young people can realistically meet their Good Life needs, an incremental, incentive-based, and short-term-focused approach has appeared to be most effective. Chapters 6 and 7 provide illustrations of how these considerations can be effectively incorporated within clinical practice. By focusing on means that are individualized and realistic, the GLM moves from being a conceptual framework to providing the conditions for the development of a tangible and achievable plan for rehabilitation.

Additionally, when constructing intervention plans, consideration needs to be given to cultural issues. To impose one's own culture and cultural interpretation of needs and means could be counterproductive to the effectiveness of rehabilitation, since it might not be meaningful or motivational to the recipient. For example, the importance that an individual places on *sexual health,* and the means that he or she uses to achieve it, may be largely dependent on the beliefs, norms, and values that exist within his or her own religious and cultural affiliations. This could include attitudes toward sexual relationships prior to marriage, the acceptability of masturbation, and practices such as monogamy. Similarly group mastery and/or relatedness may have a greater priority over individual mastery and/or autonomy when an individual belongs to a culture that emphasizes collectivism rather than individualism. Also, in circumstances where an individual is raised within a local culture that differs from that of his or her parents and/or extended family, conflict may arise within the prioritization of needs, as well as the means by which needs are achieved. By way of illustration, a young person who is raised within a Westernized culture but whose parents subscribe to a communal lifestyle, such as that typified by Israeli kibbutzim, may be more likely than his or her parents to prioritize the need of being my own person. Consequently, the disparate emphasis placed on needs by the parents and the young person may result in family disharmony and a potential conflict for the young person in relation to meeting his or her needs for relatedness and for *being my own person*. In these examples, it would be important to be thoughtful about the importance the individual places on his or her differing needs and to be sensitive to what, given the cultural context, could be the most appropriate and practical way for the individual to pro-socially achieve those needs. Therefore, in respect to culture, as well as identity, development, personality, abilities, learning, strengths, opportunities, difficulties, and motivation, the importance and pursuit of needs are seen as unique to the individual (Langlands, Ward, and Gilchrist 2009) and as such the GLM is "agency-centered": The individual is central to the goal selection and the implementation of a Good Lives plan.

In adopting the GLM, with its emphasis on approach- versus avoidance-focused goals, G-map sought to move beyond some of the limitations of traditional relapse prevention approaches, for example not effectively addressing a young person's motivation in the context of therapy (Ward et al. 2007). Through its promotion of goods relevant to human life the GLM is inherently motivational (Ward and Brown 2004). Motivation is one component of McNeil's (2009) preconditions for change, the others being capacities (skills) and opportunities. The GLM encompasses all of these elements within its model of rehabilitation (Robinson 2011) and therefore intuitively should optimize the conditions for desistance from further harmful sexual behaviors to occur and increase the likelihood of other positive outcomes (Griffin et al. 2012), as well as incorporating attention to criminogenic needs (i.e., internal and external obstacles; Purvis, Ward, and Willis 2011). Research on adolescent recidivism, including samples of young people who sexually harm, provides support for the view that working with the systems around the young person reduces the risk of re-offending (Borduin, Schaeffer, and

Heiblum 2009; Schaeffer and Borduin 2005) and may help with longer-term desistance. The Good Lives framework facilitates the adoption of a systematic approach to engaging the young person's family and other key systems in the process of change, which in addition to more effectively addressing risk embodies the values of inclusively and empowerment.

While the GLM can contribute much to the field of offender rehabilitation, an important recognition is that it does not constitute a stand-alone model but is reliant on the use of other theories and approaches to realize its effectiveness and to operationalize the intervention process. In essence, the GLM primarily serves as an overarching framework that coalesces these strands. For the model to fully reach its potential for use with young people, it was G-map's view that it would benefit from revision. This included amendments to Ward's list of primary goods and to the original terminology in order to make it more accessible to a younger population. The process of revision resulted in an adapted model comprising eight needs, hereafter referred to as the adapted GLM or GLM-A. It is the GLM-A that will provide the focus for subsequent chapters on assessment, planning, treatment, transition, and evaluation.

REFERENCES

Andrews, D. A., and J. Bonta. 2010. *The psychology of criminal conduct, 5th ed.* New Providence, NJ: Lexis Matthew Bender.

Andrews, D. A., J. Bonta, and R. D. Hoge. 1990. Classification for effective rehabilitation: Rediscovering psychology. *Criminal Justice and Behaviour* 17(1):19–52.

Benson, P. 1997. *All kids are our kids: What communities must do to raise caring and responsible children and adolescents.* San Francisco: Jossey-Bass.

Bonta, J., and D. A. Andrews. 2007. Risk–Need–Responsivity model for offender assessment and treatment. *User Report* no. 2007–06. Ottawa, Ontario: Public Safety Canada.

Borduin, C. M., S. W. Henggeler, D. M. Blaske, and R. J. Stein. 1990. Multisystemic treatment of adolescent sexual offenders. *International Journal of Offender Therapy and Comparative Criminology* 34:105–13.

Borduin, C. M., C. M. Schaeffer, and N. Heiblum. 2009. A randomized clinical trial of multisystemic therapy with juvenile sexual offenders: Effects on youth social ecology and criminal activity. *Journal of Consulting and Clinical Psychology* 77(1):26–37.

Deci, E. L., and R. M. Ryan. 2000. The "what" and "why" of goal pursuits: Human needs and the self-determination of behavior. *Psychological Inquiry* 11:227–68.

Erooga, M. 2008. A human rights–based approach to sex offender management: The key to effective public protection? *Journal of Sexual Aggression* 14(3):171–83.

Erooga, M., and H. C. Masson. 2006. *Children and young people who sexually abuse others: Current developments and practice responses, 2nd ed.* New York: Routledge.

Griffin, H. I., J. A. Bickley, S. A. Price, and L. R. Hutton. 2012. *Development of a Good Lives Assessment Tool (GLAT) and preliminary findings on the primary and global needs of young people who have sexually harmed.* Manuscript submitted for publication.

Hanson, R. K. 2000. What is so special about relapse prevention? In D. R. Laws, S. M. Hudson, and T. Ward (eds.), *Remaking relapse prevention with sex offenders: A sourcebook,* 27–38. Thousand Oaks, CA: Sage Publications.

HM Government. 2004. *Every Child Matters: Change for children.* London: Department for Education and Skills.

Langlands, R. L., T. Ward, and E. Gilchrist. 2009. Applying the Good Lives model to male perpetrators of domestic violence. *Behaviour Change* 26(2):113–29.

Laws, D. R., and T. Ward. 2011. *Desistance and sexual offending: Alternatives to throwing away the keys.* New York: Guilford Press.

Lobanov-Rostovsky, C. 2010. Juvenile justice, legislative and policy responses to juvenile sexual offences. In G. Ryan, T. F. Leversee, and S. Lane (eds.), *Juvenile sexual offending: Causes, consequences, and correction, 3rd ed.,* 183–200. Hoboken, NJ: John Wiley and Sons.

Marlatt, G. A., and J. R. Gordon. 1980. Determinants of relapse: Implications for the maintenance of behavior change. In P. O. Davidson and S. M. Davidson (eds.), *Behavioral medicine: Changing health lifestyles,* 410–52. New York: Brunner/Mazel.

Maslow, A. H. 1969. The farther reaches of human nature. *Journal of Transpersonal Psychology* 1(1):1–9.

McNeill, F. 2009. What works and what's just? *European Journal of Probation* 1(1):21–40.

Pithers, W. D. 1990. Relapse prevention with sexual aggressors: A method for maintaining therapeutic gain and enhancing external supervision. In W. L. Marshall, D. R. Laws, and H. E. Barbaree (eds.), *Handbook of Sexual Assault,* 343–61. New York: Plenum.

Purvis, M. 2010. *Seeking a good life: Human goods and sexual offending.* Germany: Lambert Academic Press. Published doctoral dissertation.

Purvis, M., T. Ward, and G. M. Willis. 2011. The Good Lives model in practice: Offence pathways and case management. *European Journal of Probation* 3(2):4–28.

Reyna, V. F., and F. Farley. 2006. Risk and rationality in adolescent decision-making: Implications for theory, practice and public policy. *Psychological Science in the Public Interest* 7(1):1–44.

Robinson, A. 2011. *Foundations for offender management: Theory, law, and policy for contemporary practice.* Bristol, UK: Policy Press.

Scales, P. C., and N. Leffert. 2004. *Developmental assets: A synthesis of the scientific research on adolescent development, 2nd ed.* Minneapolis: Search Institute.

Schaeffer, C. M., and C. M. Borduin. 2005. Long-term follow-up to a randomized clinical trial of multisystemic therapy with serious and violent juvenile offenders. *Journal of Consulting and Clinical Psychology* 73(3):445–53.

Sorbello, L., L. Eccleston, T. Ward, and R. Jones. 2002. Treatment needs of female offenders: A review. *Australian Psychologist* 37(3):198–205.

Ward, T. 2002. Good lives and the rehabilitation of offenders: Promises and problems. *Aggression and Violent Behaviour* 7:513–28.

Ward, T. 2007. On a clear day you can see forever: Integrating values and skills in sex offender treatment. *Journal of Sexual Aggression* 13(3):187–201.

Ward, T., and M. Brown. 2004. The Good Lives model and conceptual issues in offender rehabilitation. *Psychology, Crime, and Law* 10(3):243–57.

Ward, T., and M. Connolly. 2008. A human rights-based practice framework for sexual offenders. *Journal of Sexual Aggression* 14(2):87–98.

Ward, T., and T. A. Gannon. 2006. Rehabilitation, etiology, and self-regulation: The comprehensive Good Lives model of treatment for sexual offenders. *Aggression and Violent Behavior: A Review Journal* 11:77–94.

Ward, T., R. E. Mann, and T. A. Gannon. 2007. The Good Lives model of offender rehabilitation: Clinical implications. *Aggression and Violent Behavior* 12(1):87–107.

Ward, T., and W. L. Marshall. 2004. Good lives, aetiology and the rehabilitation of sex offenders: A bridging theory. *Journal of Sexual Aggression* 10:153–69.

Ward, T., and S. Maruna. 2007. *Rehabilitation: Beyond the risk assessment paradigm.* London: Routledge.

Ward, T., and C. A. Stewart. 2003. Criminogenic needs and human needs: A theoretical model. *Psychology, Crime, and Law* 9:125–43.

Ward, T., P. M. Yates, and G. M. Willis. 2011. The Good Lives model and the Risk Need Responsivity model: A critical response to Andrews, Bonta, and Wormith. *Criminal Justice and Behavior* 39(1):94–110.

Wylie, L. A., and H. L. Griffin. 2012. G-map's application of the Good Lives model to adolescent males who sexually harm: A case study. *Journal of Sexual Aggression*: Online Publication.

Yates, P. M., D. A. Kingston, and T. Ward. 2008. *The Self-Regulation model of the offence and re-offence process: A workbook for the assessment and treatment of sexual offenders.* Victoria, BC: Pacific Psychological Assessment Corporation.

CHAPTER 4

Motivating and Engaging Young People

ELLEEN OKOTIE AND PAUL QUEST

Young people's motivation to change and the extent of their engagement in intervention are key determining factors for meeting therapeutic objectives. Given the typically diverse needs and often adverse life experiences of young people who display harmful sexual behavior, the obstacles to effective engagement in the therapeutic process can be extremely varied. They can include trauma, learning disabilities, attachment difficulties, and shame (Maruna and Mann 2006; Lord and Wilmott 2004). Other obstacles include factors such as the route into intervention, whether that is through child protection proceedings or criminal justice prosecution, which often result in the harmful sexual behavior being addressed therapeutically some considerable time after the incident. In addition matters dealt with in the criminal justice system may lead to the original offense being minimized as part of plea bargaining. This chapter looks at some of the difficulties facing a practitioner in trying to motivate and engage individuals in therapeutic work. We consider the usefulness of the Good Lives model (GLM) as an approach that promotes motivation and engagement and provide examples of how the model is used in practice.

Probably the best-known current approach in terms of building upon strengths in those who sexually harm has been the inculcation of motivation to not offend again. Fisher and Beech (2002), for example, note that unless individuals are motivated to use what they have learned in intervention, they will not apply their newly acquired skills and knowledge to changing their lifestyle and therefore their likelihood of recidivism will not be reduced. As for level of motivation, it is likely that most of those who have sexually harmed have an ambivalent attitude toward changing their harmful behavior.

Many will have enjoyed the behavior but not the negative consequences for themselves. Others may be reluctant to change because they have little else in their lives. Some may be unmotivated to change because they do not believe they have the ability to do so and may be very fearful of what change will involve. By demonstrating that change is possible, that there are alternatives to harmful behavior, and that a harm-free "good life" will ultimately be more rewarding than continuing to harm others, it is possible to develop a motivation to change.

In therapeutic terms, motivation (the desire to change) and engagement (active participation in the change process) are two interlinked processes. Motivation has been considered in terms of Prochaska and DiClemente's (1982) transtheoretical model of change by a number of authors (for example, Kear-Colwell and Pollack 1997; Miller and Rollnick 2002), motivation being seen as ranging from lack of acknowledgment of a problem, to beginning to acknowledge a problem and make changes, through to the maintenance of the changes bought about in intervention. Engagement is evidenced by the level of commitment, collaboration, and responsiveness an individual demonstrates in the intervention process.

Individuals' levels of motivation and engagement are often mutually influential. For example, if they experience a practitioner as trustworthy, understanding, and supportive they are more likely to accept the professional's view that they are capable of change, and the prospect of change may be less anxiety provoking. Alternatively, if they are keen to achieve change they are likely to be more open to the idea of being assisted and supported. Therefore an early-stage task for practitioners is to explore, assess motivation and engagement, and understand any resistance that is presented.

CAUSES OF LOW MOTIVATION AND ENGAGEMENT

Denial of harmful behavior is often seen as an obvious hurdle to motivation and engagement; in some cases it has been viewed as reason to exclude those who have sexually harmed from intervention programs (Blagden et al. 2013; Schlank and Shaw 1996, 1997). However, increasing understanding of the role of denial, combined with the absence of research evidence that links it to recidivism (Schneider and Wright 2004; Worling 2002) has challenged such beliefs. When denial is considered and understood it becomes clear that not only is such a response common among people confronted with having done something wrong (Maruna and Mann 2006), but it can be temporary and in many cases modifiable.

In the case of adolescents who sexually harm, most have involvement with child protection and/or criminal justice proceedings. The fear of how these systems may react—for example, by removing adolescents from home or placing restrictions on their liberty—together with the possible distress, anger, or rejection by family members may well lead to young people attempting to deny their behavior. As Freeman-Longo and Blanchard (1998) also point out, in cases of sexual harm the criminal justice system often struggles evidentially. This can result in plea bargaining when, in order to secure a conviction, the prosecution service accepts an individual's admission to a lesser charge. In such circumstances a practitioner can be presented with young people who adhere to the system's apparent minimization of their behavior.

As described in chapter 2, early approaches to working with adolescents who sexually harm were based on models designed for adults. In recent years a significantly influential model has been the Risk–Need–Responsivity model (RNR) (Andrews, Bonta, and Hoge 1990; Andrews and Bonta 2010). While the model is helpful in placing importance on the therapeutic relationship and the learning style of a participant in order to promote engagement in intervention, it has been criticized for focusing largely on criminogenic factors, the elimination of risk, and employing language that is predominantly avoidance-oriented (Ward and Maruna 2007). These drawbacks can have a significant effect on adolescents' engagement in therapeutic work as the focus is centered largely on their negative thoughts, feelings, and behaviors with the prospect of them having to refrain from activities, situations, and individuals for the foreseeable future. Since adolescents often struggle to consider the long-term future and are frequently highly emotionally driven, they often see intervention in pure RNR terms as difficult, negative, and punitive.

As noted above, feelings of shame may manifest as denial, defensiveness, or emotional distress. As Jenkins (1990) identified, adolescents who sexually harm often experience high levels of shame and embarrassment. Denial can be rooted in these feelings and can constitute a protective mechanism employed in an attempt to protect an individual's self-perception. Young people are aware of the extreme and negative views voiced by the public and media portrayals of "sex offenders." They are fearful of how they will be perceived and struggle to cope with internal acceptance of what they have done. Some are anxious that they are "mad or bad," and many experience considerable conflict in connecting their behaviors with the person they thought they were. Increasingly there is recognition that addressing the effects of shame is an important part of therapeutic intervention with young people (Marshall et al. 2009).

A heterogeneous approach to working with those who sexually harm has had an equally unhelpful effect on motivation to engage in therapeutic work. Programs have often involved manualized and group work with a view that "one size fits all." Often little attention is given to individual needs in these approaches (Scavo and Buchananan

1989), with the result that young people often feel unconnected to the therapeutic process with little to motivate them to fully participate.

While the RNR has led to improvements in considering individual needs and appropriate methods of working, it remains firmly focused on therapeutic input primarily addressing criminogenic needs. Broader issues, such as cultural needs, unless directly connected to matters of risk, are often paid scant, if any, attention. Yet matters of culture can impact on motivation to engage therapeutic work in significant ways. Cowburn (2008) identified issues such as cultural constraints in talking about sex, the influence of religious beliefs, and Western models of identity as having implications for an individual's engagement. There is some limited, though not consistent, research suggesting that ethnic matching of participant and professional should be a preference (Youth Justice Board 2010). Calverley et al. (2004) found, in a small study of probation clients, that a majority were of the view that there were advantages to having a supervisor of the same ethnicity as themselves as they would be more likely to understand the client and their culture.

As previously indicated, therapeutic engagement can be hampered by an individual's emotional fragility and self-doubt. Research has shown a link between individuals' emotional well-being (linked to a secure internal frame of reference) and their positive understanding of ethnic identity (Yasuda and Duan 2002). This has been found to have particular relevance among adolescents, as adults' ethnic identity is likely to be more strongly established (Smith and Silva 2011). For a number of young people, therefore, confusion regarding their identity, culture, and ethnicity are areas of significant need that while not evidenced as criminogenic can significantly impede their engagement with professionals. For example, a young man of mixed heritage, referred to G-map, who had been raised for most of his life in a predominantly white British environment, as a child was frequently assailed by his mother and older siblings with negative messages about his father who was of South Asian heritage. The young person had also experienced significant racism in the community. His lack of self-confidence and self-esteem, associated with a confused understanding of his ethnic identity, affected his motivation to engage in intervention. The opportunity to explore his heritage and ethnicity with a black practitioner helped him develop self-confidence and a more positive sense of self so that he was able to engage more meaningfully in his therapeutic work.

Similarly adolescents with cognitive and developmental delays require special consideration. Their motivation to change is often low, and their confidence in their ability to change is frequently poor. These difficulties emerge largely from the problems these young people have with cognitive rigidity, grasping abstract concepts (Dulaney and

Ellis 1997; Kounin, 1941; Lorsbach and Worman 1988), and low expectations of success (Cromwell 1963; Morrison and Merith 1997; Ollendick, Balla, and Zigler 1971). In motivational terms, therefore, they may struggle with recognizing the possibilities and benefits of change. Studies have shown that those with learning disabilities have a heightened motivation for social reinforcement (Balla and Zigler 1979; Royal College of Nursing 2010), so that they may present as compliant and motivated in order to please. As Langevin (2006) found, this can result in more individuals with learning disabilities who have sexually harmed appearing motivated and willing to engage in therapeutic programs than their mainstream counterparts, but in reality they are no more likely to complete them. In order to promote true engagement and motivation with this group of young people it is therefore important that full consideration is given to the language used, methods of communication, and pace of work; in addition as Beckett (2002, 177) suggests, thought should be given to the ". . . context, type of encouragement or discouragement that is offered, and the extent to which compensatory input is offered in particular areas of difficulty."

PROMOTING MOTIVATION AND ENGAGEMENT

A helpful method to motivate individuals toward change that can be used in conjunction with the Good Lives model, is motivational interviewing (Miller and Rollnick 1991). Miller and Rollnick (2002) described their model as "a method of communication rather than a set of techniques." The aim is for the practitioner and the individual to explore change together by looking at the person's past, current concerns, and goals. The practitioner remains non-directive but expresses empathy, develops discrepancy, rolls with resistance, and supports self-efficacy. Resultant decisions to make changes are therefore made by the individual and are internally driven. While the method emerged from work undertaken with people who have addictive behaviors, clinical experience and research have highlighted that its person-centered philosophy and approach have been effective when working with those who have sexually harmed (Mann and Rollnick 1996; Prescott and Porter 2011). Lambie and McCarthy (2004, 121) stated, "The use of motivational interviewing techniques is part of a 'tool kit' that allows clinicians to systematically work with adolescents toward increasing their motivation for engaging in therapy and thereby increasing the likelihood of sustained change."

Davidson, Rollnick, and MacEwan (1991) suggest that motivation is influenced by dynamic environmental and situational factors. Thus, in essence, it is a fluid process that is likely to ebb and flow in response to changes in a young person's life circumstances and emotional well-being. Practitioners must be able to recognize and respond appropriately to such conditions and support a young person whose level of motivation may be distracted and hindered by focus on other events or experiences. For example, G-map worked with a young man who expressed confusion about his sexual identity in light of his own victimization by an older male. His preoccupation with this concern significantly impacted on his emotional well-being, and he struggled to engage in therapeutic work as a consequence. In addition to providing therapeutic work that helped him to explore his feelings and reactions to his own abuse, he was supported in attending a sexuality group for young men. This provided him the opportunity to explore his sexuality in a peer group setting in a safe and appropriate way. As a result of these activities the young man's confidence in his identity substantially improved and he was able to was engage in further work to address other needs and essentials of intervention.

One of the most important elements in effectively engaging and motivating individuals who have sexually harmed is the establishment of a positive therapeutic relationship (Drapeau 2005; Marshall et al. 2003). As Rich (2006, 279) points out, "The role of the therapist is to build, or begin to build, a treatment environment which eventually will give rise to the development of both secure attachment and personal security in the client. Between the therapist and the client, this environment is embodied in the therapeutic relationship."

Positive therapeutic relationships with adolescents are built on interactions that are respectful, trusting, and open and that recognize the adolescent's capability, awareness, and maturity. The relationship should be dynamic and flexible, and practitioners need to work out the best way to interact with each individual in a variety of situations, including when a young person presents with withdrawal, boredom, or emotional dysregulation (Holmqvist, Hill, and Lang 2007; Scholte and Van Der Ploeg 2000).

Young people who have suffered insecure attachments or exposure to traumatic experiences often struggle to experience a sense of trust, safety, or connection with others. It is important to understand and take account of young people's attachment style as well as helping them to develop some internal skills and ability to manage the potential emotional impact of the work. Forming a therapeutic relationship in these circumstances is often complex and challenging and requires practitioners to demonstrate high levels of patience, empathy, and reassurance in order to build an alliance with a young person.

A positive approach to intervention, that focuses on enhancing skills, instilling prosocial attitudes, and increasing an individual's self-worth, is likely to maximize intervention benefits (Fernandez 2006; Marshall et al. 2005; Ward and Stewart 2003a, b, c). Mann et al. (2004) found that when practitioners used a more positive goal-oriented approach (as opposed to avoidance-type goals) in group intervention programs with adults who had sexually harmed, by the end of intervention the men in the group appeared to be more genuinely motivated to live life without recourse to further harmful sexual behavior.

The positive psychological approach of the GLM is particularly helpful in promoting engagement and motivation. By introducing the ideas of the GLM to young people and their families early in the therapeutic process, they can receive a message that, just like everyone else, the young people behave in ways that attempt to meet important needs. In the case of harmful behavior, they employed inappropriate means to meet some of these needs. The purpose of intervention is to help them to identify those needs and establish healthier ways to meet them. This sort of explanation helps to promote self-compassion and the reduction of shame as the young people and their families are helped to recognize that they are not unlike everyone else, that they are not "mad or bad," and that change is achievable and not difficult to understand. This introduction also lends itself to an invitation to adolescents and their families to participate in exploring with the practitioner what the young people's particular needs and strengths are and what means they tend to use to meet them. In this way the notion of engaging in an "assessment" process should appear collaborative, logical, reasonable, and positive to them.

Additionally, the emphasis of the GLM on meeting needs that are not restricted to criminogenic factors endorses therapeutic focus on aspects of the young people that may be related to difficulties in engagement, such as the effects of insecure attachment or historical trauma. The model also directs attention to where there may be conflict or lack of scope in young people's identified needs and their capacity to use appropriate means to meet their needs. For example, conflict of needs could present itself if the primary need of *having people in my life* was identified to be an important need for individuals but their emotional deregulation *(emotional health)* hinders their ability to establish and maintain healthy relationships. Helping young people to understand this process and how resolution is achievable by learning to better manage their negative feelings can prove enlightening, encouraging, and motivational. Similarly, in terms of looking at scope, Ward and Maruna (2007) refer to the importance of considering the range of an individual's primary goods and not just those directly associated with his or her harmful sexual behaviors. For example, an adolescent who has struggled in school because of behavioral difficulties may have a high level of educational need, and while this may not necessarily be viewed as reason for harmful sexual behavior it is almost certainly a significant area of need that requires attention. Such a holistic approach not only is important in enhancing the future opportunities of a positive lifestyle for each individual but also enables adolescents to recognize that those working with them consider them primarily as young people and do not view them merely as "sex offenders." This often helps to promote engagement as the young people begin to feel valued and less overwhelmed by negative feelings such as anxiety and shame.

As discussed in chapter 6, each young person in the G-map program has a Good Lives team involved in supporting him or her throughout intervention. A robust system of support around young people during and following intervention can play an important role in enhancing meaningful engagement in the process of change and is shown to be a positive factor in reducing recidivism (Borduin, Schaeffer, and Heiblum 2009; Schaeffer and Borduin 2005). A cohesive team where all, including the adolescent and his or her family, are involved in developing and reviewing the individual's Good Life plan not only provides a range of assistance to the young person but is in an optimal position to assess progress and extend the adolescent's opportunities in the community where appropriate. For many young people, this will include a progressive reduction in the level of supervision they require and an increase in the activities in which they are permitted to participate. Such extension of their independence is a powerful motivator. It is important that professionals do not fall into a predominantly risk-averse approach to working with young people. While careful risk assessment is fundamental to such decision making, unless young people are supported in community reintegration their self-confidence may well reduce and their motivation decrease.

———————————

In summary, there are several factors that can influence young people's motivation and therapeutic engagement. The GLM has proven a particularly helpful framework: Not only is the approach motivational in itself but it can incorporate models and methods that are specifically designed to improve these responses. The GLM approach helps young people contextualize their harmful behaviors as well as reduce some of the stigmatizing effects. The intrinsic simplicity of the model in its basic form allows young people, their families, and professional colleagues to fully participate in problem formulation and intervention planning. The required focus on establishing needs and developing strengths has proven to be a far more attractive proposition than the traditional concentration on risk-related deficits, and a plan of working toward achieving positive goals is significantly more appealing than one that focuses only on preventing certain thoughts, feelings, and behaviors.

———————————

REFERENCES

Andrews, D. A., and J. Bonta. 2010. Rehabilitating criminal justice policy and practice. *Psychology, Public Policy, and Law* 16(1): 39–55.

Andrews, D. A., J. Bonta, and R. D. Hoge. 1990. Classification for effective rehabilitation: Rediscovering psychology. *Criminal Justice and Behaviour* 17:19–52.

Balla, D., and E. Zigler. 1979. Personality development in retarded persons. In N. R. Ellis (ed.), *Handbook of mental deficiency, psychological theory and research*, 2nd ed., 143–168. Hillsdale, NJ: Lawrence Erlbaum.

Beckett, C. 2002. *Human growth and development*. London: Sage Publications.

Blagden, N., B. Winder, M. Gregson, and K. Thorne. 2013. Working with denial in convicted sexual offenders: A qualitative analysis of treatment professionals' views and experiences and their implications for practice. *International Journal of Offender Therapy and Comparative Criminology* 57(3):332–56.

Borduin, C. M., C. M. Schaeffer, and N. Heiblum. 2009. A randomized clinical trial of multisystemic therapy with juvenile sexual offenders: Effects on youth social ecology and criminal activity. *Journal of Consulting and Clinical Psychology* 77:26–37.

Calverly, A., B. Cole, G. Kaur, S. Lewis, P. Raynor, S. Sadeghi, D. Smith, M. Vanstone, and A. Wardack. 2004. *Black and Asian offenders on probation*. Home Office Research Study 277. London: Home Office.

Cowburn, M. 2008. *The BME male sex offender in prison: Overrepresentation and under-participation*. Paper presented to Challenging Boundaries: Social Policy Association Conference, Edinburgh, June 23–25.

Cromwell, R. L. 1963. A social learning approach to mental retardation. In N. R. Ellis (ed.), *Handbook of mental deficiency*, 41–91. New York: McGraw-Hill.

Davidson, R., S. Rollnick, and I. MacEwan. 1991. Counselling problem drinkers. In R. Miller and S. Rollnick (eds.), *Motivational interviewing: Preparing people to change addictive behaviour*. New York and London: Guilford Press.

Drapeau, M. 2005. Research on the processes involved in treating sexual offenders. *Sex Abuse* 17(2):117–25.

Dulaney, C., and N. Ellis. 1997. Rigidity in the behavior of mentally retarded persons. In W. E. MacLean (ed.), *Ellis' handbook of mental deficiency, psychological theory and research*, 175–95. Mahwah, NJ: Erlbaum.

Fernandez, Y. M. 2006. Focusing on the positive and avoiding negativity in sexual offender treatment. In W. L. Marshall, Y. M. Fernandez, L. E. Marshall, and G. E. Serran (eds.), *Sexual offender treatment: Controversial issues*, 187–97. Chichester, UK: John Wiley and Sons.

Fisher, D., and A. R. Beech. 2002. Treating the adult sex offender. In K. D. Browne, H. Hanks, P. Stratton, and C. Hamilton (eds.), *The prediction and prevention of child abuse: A handbook*. Chichester, UK: John Wiley and Sons.

Freeman-Longo, R. E., and G. T. Blanchard. 1998. *Sexual abuse in America: Epidemic of the 21st century*. Brandon, VT: Safer Society Press.

Holmqvist, R., T. Hill, and A. Lang. 2007. Treatment alliance in residential treatment of criminal adolescents. *Child Youth Care Forum* 36:163–78.

Jenkins, A. 1990. *Invitations to responsibility: The therapeutic engagement of men who are violent and abusive.* Adelaide, Australia: Dulwich Centre Publications.

Kear-Colwell, K., and P. Pollock. 1997. Motivation or confrontation: Which approach to use with child sex offenders? *Criminal Justice and Behavior* 24:20–33.

Kounin, J. S. 1941. Experimental studies of rigidity. *Character and Personality* 9:251–85.

Lambie, I., and J. McCarthy. 2004. Interviewing strategies with sexually abusive youth. In R. Geffner, K. Crumpton, T. Geffner, and R. Falconer (eds.), *Identifying and treating youth who sexually offend: Current approaches, techniques and research,* 107–23. New York, London, and Victoria, AU: Haworth Maltreatment and Trauma Press.

Langevin R. 2006. Acceptance and completion of treatment among sex offenders. *International Journal of Offender Therapy and Comparative Criminology* 50:402–17.

Lord, A., and P. Willmot. 2004. The process of overcoming denial in sexual offenders. *Journal of Sexual Aggression* 10:51–61.

Lorsbach, T. C., and L. J. Worman. 1988. Negative transfer effects in learning disabled children: Evidence for cognitive rigidity? *Contemporary Educational Psychology* 13(2):116–25.

Mann, R., and S. Rollnick. 1996. Motivational interviewing with a sex offender who believed he was innocent. *Behavioural and Cognitive Psychotherapy* 24:127–34.

Mann, R. E., S. D. Webster, C. Schofield, and W. L. Marshall. 2004. Approach versus avoidance goals with sexual offenders. *Sexual Abuse: A Journal of Research and Treatment* 16:65–75.

Marshall, W. L., L. E. Marshall, G. A. Serran, and M. D. O'Brien. 2009. Self esteem, shame, cognitive distortions and empathy in sexual offenders: Their integration and treatment implications. *Psychology, Crime, and Law* 15(2):217–34.

Marshall, W. L., G. A. Serran, Y. M. Fernadez, R. Mulloy, R. E. Mann., and D. Thornton. 2003. Therapist characteristics in the treatment of sexual offenders: Tentative data on their relationship with indices of behaviour change. *Journal of Sexual Aggression* 9(1):25–30.

Marshall, W. L., T. Ward, R. E. Mann, H. Moulden, Y. M. Fernandez, G. Serran, and L. E. Marshall. 2005. Working positively with sexual offenders: Maximising the effectiveness of treatment. *Journal of Interpersonal Violence* 20:1096–114.

Maruna, S., and R. E. Mann. 2006. A fundamental attribution error? Rethinking cognitive distortions. *Legal and Criminological Psychology* 11:155–77.

Miller, W. R., and S. Rollnick. 1991. *Motivational interviewing: Preparing people to change addictive behavior.* New York: Guilford Press.

Miller, W. R., and S. Rollnick. 2002. *Motivational interviewing: Preparing people for change,* 2nd ed. New York: Guilford Press.

Morrison, G. M., and A. C. Merith. 1997. Risk, resilience, and adjustment of individuals with learning disabilities. *Learning Disability Quarterly* 20(1):43–60.

Ollendick, T., D. Balla, and E. Zigler. 1971. Expectancy of success and the probability learning of retarded children. *Journal of Abnormal Psychology* 77:275–81.

Prescott, D. S., and J. Porter. 2011. Motivational interviewing in the treatment of sexual offenders. In D. P. Boer, R. Eher, L. A. Craig, M. H. Miner, and F. Pfäfflin (eds.), *International Perspectives on the Assessment and Treatment of Sexual Offenders: Theory, Practice, and Research,* 373–96. Chichester, UK: John Wiley and Sons.

Prochaska, J. O., and C. C. DiClemente. 1982. Transtheoretical therapy: Toward a more integrative model of change. *Psychotherapy: Theory Research, and Practice* 19:276–88.

Rich., P. 2006. *Attachment and sexual offending: understanding and applying attachment theory to the treatment of sexual offenders.* Chichester, UK: John Wiley and Sons.

Royal College of Nursing. 2010. *Mental health nursing of adults with learning disabilities: RCN guidance.* London: Royal College of Nursing.

Scavo, R., and B. D. Buchanan. 1989. Group therapy for male adolescent sex offenders: A model for residential treatment. *Journal of the American Association of Children's Residential Centers* 7(2):59–74.

Schaeffer, C. M., and C. M. Borduin. 2005. Long-term follow-up to a randomized clinical trial of multisystemic therapy with serious and violent juvenile offenders. *Journal of Consulting and Clinical Psychology* 73:445–53.

Schlank, A. M., and T. Shaw. 1996. Treating sexual offenders who deny their guilt: A pilot study. *Sexual Abuse: A Journal of Research and Treatment* 8(1):17–23.

Schlank, A. M., and T. Shaw. 1997. Treating sexual offenders who deny: A review. In B. K. Schwartz and H. R. Cellini (eds.), *The sex offender: New insights, treatment innovations and legal developments,* vol. 2, 6.1–6.7. Kingston, NJ: Civic Research Institute.

Scholte, E. M., and J. D. Van Der Ploeg. 2000. Exploring factors governing successful residential treatment of youngsters with serious behavioural difficulties: Findings from a longitudinal study in Holland. *Childhood* 7:129–53.

Schneider, S. L., and R. C. Wright. 2004. Understanding denial in sex offenders: A review of cognitive and motivational processes to avoid responsibility. *Trauma, Violence, and Abuse* 5(1):3–20.

Smith, T. B., and L. Silva. 2011. Ethnic identity and personal well-being of people of colour: A meta-analysis. *Journal of Counselling Psychology* 58:42–60.

Ward, T., and S. Maruna. 2007. *Rehabilitation: Beyond the risk assessment paradigm.* London: Routledge.

Ward, T., and C. A. Stewart. 2003a. The treatment of sex offenders: Risk management and good lives. *Professional Psychology: Research and Practice* 34:353–60.

Ward, T., and C. A. Stewart. 2003b. Criminogenic needs and human needs: A theoretical model. *Psychology, Crime, and Law* 9:125–43.

Ward, T., and C. A. Stewart. 2003c. The relationship between human needs and crimogenic needs. *Psychology, Crime, and Law* 9:219–24.

Worling, J. R. 2002. Assessing risk of sexual assault recidivism with adolescent sexual offenders. In M. C. Calder (ed.), *Young people who sexually abuse: Building the evidence base for your practice,* 365–75, Lyme Regis, UK: Russell House Publishing.

Yasuda, T., and C. Duan. 2002. Ethnic identity, acculturation and emotional well-being among Asian Americans and Asian international students. *Asian Journal of Counselling* 9(1):1–26.

Youth Justice Board. 2010. *Exploring the needs of young black and minority ethnic offenders and the provision of targeted interventions.* London: Youth Justice Board for England and Wales.

CHAPTER 5

Assessment

HELEN GRIFFIN AND LAURA WYLIE

Assessment is fundamental to achieving an informed and responsive approach to working with young people with harmful sexual behavior and provides the foundation for all subsequent intervention. It has implications for intervention outcomes, the efficient use of resources and, critically, public protection. Assessment is not a discrete process, but should permeate every aspect of working with young people, as well as being sufficiently dynamic to reflect the evolving nature of adolescent development and the progress of the individual. A departure from a purely adult-based assessment model is necessary for adolescents (Miner 2002; Rasmussen 2004) since young people occupy a different position within their families and communities (Rich, 2003), undergo greater developmental change (Calder 2001; Rich 2003), and typically have less established sexual preferences, attitudes, and interests (Bourgon, Morton-Bourgon, and Madrigrano 2005; Seto, Lalumière, and Blanchard 2000; Seto et al. 2003). The remit of a specialist assessment can vary according to the needs of the organization and the young person's presenting difficulties, although it commonly includes an evaluation of risk, motivation, context, intervention needs, placement needs, and likelihood of future recidivism (Grant 2006; Will 1999). In addition to consideration of risk, the benefit of assessing the young person's strengths has more recently been acknowledged (Griffin et al. 2008; Griffin and Harkin 2012). Hackett (2006) differentiated between a "risk reduction" and "resilience development" assessment framework. He observed that whereas both can meet the same objective of preventing further abuse, a "risk reduction" approach is likely to lead to a focus on deficits and requires the avoidance or elimination of behaviors. Alternatively, a resilience-based assessment, which focuses on competencies, is more likely to encourage the young people and their families to actively engage in the process of identifying goals. According to Rich (2011, 439) "treatment and rehabilitation built on correcting deficits is not likely to be as successful or affirming as treatment built on highlighting and reinforcing strengths." Thus, it would appear that for intervention to be most effective in reducing crime and protecting the public, it needs to be informed by an assessment process that incorporates risks, resilience, and strengths.

As previously noted, the Good Lives model (GLM) as an overarching framework facilitates this dual focus on risks and strengths, while affording a provisional overview of the possible motivating factors for a given harmful act. Moreover, by incorporating criminogenic needs, through considering the internal and external obstacles experienced by the young person (Purvis, Ward, and Willis 2011), the GLM provides some measure of dynamic risk assessment. For example, social isolation is a risk factor that is supported by research pertaining to adolescent sexual recidivism (Print et al. 2007) and is likely be an obstacle to meeting the need of *having people in my life*. As a rudimentary indication of future risk, if young people continued to be unable to adequately meet the needs assessed as being relevant to their harmful behavior, the implication is that they are likely to commit further harmful acts. However, the GLM does not adopt a structured or actuarial approach to risk assessment, it does not provide insight into how people might commit further harm or their likely victim preferences, and it does not specifically attend to predisposing, trigger, or maintenance factors. Therefore, although the GLM makes a positive contribution to the assessment process, it is necessary to use other models alongside it, in order to achieve a more holistic and comprehensive assessment of pathways, risks, and needs. In this chapter we focus on G-map's adapted Good Lives model (GLM-A), but out of necessity include reference to additional models that augment the assessment process. Figure 5.1 illustrates an assessment process where the GLM is an instrumental component in reaching a clinical formulation.

Figure 5.1 The Assessment Process

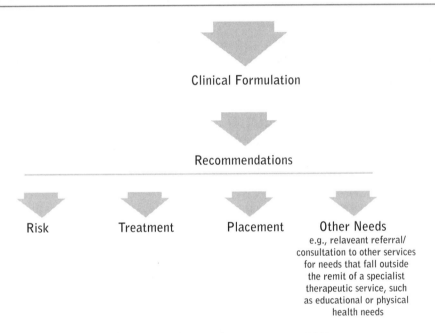

ASSESSMENT

Problem Formulation: This would involve consideration of pathways to harmful sexual behavior and includes the Good Lives assessment.

Psychometric Assessment: This could help to inform the problem formulation, risk assessment, indentify possible tratment targets, and facilitate pre-and post-treatment comparison.

Risk Assessment: This may include the use of clinical risk assesment and actuarial or empirically guided risk instuments and a clinical assessment to consider the risk of re-offending and potential level of harm.

Clinical Formulation

Recommendations

Risk   Treatment   Placement   Other Needs
                                                    e.g., relaveant referral/
                                                    consultation to other services
                                                    for needs that fall outside
                                                    the remit of a specialist
                                                    therapeutic service, such
                                                    as educational or physical
                                                    health needs

GATHERING THE INFORMATION

The validity and reliability of the assessment information is likely to be enhanced by the use of diverse assessment methods from a variety of sources (Beckett 1994), including clinical interviews and file reviews. Interviews with multiple informants are more likely to provide a "complete picture" to assist case formulation and the assessment of needs (Rich 2003). Young people can make an invaluable contribution to the assessment process, since, from a social psychological perspective, it is their personal interpretation of actions, events, and experiences that precipitates their behavior (Taylor 1998). This view is consistent with the ethos of the GLM, which is "agency-centered" and emphasizes the importance of considering individuals' value base and self-identity, in order to accurately interpret their behavior within the context of a holistic rehabilitation approach (Laws and Ward 2011). Clinical interviews with the young person can provide important information on motivation and engagement, social functioning, harm-supportive attitudes and beliefs, and level of responsibility (Beckett 1994). Self-report has some well-documented limitations, including the distortion of information through deliberate falsification or defensiveness (Ward 2003). However, Worling (2012) comments on emerging support for the validity of self-report methods with adolescents who sexually harm to elicit information on sexual interests and arousal. The usefulness of interview data can be enhanced by having a context in which to situate it—for example, through prior consultation of case files. Case files can provide a rich source of information, offering a snapshot of the individual's circumstances at various points in time (Griffin and Vettor 2012). However, by their very nature, they can be prone to errors, omissions, and ambiguities (Cockburn 2000; Rich 2003) and the information presented by professionals has the potential to be biased and/or subjective (Hayes and Devaney 2004).

In summary, it appears prudent to gather information using diverse methodologies and from a range of sources. It is particularly pertinent to young people that the assessment process includes family (Calder 2001) and other relevant agencies (Vizard 2002). The process outlined in this chapter, whether explicit to the GLM-A, focused on predisposing factors, or related to risk of recidivism, should be based on multiple sources of information, including file reviews, professional meetings, observations from professionals and caregivers, interviews with parents/caregivers, and interviews with the young person.

CLINICAL FORMULATION

The information gathered in the course of the assessment process can often be unwieldy and requires careful refinement and organization so that it can efficiently inform intervention planning and other service provision. Clinical formulation, often interchangeably referred to as "case formulation," is a means of integrating key information in a manner that facilitates the development of a testable hypothesis. How a clinical formulation is organized and what it incorporates will largely be dictated by the psychological model underpinning it. It is essential that clinical formulation is grounded in theory and supported by evidentiary sources (Eells and Lombart 2011). In general, a clinical formulation will assist the practitioner to: (1) elucidate the problem; (2) explain the onset and maintenance of the problem; and (3) develop an individualized intervention plan (Sturmey 2010). As well as integrating all of the key elements highlighted above, an intervention plan should also attend to risk and resilience factors pertinent to the individual and consider how these may interact with maintenance factors to potentially mediate the effects of the problem behavior.

In the context of young people with harmful sexual behavior, theoretical models typically include attachment, psychodynamic, cognitive, behavioral therapy, humanistic, and applied behavior analysis. The GLM can also provide a theoretical foundation to case formulation; according to Willis, Yates, Gannon, and Ward (2012, 2), when compared with relapse prevention approaches, the GLM also has a "stronger theoretical basis supporting its integration in sex offender treatment programs."

Clinical formulation relies on robust assessment and should, where possible, be undertaken collaboratively with the young people and their support networks. In G-map's work, clinical formulation is informed by a number of components, namely problem formulation, risk assessment, and psychometric assessment. Moreover, as a working hypothesis, clinical formulation is dynamic in nature, and may require revision in response to new information.

PROBLEM FORMULATION

Problem formulation is an important aspect of the overall clinical formulation. It involves consideration of pathways to harmful sexual behavior, incorporates the Good Lives assessment, and can also include a description of the harmful behavior process attained via reference to models of sexual recidivism.

Pathway to Behavior

There is broad consensus that human behavior, in all its complexity, is influenced by a multitude of variables, and can never be attributed to a singular cause (Calder 2001; Rich 2003). By this token, harmful sexual behavior does not have a universal cause and needs to be understood at an individual level. Furthermore, there is a general acceptance that pathways relevant to adults who sexually harm do not readily transfer to young people (see chapter 2). An important component of the assessment process is the development of a working hypothesis of how predisposing factors or distal antecedents interact with both environmental triggers (proximal antecedents) and protective factors to precipitate the occurrence of harmful sexual behavior. Information to consider when formulating a young person's pathway to harmful sexual behavior is likely to include family background and functioning; attachment history; personality traits; the young person's developmental history, comprising social, emotional, physical, cognitive, sexual, and behavioral domains; educational history; trauma history; and psychiatric and psychological diagnoses.

As noted above, a wide range of models and approaches to case formulation is available to practitioners (Flitcroft et al. 2007). Bickley (2012) proposed a model for use in exploring pathways to harmful sexual behavior that illustrates the role of predisposing, precipitating, maintaining, and protective factors, and the interplay among them (see figure 5.2).

Figure 5.2 Comprehensive assessment framework for young people who sexually abuse
Source: Bickley 2012. Printed by permission of James A. Bickley.

PERSONAL PREDISPOSING FACTORS

Biological/Developmental Factors
- Hormonal imbalance/neurological problems

Psychological Characteristics
- Limited cognitive abilities/intellectual disability
- Personality (e.g., difficult temperament)
- Low self-esteem
- Impulsiveness/external locus of control

Behavioral/Interpersonal Difficulties
Early onset of severe behavioral problems
Diagnosis of Conduct Disorder or ADHD
- History of interpersonal aggression, sexually inappropriate behavior, or antisocial behavior
- School problems
- Substance misuse

CONTEXTUAL PREDISPOSING FACTORS

Parent-Child Factors in Early Life
- Attachment problems/discontinuity of care
- Authoritarian/permissive/neglectful parenting
- Inconsistent parental discipline/poor boundaries

Exposure to Family Problems in Early Life
- Marital discord or family violence
- High-stress family environment
- Exposure to family anti-social behavior

Stresses in Early Life
- Child abuse: sexual/physical/emotional/neglect
- Exposure to sexually inappropriate behavior
- Bereavements/losses or separations
- Social disadvantage
- Bullying/peer victimization

PRECIPITATING FACTORS
- Acute life stresses
- Lifecycle transitions
- High risk thoughts/feelings/situations
- Opportunity/access to potential victim

PERSONAL MAINTAINING FACTORS

Harmful Sexual Behavior (HSB) Specific
- Deviant sexual interests/behaviors
- Obsessive sexual interests/behaviors
- Attitudes supportive of HSB
- Limited awareness of HSB pattern/process
- Poor awareness of the consequences of HSB

Sexual Development
- Limited sexual knowledge or lack of understanding of appropriate/inappropriate sexual behavior
- Poor sexual scripts/sexual relationship skills
- Negative view of own sexual identity
- Lack of appropriate outlet for sexual satisfaction

Self Concept and Social Functioning
- Low self-esteem, poor self-concept/self-efficacy
- Dysfunctional attributional style and negative automatic thoughts
- Anti-social attitudes and behaviors
- Limited pro-social interpersonal skills
- Disordered personality development

Self-Management Skills
- External locus of control
- Poor emotion regulation/arousal control
- Poor behavior regulation/impulsivity/hyperactivity
- Limited problem-solving or decision-making ability
- Substance misuse/dependency

Intervention System Factors
- Denial/ambivalence about HSB
- Fear of change/consequences of disclosure
- Cognitive difficulties or mental health needs

PERSONAL PROTECTIVE FACTORS

Harmful Sexual Behavior (HSB) Specific
- Appropriate sexual interests/behaviors
- Attitudes that fail to support HSB (e.g., internal inhibitors)
- Raised awareness of HSB pattern/process
- Awareness of the consequences of HSB
- Demonstrates remorse/empathy

Sexual Development
- Appropriate sexual knowledge, attitudes, sexual scripts, and relationship skills
- Positive view of own sexual identity
- Appropriate outlet for sexual satisfaction

Self Concept and Social Functioning
- Positive view of self/appropriate self-efficacy
- Positive future goals and interests
- Optimistic attributional style
- Pro-social attitudes and behaviors
- Effective interpersonal skills
- Appropriate personality development/adjustment

Self-Management Skills
- Internal locus of control
- Effective emotional regulation
- Appropriate behavioral control
- Good problem-solving or decision-making ability

Intervention System Factors
- Open about HSB and willingness to change
- Motivated to engage in intervention
- No current health needs or cognitive problems

CONTEXTUAL MAINTAINING FACTORS

HSB Specific
- Family/care provider attitudes or behaviors supportive of HSB
- Family/care provider lack victim awareness/empathy
- Exposure to media/societal/social influence supportive of HSB
- Opportunities for HSB

Sexual Attitudes and Practices
- Lack of appropriate family/care provider sexual boundaries
- Lack of family/care provider knowledge about developmentally appropriate sexual behavior
- Poor family/care provider attitudes toward sex and sexuality
- Limited communication about sexual matters

Family Functioning
- High stress family/care provider environment
- Poor family/care provider communication
- Problematic parent/care provider relationships
- Caregiver inconsistency/inadequate parenting
- Lack of family/care provider support/availability

Environmental Conditions
- Social isolation/lack of support network
- Lack of intimate peer relationships
- Lack of appropriate supervision/monitoring
- Negative peer associations and influences
- Poor educational/employment opportunity
- Social disadvantage

Intervention System Factors
- Family deny/ambivalent about resolving problem
- Family reject formulation and intervention plan
- Lack of co-ordination among professionals
- Unsafe or unsupportive environment for change

HARMFUL SEXUAL BEHAVIOR
- Nature of HSB
- Severity of HSB
- Victim characteristics
- Circumstances of HSB
- Onset, duration, and frequency of HSB
- Pattern of HSB
- Escalation of SHB

CONTEXTUAL PROTECTIVE FACTORS

HSB Specific
- Family/care provider attitudes or behaviors challenging of HSB
- Family/care provider awareness of victim's perspective
- Media/societal/social influence challenging of sexual offending
- No/limited opportunities for HSB

Sexual Attitudes and Practices
- Appropriate family/care provider sexual boundaries
- Good family/care provider knowledge about developmentally appropriate sexual behavior
- Positive family/care provider attitudes toward sex and sexuality
- Effective communication about sexual matters

Family Functioning
- Flexible family organization/clear communication
- Positive parent/care provider relationships
- Consistent/effective and appropriate parenting
- Adequate family/care provider support and availability

Environmental Conditions
- Good social and support network
- Appropriate intimate peer relationships
- Effective supervision/monitoring
- Positive peer associations and influences
- Good educational/employment opportunity
- Opportunity to make positive contributions

Intervention System Factors
- Family accepts and is committed to resolving problem
- Family accepts formulation and intervention plan
- Good co-ordination among professionals
- Safe and supportive environment for change

Predisposing factors can be personal (i.e., biological/developmental factors, psychological characteristics, and behavioral/interpersonal difficulties) or contextual (i.e., early life experiences relating to parent–child factors, family problems, and exposure to stressors). Personal factors may include features internal to the young people that influence their functioning, such as cognitive development or temperament. In relation to contextual factors, some early life experiences can impede young people's ability to develop secure attachments, a sense of emotional safety, self-regulation skills, and positive social relationships, which may ultimately result in a poor or fragmented sense of self, inadequate emotional and behavioral self-management, and limited social skills. They may also give rise to harmful behavior-supportive thoughts, beliefs, and/or interests. Therefore, although these factors occur relatively early in life, it might take years before their effects can be more fully observed. By contrast, precipitating factors constitute the triggers to the harmful sexual behavior and occur shortly before the problem. Precipitating factors can include events that trigger emotional distress (such as loneliness and rejection), victim access, misuse of drugs and alcohol, and high states of arousal. Predisposing factors in combination with precipitating factors provide the pathway to harmful sexual behavior. However, according to this model, once the behavior has been established, factors in the here and now may come into play to maintain or mitigate against it. Maintaining factors can reinforce the harmful sexual behavior and can also be personal (e.g., cognitive distortions supportive of the behavior) and contextual (e.g., the young person lacking a social support network). Similarly protective factors, which are factors that could help offset risks, can be both personal and contextual. Here, personal factors can include developmentally appropriate sexual knowledge and pro-social attitudes, whereas contextual factors might take account of a young person having an emotional confidant or good educational opportunities.

Assessment Using the GLM-A

Some models contextualize harmful sexual behavior with reference to the complex interplay between proximal and distal factors, as well as helping to elucidate the obstacles and resources relevant to the young person. While the GLM/GLM-A do not in themselves facilitate exploration of the interplay between these factors, they can help to assess the pathways to harmful sexual behavior through their acute focus on what fundamental needs drive the young person's behavior. Moreover, through their consideration of obstacles and resources, both at the time of the inappropriate or harmful behavior and in the present, the GLM/GLM-A provides insight into why needs could not be met historically and, importantly, inform the process of change.

A Good Lives assessment of the needs young people were meeting through their harmful sexual behavior requires the gathering of information specific to the time of the event. This encompasses the prioritization of needs, the means by which the young people met their needs, the appropriateness of them, associated internal and external obstacles and resources (factors that enable and get in the way of the need being attained), conflict (where it is difficult for needs to co-exist because they are at odds with one another), and lack of scope (where a number of important goods are not pursued or are ignored; this can also lead to conflict between goods). For illustrative purposes, table 5.1 provides a semi-structured interview that can assist with the collation of information required for a GLM-A assessment. It is noteworthy that Yates, Kingston, and Ward (2009) also recommend a semi-structured interview format to assess "primary goods" pertaining to the original GLM.

To support young people in talking about themselves and identifying positive qualities it is important that the assessor uses supplementary information that helps to elucidate the young people's strengths and interests. This offsets the possibility that the interview, by virtue of asking the young people to focus on their lack of opportunities and resources, could evoke a sense of inadequacy or failure. While the semi-structured interview should draw out relevant information pertaining to needs, means, and scope, it does not specifically focus on issues of conflict. However, on the basis of the information gleaned, the assessor should be able to make inferences about whether needs were in conflict. Young people can experience the semi-structured interview format as quite onerous, and therefore the assessor may choose to use more creative ways to elicit the required information. Alternative ways of collecting the information include the use of photographs, images, drawings, storyboarding, time lines, and cartoon strips; these have the additional benefit of eliciting more responsiveness from young people with a preference for visual learning as well as those with intellectual disabilities. Moreover, as the assessor becomes more familiar with the various elements of the GLM-A the information can be gathered more informally, including via general conversations and exchanges with young people and their network, as well as through pieces of work such as Old Life/New Life, which is covered later in this chapter. As previously noted, while the young people's accounts can be important to the GLM-A assessment, other sources of information such as case records, anecdotes from family, and caregiver observations should also be considered.

Table 5.1 GLM—A semi-structured interview covering the time of the harmful sexual behavior

NEED	DEFINITION	EXAMPLE QUESTIONS
Having Fun	*Having fun* might be defined as play, thrill, amusement, enjoyment, entertainment, and excitement. Examples of how this need could be attained might include: going to a theme park; playing sport; going to the theatre; reading a book.	What did you do to have fun at this time? (The following can act as prompts: what did you do that gave you a sense of thrill and excitement? What were your favorite games/play activities? Did you enjoy doing new things, and if so, what?) How easy was it for you to have fun? *(What helped?)* What got in the way of you having fun? *(What were the obstacles? How able were you to overcome these obstacles?)* Was having fun important to you? *On a scale of 1 (not important to me at all) to 5 (very important to me), how important was having fun to you?* Do you think the things you did to have fun were appropriate? *(If applicable: What was not appropriate and why? Did you try to change or give up anything that wasn't ok? If so, what helped or got in the way?)* Did you focus so much on having fun that it got in the way of doing other things? Do you think that this need was relevant to your harmful sexual behavior? If so, how?
Achieving	*Achieving* may be defined as knowledge, learning, talents, fulfillment, competence, and status. Examples of how this need could be attained might include: passing an exam; learning to ride a bike; painting a picture; scoring a goal in sport; or being popular among friends.	What were your achievements? *(What were you good at? What were your talents? Were you popular? Were you respected by other people?)* How easy was it for you to achieve? *(What skills, talents, and supports did you have to help?)* What got in the way of you achieving? *(What were the obstacles? How able were you to overcome these obstacles?)* Was achieving important to you? *On a scale of 1 (not important at all) to 5 (very important to me), how important was achieving to you?* Do you think the things you did to achieve were appropriate? *(If applicable: What was not appropriate and why? Did you try to change or give up anything that wasn't ok? If so, what helped or got in the way?)* Did you focus so much on achieving that it got in the way of doing other things? Do you think that this need was relevant to your harmful sexual behavior? If so, how?

NEED	DEFINITION	EXAMPLE QUESTIONS
Being My Own Person	*Being my own person* might be defined as independence, self-motivation, making decisions, self-reliance, expressing self-identity, empowerment, life skills, internal locus of control, and self-actualization. Examples of how this need could be attained might include: choosing to dress in a particular style; self-care skills; setting future goals; stubbornness; or financial independence.	What did you do to be your own person (e.g., having goals, being independent)? *(What did you want out of life? What plans were you making for the future? What steps had you taken to help you get there? How able were you to make decisions for yourself? How much control did you have over your life? How independent were you?)* How easy was it for you to be your own person? *(e.g., having goals, being independent)?* What got in the way of being your own person? *(What were the obstacles? How able were you to overcome these obstacles?)* Was being your own person important to you? *On a scale of 1 (not important at all) to 5 (very important to me), how important was being your own person to you?* Do you think the things you did to be your own person (e.g., your goals and decisions) were appropriate? *(If applicable: What was not appropriate and why? Did you try to change or give up anything that wasn't ok? If so, what helped/got in the way?)* Did you focus so much on being your own person that it got in the way of doing other things? Do you think that this need was relevant to your harmful sexual behavior? If so, how?
Having People in My Life	*Having people in my life* might be defined as relationships with family, peers, community, romantic, and intimate relationships. It can also refer to the young person availing of an emotional confidant. Examples of how this need could be met include: making friends; attending youth club; joining a football team; having a boyfriend/girlfriend; spending time with family; or talking to a trusted friend about a problem.	What relationships did you have at this time? *(Refer to relationships with family, friends, community, or a boyfriend/girlfriend).* How would you describe these relationships? *(Note to assessor: Attempt to gauge information on closeness/ intimacy.)* Did you have someone that you could talk to about your feelings and get support from? *(Was this person always available?)* How easy was it for you to make and keep relationships? *(What helped?)* What got in the way of you having relationships? *(What were the obstacles? How able were you to overcome these obstacles?)* Was having people in your life important to you? *On a scale of 1 (not important at all) to 5 (very important to me), how important was having relationships to you?*

continues on the next page

Table 5.1, continued

NEED	DEFINITION	EXAMPLE QUESTIONS
Having People in My Life (continued)	It refers more to close relationships where the young person spends time with others and can feel supported by them, rather than superficial relationships.	Do you think all of your relationships were appropriate? *(If applicable: What was not appropriate and why? Did you try to change or give up any relationships that weren't ok? If so, what helped or got in the way?)* Did you focus so much on relationships that it got in the way of doing other things? Do you think that this need was relevant to your harmful sexual behavior? If so, how?
Having a Purpose and Making a Difference	*Having a purpose and making a difference* might be defined as ascribing to positive social values and codes of behavior, conforming to societal norms, spirituality, and making a positive contribution are ways in which this need can be realized. Specific examples could include: donating money to charity; doing things for others without expecting reward; respecting others; lawful behavior; or having a belief in or an appreciation of something outside of oneself.	What did you do to have a purpose and make a difference at this time? *(What things did you do that were helpful, generous, or respectful? How able were you to follow rules? Were you spiritual or religious? What beliefs did you have which gave a sense of meaning to your life?)* How easy was it for you to have a purpose and make a difference? *(Was it easy for you to be helpful, generous, respectful, spiritual, or religious)? (What helped?)* What got in the way of your having a purpose and making a difference? *(What were the obstacles? How able were you to overcome these obstacles?)* Was having a purpose and making a difference important to you? *On a scale of 1 (not important at all) to 5 (very important to me), how important was having a purpose and making a difference?* Do you think the things you did have a purpose and make a difference were appropriate? *(If applicable: What was not appropriate and why? Did you try to change or give up any of the things that were not ok? If so, what helped/got in the way?)* Did you focus so much on helping others, following rules, spirituality, or religion that it got in the way of doing other things? Do you think that this need was relevant to your harmful sexual behavior? If so, how?

NEED	DEFINITION	EXAMPLE QUESTIONS
Being Healthy	*(Note to assessor: Consider alternative information sources regarding the young person's level of hygiene, physical appearance, level of sexual education, formal diagnoses)*	The things about me that get in the way of meeting my needs:
Emotional Health	*Emotional health* includes emotional safety, emotional regulation, mental health, and well-being. Examples of how this can be achieved include: using calming self-talk; empathizing with another person; living in an environment that is free from conflict; seeking support to manage difficult feelings; or restoring a sense of well-being through exercise.	What did you do to be emotionally healthy? *(i.e., manage your feelings, feel safe, keep healthy in your mind)* How easy was it for you to feel safe, keep a healthy mind, and manage your feelings? What got in the way of you feeling safe, keeping a healthy mind, and managing your feelings? *(What were the obstacles? How able were you to overcome these obstacles?)* Was feeling safe and being able to cope with difficulties important to you? *On a scale of 1 (not important at all) to 5 (very important to me), how important was emotional health to you?* Do you think the things you did to be emotionally healthy were appropriate? *(If applicable: What was not appropriate and why? Did you try to change or give up any of the things that were not ok? If so, what helped/got in the way?)* Did you focus too much on your emotional health that it got in the way of doing other things? Do you think that this need was relevant to your harmful sexual behavior? If so, how?
Sexual Health	*Sexual health* includes sexual competency and satisfaction. It may include sexual knowledge, sexuality, sexual development, sexual confidence, and sexual pleasure and fulfillment.	How did you meet your sexual health needs at this time? *(How much sexual knowledge did you have? What sexual experiences did you have? How confident did you feel with sexual experiences and your sexual identity? How did you experience puberty? How satisfying were your sexual experiences?)*

continues on the next page

Table 5.1, continued

NEED	DEFINITION	EXAMPLE QUESTIONS
Sexual Health (continued)	This need might be attained through the following more specific examples: sexual education classes at school; having a positive sexual identity; having a positive experience of puberty; speaking to supportive others about sexual anxieties; use of masturbation; or sexual experiences.	How easy was it for you to meet your sexual health needs? *(What helped?)* What got in the way of you meeting your sexual health needs? *(What were the obstacles? How able were you to overcome these obstacles?)* Was meeting your sexual health needs important to you? *On a scale of 1 (not good at all) to 5 (very good), how important was this to you?* Do you think the things you did to meet your sexual health needs were appropriate? *(If applicable: What was not appropriate and why? Did you try to change or give up anything that wasn't ok? If so, what helped/got in the way?)* Did you focus so much on your sexual health needs that it got in the way of doing other things? Do you think that this need was relevant to your harmful sexual behavior? If so, how?
Physical Health	*Physical health* includes sleep, diet, exercise, hygiene, physical safety, and physical functioning. Examples of how a young person might meet this need are: getting sufficient rest; eating fruit and vegetables; going to the gym; bathing regularly; or being free from physical harm.	What did you do to meet your physical health needs at this time? *(i.e., eat healthily, look good, keep fit, have a good sleeping pattern, manage any illness or physical disability, or keep safe from physical harm)* How easy was it for you to meet your physical health needs? *(What helped?)* What got in the way of you meeting your physical health needs? *(What were the obstacles? How able were you to overcome these obstacles?)* Was meeting your physical health needs important to you? *On a scale of 1 (not good at all) to 5 (very good), how important was this to you?* Do you think the things you did to meet your physical health needs were appropriate? *(If applicable: What was not appropriate and why? Did you try to change or give up anything that wasn't ok? If so, what helped/got in the way?)* Did you focus so much on your physical health needs that it got in the way of doing other things? Do you think that this need was relevant to your harmful sexual behavior? If so, how?

Source: Adapted from interview schedule developed by Griffin and Price 2009.

Young people might display harmful sexual behavior as a direct means of meeting a need or needs, or they could display harmful sexual behavior as an indirect consequence of trying to meet separate and distinct needs (see figure 5.3). These two potential pathways to committing harmful sexual behavior have achieved some empirical support (see Purvis 2010). An example of a direct route in relation to the need of *having people in my life* could be the use of harmful sexual behavior in order to gain a sense of intimacy. An indirect route in relation to the same need could be young people seeking affirmation and affection from a parent, but instead experiencing rejection. Resultantly the young people, in the absence of having an emotional confidant, use drugs to help regulate the affect associated with their sense of rejection and lack of support. This creates a ripple effect in that the young people's difficulties, combined with the use of drugs, leads to a continued deterioration in their emotional state and relationships, and has a disinhibiting effect on their behavior. As a consequence of these spiraling difficulties the young people experience low mood, loneliness, a sense of detachment, and disinhibition, which leads to their sexually harmful behavior. Thus in this latter example, the harmful behavior is not a means by which individuals directly sought to meet the need of *having people in my life*.

Figure 5-3 additionally demonstrates that the needs that underpin the sexual harm can have a role in the maintenance/reinforcement of the behavior. Using the example of a young person seeking to meet the need of *intimacy* through sexually harmful behavior, the need of *having people in my life* may be relevant to both the onset and maintenance of the behavior. In this case the fact that the harmful sexual behavior allowed an individual to achieve feelings of closeness is reinforcing in itself, thereby increasing the likelihood that the behavior will be repeated in the future at times when the young person feels lonely and isolated. Furthermore, it is possible that in the course of meeting intimacy needs through harmful sexual behavior the young person also experiences a sense of sexual gratification. Therefore, while this factor did not originally precipitate the onset of their harmful sexual behavior, it could become integral to its continuation.

*Figure 5.3 Pathways into harmful sexual behavior using the GLM-A
(Adaptation of the Goods Etiological Theory, Purvis et al. 2011)*

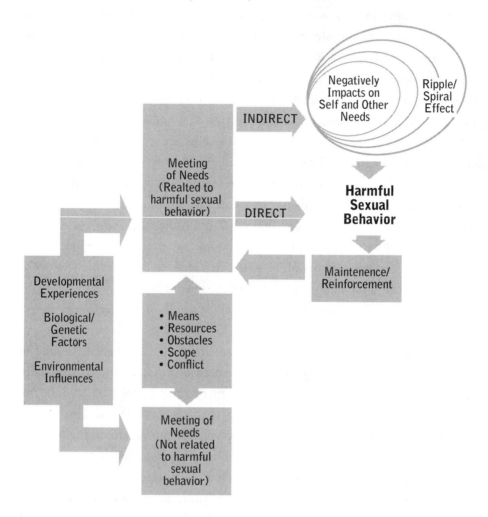

In addition to understanding the needs associated with the harmful sexual behavior of young people, whether directly or indirectly, a key facet of assessment is to establish a picture of how and to what extent they are meeting their needs presently. Moreover, there are often lengthy gaps between the original harmful behavior and the assessment period, during which time the young people may have altered their preferences and prioritization in relation to needs. Also, the resources young people have to meet their needs and the obstacles they face may have changed over time. If an assessment of the young people's present circumstances indicates that they continue to have difficulties meeting their needs in a coherent way, it could lead to further inappropriate or harmful behavior. Such difficulties could include: lack of scope; needs in conflict; insufficient internal and/or external capacity to meet needs appropriately; internal and/or external obstacles preventing needs, particularly priority needs, from being met appropriately. With adaptations to tense, the interview in table 5.1 could offer a way to gather information about a young person at the time of assessment in addition to furnishing details about the progression of the harmful sexual behavior.

A useful way for assessors to check their initial hypotheses pertaining to the needs met by a young person's harmful sexual behavior is to use an exercise such as Old Life/New Life. Old Life/New Life could also enable assessors to ascertain the young person's previous and current prioritization of needs, means, resources, obstacles, scope, and conflict. Old Life/New Life is G-map's adaptation of a strengths-based model called Old Me/New Me developed by Haaven, Little, and Petre-Miller (1990), and employed widely with intellectually disabled as well as mainstream individuals who sexually harm, to positive effect (for example, see Mann et al. 2004). The original model encouraged individuals to consider how they presented at the time of their harmful actions, including their associated thoughts, feelings, and behaviors, and to contrast that with a conceptualization of the kind of people they aspire to be and the needs they prioritize, that is, their "non-harming" selves. Individuals set "New Me" goals as a means of achieving their desired "good life." In order to reflect the important role that families and significant others play in young people's development, and thus embrace a more systemic approach, G-map elected to shift from the more individually centered concepts of Old Me/New Me to the broader concepts of Old Life/New Life. G-map's Old Life/New Life represents the journey that adolescents make from "Old Life"—that is, life prior to and at the time of displaying harmful sexual behavior—to "New Life," namely what they want in their future. A further departure from the original model is the representation of the journey as a road map for change, as illustrated in figure 5.4. Further details of G-map's general use of this model are provided by O'Callaghan (2004).

Figure 5.4 A basic representation of the Old Life/New Life Model

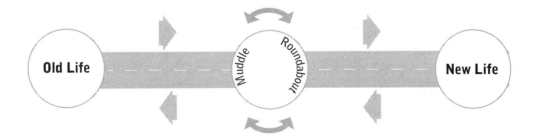

With specific regard to how it can be linked to GLM-A, Old Life depicts the young people's means, resources, and obstacles, as well as helping to identify their prioritization of needs via exploration of their motivations and aspirations, prior to and at the time of their harmful sexual behavior. Conversely, New Life symbolizes the young people's good life goals and allows for exploration of how these might relate to their primary needs. The assumption is that the needs that appear most important to the young people regarding their New Life aspirations will reflect the primary needs their harmful sexual behavior was meeting. While their New Life goals may incorporate additional needs not considered to have been related to their harmful behavior, G-map's clinical practice to date has shown that there is a distinct correlation between the harmful-behavior-related needs and the core needs young people hope to meet through a variety of means in their New Life. As such it offers a degree of reassurance that the identified harmful-sexual-behavior-related needs are likely to be correct as they generally reflect with some consistency the needs an individual is most concerned with meeting.

When using this tool with young people they are invited to think about the personal significance of each of their identified New Life goals. For example, in the above example a young person may be asked, "If you did have lots of girlfriends, what would that mean to you?" and the young person may respond that it would mean that he would be popular (i.e., the primary need of *achieving*), have people he could be close to (i.e., *having people in my life*), and have sex *(sexual health)*; similarly, "having a family of my own" may relate to a need for belonging (i.e., *having people in my life*). This can help frame the young person's New Life aspirations within the context of Good Lives needs and allows the focus of further discussion to be on the expressed needs rather than the material goods.

The concept of "Muddle Roundabout" can be used to represent the consequences for young people of their harmful behavior and obstacles they currently face that they need to overcome in order to continue their journey toward New Life (or good life). Muddles could include having to live away from home, exclusion from school, restrictions on liberty, etc. The road to New Life is viewed as being "under construction" and is dependent on the young people working to develop building blocks to complete the road. Old Life/New Life provides an opportunity to illustrate to the young people how aspects of Old Life meant that important needs were either unmet or met through inappropriate means as a result of barriers and/or a lack of resources, and how this could have precipitated their harmful sexual behavior. In this sense it allows young people to be involved in the process of hypothesis testing, and thus provides a collaborative method of working. Moreover, it can help the young people to understand the rationale for intervention in that they will require improved resources to achieve alternative and appropriate ways of meeting their needs in New Life in order to desist from harmful behavior and enhance well-being. In addition to providing a way of checking and conveying the Good Lives hypothesis, the Old Life/New Life model facilitates the drafting of a Good Lives plan, via the "under construction" part of the model, and offers a means of monitoring progress.

Figure 5.5 An example of goals for New Life and the needs they represent

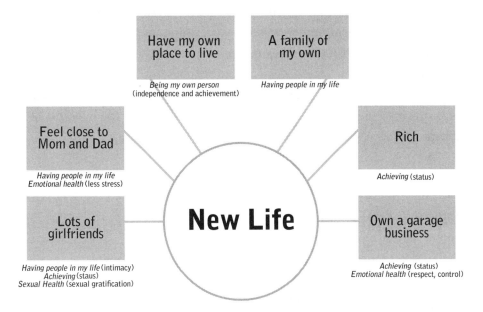

Further methods of checking the initial hypothesis can include: gathering good-quality observations to highlight the needs that are most important to a young person; lifeline work to assist with understanding the needs that were most prevalent in Old Life; and, where appropriate, exploration of the young person's thoughts, feelings and behaviors at the time of the harmful event(s) in order to assist understanding of the motivations underpinning the harmful behavior.

Understanding the Process of the Harmful Sexual Behavior

As well as understanding the young people's pathway to harmful sexual behavior (including predisposing, precipitating, and maintenance factors) and their Good Lives needs (including resources and obstacles), there continues to be a role for understanding the process of the harmful sexual behavior, that is, the "how" of the behavior (Bickley 2008). Practitioners can employ creative techniques such as storyboarding to elicit the information and to help young people recount the sequence of events concerning their harmful sexual behavior. Finkelhor's (1984) Four Preconditions model of child sexual abuse posits that there are four conditions underpinning sexually harmful behaviors: motivation to sexually harm; overcoming internal inhibitors; overcoming external inhibitors; and overcoming the resistance of the child. While this model has been superseded by more complex models, with minor adaptation such as the simplification of language or use of visual and concrete representations, its simplicity has some value when working with adolescents. It can assist them to gain insight into their harmful behavior, including being able to recognize risky situations, thoughts, and feelings, and so offers a foundation for the development of future self-management strategies. However, young people who have high levels of shame regarding their harmful sexual behavior can also experience these models somewhat negatively as a consequence of their explicit focus on the harmful behavior. Practitioners should consider the appropriateness of whether and when to use behavior-process models in developing an understanding of the harmful behavior when working with individual young people.

OTHER AREAS FOR ASSESSMENT

Psychometric Assessment

Psychometric testing is a well-established method of information gathering and assessment (Hammond 2006). With young people who have exhibited harmful sexual behavior it can be useful to include psychometric assessment of the following areas: social adequacy, locus of control, coping strategies, emotional reactivity, trauma, sexual attitudes and interests, sexual knowledge, family dynamics, executive functioning, behavioral functioning, strengths, and resilience. Psychometric assessment allows an individual's characteristics and attitudes to be compared against large samples and provides an indication of where he or she is situated in relation to the normal range. The completion of a battery of psychometric tools before and after intervention can also provide a measure of therapeutic progress (Beckett 1994), thus assisting with the evaluation of how a Good Lives approach may effectively promote change. A further advantage of psychometric assessment is that it enables the young people and key members of their support network to contribute to a process that is underpinned by an empirical base and can therefore usefully inform, supplement, or challenge clinical judgment. In this respect, it is consistent with the ethos of the GLM, which advocates consulting with the individuals to ascertain their perceptions, interpretations, and priorities. An obvious disadvantage of psychometric assessment is its typical reliance on self-report and consequently the potential for results to be distorted due to impression management and/or lack of self-insight (Medoff 2003; Paulhus

1999). Furthermore, the effectiveness of psychometric testing is often dependent on the individual's level of comprehension. This is particularly pertinent for young people with intellectual disabilities (Clare 1993), who appear to be overrepresented among populations of young people with inappropriate or harmful sexual behavior (Griffin and Vettor 2012). Additionally young people with intellectual disabilities can encounter problems with self-report (Keeling, Beech, and Rose 2007), recalling sexual thoughts and feelings (Gilby, Wolf, and Goldberg 1989), and acquiescent responding (Clare and Gudjonsson 1993).

Risk Assessment

The GLM-A enables "risk" to be assessed in respect to whether the young people's present circumstances allow them to positively meet needs that have been, or could be, related to further inappropriate or harmful behavior. However, it does not quantify risk, and therefore fails to differentiate among young people in terms of the level of supervision and intervention that may be required to prevent further sexually harmful behavior and protect the public. It is this emphasis on managing risk and reducing crime that underpins what Ward and Stewart (2003) refer to as a "risk management" model. The Risk–Needs–Responsivity model (RNR) (Andrews and Bonta 2010; Andrews, Bonta, and Hoge 1990; Bonta and Andrews 2007) is an example of a risk management model and is discussed in more detail below. An alternative approach to rehabilitation focuses on enhancing the individual's well-being and capabilities, with risk reduction following as a natural consequence. The GLM represents a good example of what Ward and Stewart (2003) refer to as an "enhancement model." Ward and Stewart (2003) suggested that models such as the RNR and GLM can co-exist, and Wilson and Yates (2009) asserted that rehabilitation may be most effectively achieved through integrating these models.

"Risk" represents the first of the principles contained within the RNR model, and relates to making interventions proportionate to the likelihood of further harmful sexual behaviors. Some research has indicated that intervention with low-risk individuals can be counterproductive (Andrews and Dowden 2006); in view of this, and in the interests of a cost-effective criminal justice system, the model stipulates that services provide minimal interventions to those considered low-risk and intensive interventions to those viewed as high-risk. The second principle in this model is "need" (criminogenic needs), which refers to targeting the dynamic risk factors that have a direct association with the harmful behavior. The GLM also attends to criminogenic needs (Purvis et al. 2011) in that it considers the obstacles to achieving primary needs; however, in the absence of delineating risk factors within the conventional check-box-type format characteristic of actuarial and empirically guided risk assessments, it may be experienced as less pragmatic. Earlier research indicated that using unstructured clinical judgment alone can be little better than chance at predicting recidivism (Andrews 1996). This highlights the importance of using actuarial or research-informed risk assessment instruments alongside clinical judgment in order to achieve more accurate, objective, and structured predictions of risk that are underpinned by an empirical foundation. While there are a number of actuarial instruments available for use with adults who have sexually harmed, there are currently no validated actuarial models for use with young people (Print et al. 2010). To inform its risk assessment, G-map employ the AIM2 initial assessment model (Print et al. 2007), which reflects the risk and need principles of the RNR model. The assessment of the third principle, namely responsivity (i.e., adapting interventions to the individual characteristics of the young person, including learning style, culture, motivation, personality, abilities, and strengths), is embedded within GLM-A in addition to G-map's wider practice, although is not specifically addressed within the AIM2 assessment model.

AIM2 is an empirically guided clinical judgment model for the assessment of recidivism. It was initially intended for use with young males of mainstream educational ability, although more recently has received support regarding its ability to predict sexual recidivism in adolescents with intellectual disabilities (Griffin and Vettor 2012). It comprises 75 assessment items organized into four domains: sexually and non-sexually harmful behaviors, developmental, family, and environmental. It consists of static and dynamic "concerns" and "strengths" factors, and therefore attempts to focus practitioners on the young people's resiliency and protective resources, in addition to their deficits and pathology. Risk and protective factors are believed to interact across time in complex ways (Bremer 2006) that Griffin et al.'s (2008) adaptation of Beech and Ward's (2004) etiology of sexually harmful behavior begins to interpret. Within the context of young people who sexually harm, Griffin and colleagues (2008) made the observation that some of the young people's strengths functioned as protective factors, in that they mitigated the effects of risk by first reducing "trait psychological problems" (e.g., the availability and use of an emotional confidant could reduce the young people's propensity to self-soothe via maladaptive strategies such as harmful sexual behavior), and second directly addressing triggering factors (e.g., the promotion of a range of constructive and pro-social activities could reduce the likelihood that the young person will remain preoccupied with sex). This etiological model illustrates the importance of considering both risk and protective factors in the assessment of adolescents with harmful sexual behavior and thus can be viewed as a useful adjunct to the GLM-A.

It is noteworthy that AIM2 includes factors that do not necessarily have a strong and direct link to sexual recidivism but are nonetheless considered relevant—for example, a history of non-sexual aggression. While their inclusion provides for a more holistic approach to assessment, they are weighted in such a way that those with a stronger evidence base receive a higher score. On the basis of all assessment items the young people receive a score that reflects their concerns and strengths and that places them in a "high," low," or "medium" category. Additionally, a "Level of Supervision" scale is used to inform decisions about the degree of external risk management required. This comprises a subset of factors that were able to differentiate between sexual recidivists and non-recidivists in a small-scale retrospective empirical study (see Griffin et al. 2008). The AIM2 assessment model therefore guides the practitioner's decision making in relation to the young people's "risk" and "need," although to date it has not been subjected to full-scale scientific validation.

Alternative assessments used to assess young people's risk of recidivism include the Juvenile Sex Offender Assessment Protocol-II (JSOAP-II; Prentky et al. 2000; Prentky and Righthand 2003) and the Estimate of Risk of Adolescent Sexual Offender Recidivism, Version 2 (ERASOR 2.0; Worling and Curwen 2001). The JSOAP-II is a checklist comprising 28 factors subsumed within four subscales, two of which correspond to static domains (i.e., sexual drive/preoccupation and impulsive/antisocial behavior) while the other two correspond to dynamic aspects of risk (i.e., intervention and community stability/adjustment), the latter allowing for the additional function of assessing change as a result of intervention. The JSOAP-II is intended for use with males in the age range of 12 to 18 years who have exhibited harmful sexual behavior and who may or may not have received criminal sanctions. The ERASOR 2.0 is another empirically guided assessment tool and has the specific function of assessing short-term recidivism risk in adolescents of the same age range who have previously committed a sexual assault. It incorporates 25 items that similarly reflect both static and dynamic facets of sexual risk. The risk factors are arranged into five categories: (1) sexual interests, attitudes, and behaviors; (2) historical sexual assaults; (3) psychosocial functioning, (4) family/environmental functioning; and (5) treatment. Assessment outcomes of "high," "moderate," or "low" are obtained.

While empirically guided and actuarial risk assessments permit an evaluation of the likelihood that harmful sexual behavior will recur—or as Rich (2009) termed it, the "will he or won't he"—it does not predict:

- Why the behavior occurs;
- When the behavior is most likely to occur;
- What particular behaviors are likely to occur;
- Where the behavior is likely to take place;
- Who is at risk; or
- How the behavior is likely to manifest.

These considerations provide a context to risk and therefore constitute an important part of any comprehensive risk assessment, allowing for the implementation of appropriate interventions and public protection measures. The "why" and "when" referred to above have previously been addressed in discussions pertaining to pathways and the GLM-A. The "what," "where," "who," and "how" help further elucidate the circumstances of any future harmful behaviors, making the risk assessment more prescriptive to the individual. Collectively issues to consider could include the type of sexual behavior (e.g., rape, indecent exposure, or child abuse images); the intrusiveness of the behavior and resultant harm; whether the behavior is likely to take place in a public or private setting; whether the behavior is likely to be directed at a child, peer, or adult, or if the victim is likely to be familial or extra-familial; whether the behavior is likely to be planned or opportunistic; whether it is likely to be precipitated by drugs/alcohol or initiated in the context of a game or dare; and whether victim compliance is gained through aggression, coercion, or manipulation. This list is by no means exhaustive, but highlights some of the issues that assessors may wish to consider in arriving at a more individualized and pragmatic risk formulation.

Having a tailored assessment of risk enables practitioners to make more considered judgments regarding the opportunities young people are given to enhance their well-being and reduce risk. This helps to avoid an approach to risk management that is homogeneous and overly restrictive, thereby allowing practitioners to make safe and reasonable decisions. For example, in the absence of any indicators or evidence of risk toward peers, it might be appropriate and safe for young people to attend a youth club where they can achieve a sense of belonging and practice their interpersonal skills. However, it is important to stress that predicting future behavior is highly complex and susceptible to many pitfalls. The questions for consideration highlighted above help to individualize approaches to risk management and intervention, but should not be unduly relied upon. For example, even where a young person has, to date, exclusively sexually harmed children, it does not exclude the possibility of future cross-over in behavior to include peers or adult victims. In this instance the previous behavior pattern merely serves to guide our thinking, and needs to be supported by cross-reference to as many available sources of information as possible, as well as being subject to continuing review via re-assessment. In a study of adults who sexually harmed, Cann, Friendship, and Gozna (2007) found that one-quarter of their sample demonstrated cross-over behavior with respect to a victim's age, gender, or relationship. The dynamic nature of behavior means that risk is not static and thus the assessment process must be able to reflect this (Craig, Browne, and Stringer 2004). This is particularly true for adolescents: Change and flux are defining features of their developmental stage.

CASE ILLUSTRATIONS

The rationale for the case illustrations in this section is to provide the reader with practical examples of how a Good Lives approach can inform formulation, risk assessment, and intervention planning, and can work effectively alongside other models and assessment tools. The first case illustration is designed to be comprehensive in order to guide the reader through the various steps of the process. In reality it is not always possible to obtain this amount of detail at the time of assessment, reflecting the need for continual assessment. The remaining case illustrations are intended to consolidate understanding of the process without being overly exhaustive.

The selection of case illustrations is intended to reflect the heterogeneity of this population, and thus includes different genders, ethnicities, ages, levels of cognitive functioning, and risk and resilience factors. It also reflects a range of harmful-sexual-behavior-related needs that are illustrative of those presented by G-map's service users.

For the purposes of continuity, the same case illustrations are threaded through chapters 5, 6, 7, and 8, charting the journey of the young people through the therapeutic process.

Case A: Joe

Background

Age: 16 years

Ethnic origin: White British

Cognitive functioning: Intellectual disability

Brief details of harmful sexual behavior: At the age of 15 Joe anally raped his 11-year-old brother in the family home. The behavior occurred on several occasions over a seven-month period. The behavior ended after Joe's brother confided in a friend's parent, who subsequently told Joe's parents. The police were informed and Joe received a two-year supervision order. At the point of investigation Joe was removed from the family home and placed in a local authority children's home.

Brief summary of background information: Joe's mother had been diagnosed with mental health difficulties, i.e., depression. Additionally a volatile and ambivalent relationship between his parents resulted in numerous temporary separations, and Joe spent brief periods living with different members of his extended family. He therefore had multiple house moves in the first 10 years of life that disrupted his primary education.

Joe's parents divorced when he was seven years old. Coinciding with the divorce of his parents he self-harmed for a short period. Joe had some strategies to regulate his emotions, although he was only able to employ them when faced with minor stresses.

Following divorce from her husband, Joe's mother had a number of short-term relationships with male partners. At the age of nine Joe was exposed to domestic violence perpetrated by one of his mother's partners.

At the age of 15 Joe found out that the man he regarded as his father was not his biological father. The upset this evoked was exacerbated by the fact that the man was the biological father of his younger brother.

Joe had an insecure attachment style (ambivalent). He had received inconsistent parenting and there had been poor enforcement of boundaries in the family home. He has an enmeshed relationship with his brother.

Joe had a mild intellectual disability (full-scale intelligence quotient of 68) that was not diagnosed until he was 16 years old. Despite being a boy who is physically attractive, his self-esteem is poor. He has been bullied throughout his time in secondary school and has significant difficulties developing and maintaining peer relationships. At the age of 15, Joe was sexually harmed by a peer who had befriended him.

Joe's behavior was generally pro-social, and he had an internal locus of control. He had positive interests including music, playing computer games, and watching football.

Joe's experience of going through puberty was generally positive and he had received good-quality input on sexual education from the school nurse. His sexual knowledge was developmentally appropriate.

Summary of Good Lives Information: Time of the Harmful Sexual Behavior

This section is based on the information obtained from the GLM-A semi-structured interview (illustrated in table 5.1) pertaining to the time of Joe's harmful sexual behavior.

Having Fun

Joe enjoyed playing computer and board games with his brother and also recalled having fun on family holidays within the United Kingdom. He also took pleasure in playing the keyboard and liked to write his own songs. Joe had few opportunities outside the home environment to have fun. Obstacles to this were that his parents did not fund or promote recreational pursuits and Joe did not have friendships or peer associates with whom to engage in fun activities. However, he reported getting along well with and having similar interests to his brother, and believed this helped him to have fun. The way in which Joe attempted to meet his need for fun appeared to be appropriate; he attached a moderate importance to having fun and did not appear to focus on it to the exclusion of other needs.

Achieving

Joe recalled limited opportunities to achieve, and generally had a poor sense of status. However, he felt competent in a small number of self-care and independence tasks, such as having good personal hygiene, and being able to travel to school without assistance. He also appeared to derive a sense of achievement from his role as an older brother and actively tried to mentor his brother through actions such as accompanying him to school and assisting him in using the home computer. His motivation to achieve and willingness to attempt new things were notable strengths. Obstacles to attaining a sense of achievement included his undiagnosed intellectual disability that resulted in Joe feeling marginalized and inadequate in the mainstream school setting. While status was of low importance to Joe, he had a strong wish to achieve more generally and overall regarded it as having moderate importance. He recalled that the experience of "getting away with" the sexual harm of his brother and "no one catching me out" felt good and indicated that this gave him a sense of success. Joe did not appear to focus on achievement to the detriment of other needs.

Being My Own Person

As outlined above, activities such as traveling independently to school and attending to self-care tasks provided Joe with some degree of independence. Additionally, he purported to be good at saving and budgeting for new computer games and presents for his family. He was also inclined to see himself as being responsible for events that happened in his life, reflective of an internal locus of control. However, he had a poor sense of self and sought constant reassurance from adults, reflecting his low self-esteem and tendency to defer to others when making everyday decisions. Overall Joe attached a low priority to the need of *being my own person,* and there were no indications that he attempted to meet it in inappropriate ways or focused unduly on it.

Having People in My Life

Joe experienced a dearth of peer-aged social interaction and sought to meet his need for belonging exclusively within the family. His parents were frequently preoccupied and often emotionally unavailable to him. He recalled that his mother would occasionally be very interested and involved in his life, but this was typically followed by periods of disinterest coinciding with her depression and/or her prioritization of relationships with partners. Joe identified that his relationship with his brother more consistently provided him with a sense of warmth, comfort, and support. He recalled experiencing an acute sense of rejection upon learning the truth about his non-biological father. It was his view that his "father" began to treat him differently and to favor his brother, increasingly marginalizing him within the family. Joe had a strong desire for love and affirmation from others and frequently tried to please in order to gain acceptance. He recalled having one "best friend" when he was aged 15, however the boy subsequently sexually assaulted him. Joe sometimes sought to meet this need through inappropriate means such as making false allegations and telling untruths in order to gain adult attention and support. He had some, albeit limited, resources to meet his need for belonging such as his sociable nature, illustrated by him instigating conversations with adult strangers in shops and on buses, and the stability and support gained from the sibling relationship. Obstacles to meeting the need included a lack of opportunities to form friendships, compounded by multiple house and education moves in early childhood, his poorly developed interpersonal skills, being bullied over a prolonged period, and his tendency to engage in attention-seeking behaviors. Joe attached high importance to having people in his life and recognized that he focused heavily on this. However, he did not believe that the need was associated with his harmful sexual behavior.

Having a Purpose and Making a Difference

Overall, Joe identified limited means and associated resources through which to meet this need. He was not religious and displayed little interest in the world outside of his immediate surrounds. He recalled having participated in a charity run at school, and viewed himself as generous on the basis that he often bought gifts for his family, consistent with his motivation to please others. In addition Joe generally had a pro-social orientation and liked to follow rules. A significant obstacle to meeting this need was his limited social awareness, which resulted in his more insular outlook. While he attached moderate importance to pleasing others, on the whole this need was of low priority to Joe. There were no indications that he attempted to meet the need of having a purpose and making a difference through inappropriate means, or that he focused unduly on it.

Emotional Health

Resources that enabled Joe to meet the need of *emotional health* included his motivation to approach others to elicit help, his use of music to self-soothe, and the use of computer games as a distraction. In the absence of having a range of confidants, Joe was overly reliant on talking to his brother as a means of regulating his emotions. In response to minor difficulties Joe reported being able to maintain positive emotional health. However, when confronted with more pronounced emotional challenges, such as the divorce of his parents, he resorted to maladaptive and inappropriate strategies, exhibiting low-level self-harming behaviors. Prior to displaying the harmful sexual behavior toward his brother, Joe recounted experiencing a high level of personal distress that he linked to the ongoing bullying by his peers, his own sexual victimization, and ultimately his sense of rejection upon learning about his non-biological father. Joe viewed this need as being of high importance to him, but did not appear to focus excessively on it.

Sexual Health

Joe believed that prior to his sexual victimization he had a positive sexual identity. He experienced puberty as unproblematic and identified himself as heterosexual, with aspirations of having a girlfriend and eventually getting married and having children. His sexual knowledge was developmentally appropriate and he reported masturbating to images in his mother's fashion and homemaking magazines. He also demonstrated a good understanding of the concepts of public and private boundaries and behaviors. An obstacle to Joe meeting this need more fully was the lack of opportunities available to him to form age-appropriate relationships with females. He indicated that in relation to his own sexual victimization he found it difficult to reconcile the fact that the behavior had been instigated by a peer who had provided him with a much-desired sense of closeness and trust. Joe did not wish to discuss the details of this event. However, he recognized that the sexual behavior toward his brother was inappropriate. He did not believe that he focused on sexual health to the detriment of other needs and perceived it as of moderate importance to him.

Physical Health

Joe reported enjoying good physical health, although he acknowledged that he engaged in limited exercise. He described a relatively healthy diet and good personal hygiene. He suggested that historically his sleep pattern had been good but noted recent sleep disturbance linked to his sexual victimization. Joe did not appear to recognize his physical attractiveness as a resource. An obstacle to meeting this need was the lack of encouragement from his parents to be physically active and eat healthily, given that they had a sedentary lifestyle and were poorly inclined to cook nutritious foods. Additionally, Joe had limited motivation to pursue physical health goals, and his neglect of this area was due to the low priority he attached to this need. The limited means Joe used to meet this need appeared to be appropriate.

Conflict Among Needs

The information gathered suggested that Joe's emotional health needs were sometimes in conflict with his belonging needs. For example, when he felt anxious, rejected, or lonely, he sometimes exhibited attention-seeking behaviors, such as telling lies about others or himself, in order to gain affirmation and assurance that he was cared for. However, this behavior inadvertently resulted in others being more dismissive and rejecting of him, thus reinforcing his sense of isolation.

Scope

Joe had limited scope of primary needs, in that he placed emphasis on the need of *having people in my life,* neglecting the needs of *physical health, being my own person,* and *having a purpose and making a difference.* Moreover, his focus on meeting his need for having people in his life through his relationship with his brother meant that when his harmful behavior was discovered this relationship became fractured and he lacked the means to meet his belonging needs, consequently experiencing emotional loneliness.

Problem Formulation

This formulation uses information gathered from a range of sources pertaining to Joe's Good Lives assessment and pathway to harmful sexual behavior.

Joe's poor attachment history, including disrupted parental attachments and experiences of loss and rejection, adversely affected his sense of belonging *(having people in my life).* The instability and inconsistency he experienced from his primary caregivers gave rise to a sense of insecurity that manifested in exaggerated proximity-seeking behaviors and a strong desire for affirmation, consistent with an ambivalent attachment style. Joe's sense of belonging was further eroded by his extensive experiences of bullying and marginalization by peers, in the context of both school and the community. These circumstances were further exacerbated by his poor interpersonal skills combined with a lack of social opportunities. Finding it difficult to achieve a sense of closeness and intimacy with his parents and peers, Joe became reliant on his younger brother to meet his affiliative needs, leading to an enmeshed relationship. This pattern was only interrupted by Joe developing a relationship with a male peer who was new to the local community, and in whom he began investing emotionally. When the peer exploited his relationship with Joe and sexually harmed him, his sense of rejection was amplified. In close succession, Joe learned that the man he regarded as his father was not his biological father, precipitating a sense of abandonment. This was augmented by his belief that he would lose his place within the family, including access to his "father" and the close connection he had forged with his brother. The impact of these events was magnified by the fact that achieving a sense of belonging and connectedness to others was an "overarching need" (i.e., what was most important to Joe and reflective of his personal identity), thus constituting a significant impetus to his behavior. Joe's harmful sexual behavior appeared to be an attempt to re-establish a sense of intimacy with his brother and to meet his belonging needs more generally.

Joe's fragmented sense of belonging and feelings of isolation were detrimental to his emotional state. When combined with the trauma resulting from his own sexual victimization, and the perceived loss of his "father," Joe felt overwhelmed by his emotions. Feeling unable to talk to his brother, formerly his emotional confidant, about his feelings of loss and abandonment pertaining to both the sibling and paternal relationships, and lacking sufficient alternative resources, Joe could not regulate his affect appropriately. His existing tendency to engage in proximity-seeking behaviors and to use maladaptive coping strategies as a means of managing acute distress resulted in him using harmful sexual behavior as a means of self-soothing.

Joe's sexual victimization by a peer, which involved anal rape, took place in the context of what he believed to be a close and trusting relationship. It is hypothesized that the experience distorted Joe's perception of sex and intimacy, leading to these concepts becoming blurred and intertwined. His concrete thinking style, consistent with his intellectual disability, meant that, in the absence of his peer receiving any negative consequences for his harmful behavior, Joe failed to comprehend the seriousness of perpetrating sexual harm. These factors, in combination, gave rise to Joe attempting to meet his needs through harmful sexual behavior.

Therefore, in summary, Joe's harmful sexual behavior provided a means through which he could meet his belonging and emotional health needs. The obstacles and lack of resources associated with these needs formed a direct route to Joe's harmful sexual behavior. Additionally these needs maintained Joe's behavior by virtue of the fact that the sexual contact provided an ongoing outlet for self-soothing as well as facilitating a sense of closeness, both of which were self-reinforcing. Joe also derived a sense of achievement through "getting away" with the sexually harmful behavior toward his brother, which in the context of his poor sense of achievement more generally represented a significant motivating factor for the continuation of his harmful sexual behavior.

Summary of Good Lives Information: Current Circumstances

This section provides a brief overview, drawn from the GLM-A semi-structured interview (illustrated in table 5.1), regarding Joe's circumstances at the time of assessment, in addition to other sources of information including caregiver observations.

Having Fun

This information was consistent with what Joe reported was true at the time of the harmful sexual behavior. Part of the reason Joe was not engaging in additional activities linked to the need of *having fun* was that residential staff were concerned about introducing new activities prior to a specialist risk assessment being undertaken.

Achieving

By the time of the assessment Joe's special learning needs were recognized. He was in receipt of educational input in his residential placement that was geared toward providing him with a range of opportunities in which he could achieve. Joe was subject to greater levels of encouragement from residential staff to engage in and achieve independence and to complete self-care tasks. There was little variation regarding scope, prioritization, and conflict.

Being My Own Person

While Joe had greater opportunities and encouragement to undertake self-care and independence tasks, compared with the time of his harmful sexual behavior, he was subject to more restrictions regarding his freedoms in the community. Otherwise, Joe's meeting of this need was consistent with the time of the harmful sexual behavior, in respect to his internal locus of control, deferment to others for decision making, scope, conflict, and prioritization.

Having People in My Life

Up to and including the assessment period, Joe had few visits from his parents, linked to travel costs and difficulties arranging child care for his brother. He was permitted weekly telephone contact with his parents but this had been inconsistent, with parents sometimes omitting to call. Joe was not allowed contact with his brother or other family members at that time. The limited family contact was currently a source of great distress for Joe and he had indicated that he often felt rejected by his family and "like a stranger." He reported a particular sense of loss concerning the absence of contact with his sibling, whom he viewed as "getting on in his life without me." Residential staff encouraged Joe to develop interaction with his peers in-house, but being unable to join in with community-based activities and trips in the absence of a risk assessment meant that he sometimes felt excluded and "left out." Since his admission to the unit Joe had been subject to some low-level bullying by peers. He reported it to staff who intervened, with some resultant improvement. He also befriended a 15-year-old male resident, but the indications were that this was of a superficial nature and not necessarily reciprocal. Joe wanted more friends and believed that having a girlfriend might help him to "fit in." He continued to attach high importance to the need of *having people in my life* and to focus disproportionately on this.

Having a Purpose and Making a Difference

This information was consistent with what Joe reported was true at the time of the harmful sexual behavior.

Emotional Health

Joe continued to exhibit difficulties with emotional regulation and to be reliant on a restricted range of self-soothe strategies. He gradually adjusted to his new environment and developed a positive relationship with his male caseworker, whom he began to use as an emotional confidant. However, he developed some reliance on this staff member to the extent that he only felt emotionally safe when he was on duty. Joe periodically exhibited high levels of anxiety and distress, particularly in advance of family contact, and in response to triggers such as low-level bullying by peers. He self-harmed by making superficial scratches on his arm during his first week in residence, but this did not recur. Joe continued to attach a high level of importance to the need of *emotional health,* and was of the view that he had been more focused on this need since his admission to residential care.

Sexual Health

This information was consistent with what Joe reported was true at the time of the harmful sexual behavior.

Physical Health

Joe responded positively to having more opportunities and encouragement to meet the need of *physical health* in the residential setting, including participating in an in-house healthy eating initiative and using the unit's gym. At the time of assessment, he had limited opportunities to participate in contact sports or off-site activities due to staff awaiting the completion of a risk assessment. He reported a disturbed sleep pattern since his admission, which he attributed to the very limited opportunities for family contact and subsequent "worries about my family." Overall Joe indicated that at the time of assessment he attached moderate importance to the need of *physical health.*

Summary of Other Assessment Outcomes

Table 5.2 below provides an overview of the assessment outcomes for Joe.

Table 5.2 An overview of assessment outcomes for Case A—Joe

GOOD LIVES NEEDS LINKED TO HARMFUL SEXUAL BEHAVIOR	PSYCHOMETRIC ASSESSMENT	OUTCOMES FROM RISK ASSESSMENT TOOL
• Emotional health • Having people in my life • Achieving*	• Low levels of resilience • Good sexual knowledge • Internal locus of control • Poor level of self-esteem • High levels of emotional reactivity • High degree of emotional loneliness • Cognitive distortions • Problems in general family functioning	• Medium concern/low strength • Medium level of supervision required • Higher risk to male children • No known risk to strangers, peers, or adults • Sexually harmful behavior took place in a private place • Risk of serious sexually harmful behaviors

*Exclusively a maintenance role

Overall Clinical Formulation and Recommendations

This section provides a synopsis of the overall clinical formulation and recommendations for Joe as they appeared in his therapeutic assessment report.

Joe's social and emotional development, including his attachment relationships, have been adversely affected by factors such as domestic violence, inconsistent parenting, loss and rejection, limited social opportunities, bullying, and sexual victimization. Having an intellectual disability is likely to have exacerbated these difficulties, and having been un-diagnosed until he was 16 years of age may have increased his vulnerability in relation to the impact of these adversities. This combination of factors has resulted in Joe lacking sufficient internal and external resources to meet some of his primary needs, as well as encountering internal and external obstacles. Our assessment is that Joe used harmful sexual behavior as a means of meeting his needs for *emotional health* and *having people in his life.* Alongside the need of *achieving,* these needs were also integral to the maintenance of Joe's harmful sexual behavior.

The outcomes of the risk assessment employed indicated that Joe has a medium level of concerns and a low level of strengths. A requirement for a medium level of supervision is indicated to prevent further harmful behavior. Key concerns that have been elucidated through the risk assessment and psychometric testing include: that he has sexually harmed males; that this behavior included penetration; that he has difficulties emotionally regulating; and that he holds a number of harm-related cognitive distortions—for example, he was of the view that while his behavior was wrong it did not hurt his brother. Joe's strengths were limited but included his developmentally appropriate sexual knowledge and some positive interests, such as music. It is important to stipulate that the risk assessment has been completed on the basis that Joe is resident within a fully-supervised residential setting, and therefore the assessed level of concern would likely increase, and/or strengths decrease, if Joe were to return to the care of his parents in advance of the necessary interventions. While it is the assessor's view that Joe does not require one-to-one supervision at all times, he currently requires full supervision when in high-risk situations, which, on the basis of existing assessment information, would be when he is in the company of others more vulnerable than himself. This could include children or more vulnerable peers who would most likely be known to him. Joe is more likely to engage in harmful sexual behavior when he is feeling emotionally lonely, distressed, or rejected, and the behavior could be at the most serious and intrusive end of the spectrum.

The assessment that Joe continues to have difficulties regulating his emotions and meeting his belonging needs highlights the requirement for appropriate supervision and intervention to be implemented to prevent further harmful behaviors. However, it is positive that Joe presently has increased access to opportunities through which he can appropriately gain a sense of achievement. It is probable that as he begins to respond to a program of intervention and is able to demonstrate an ability to positively manage his behavior, his requirement for external risk management will reduce. Any reductions in supervision levels should be carefully risk-assessed and informed by progress he makes on factors related to his harmful sexual behavior.

Based on our assessment to date, our provisional recommendations include that Joe should undertake a program of therapeutic work to address his harmful sexual behavior. The program should incorporate the following elements, although the list is by no means exhaustive:

- Emotional regulation and distress tolerance work in order to support Joe in developing a sense of emotional safety, and coping with distress

- Attachment; working with Joe's care environment to help him develop a more functional style of relating to others, including the use of attunement exercises

- Relationships; including supporting Joe to develop appropriate peer interaction skills

- Victim-centered work to enable Joe to process his own victimization experience and to keep safe in the future

- Support Joe to develop an understanding of his pathway into harmful sexual behavior, develop self-management skills, and address his cognitive distortions

- Self-identity and self-compassion work to enhance Joe's self-esteem

- Problem solving, particularly in a social context

- Family work will represent an important element of any therapeutic program of work. Information obtained from the assessment highlights that it would be particularly important to look at family functioning difficulties that have affected Joe and represented obstacles to him meeting his need to belong and achieve closeness in positive and adaptive ways.

In addition to a specific program of therapeutic work, the following interventions have been provisionally assessed as foundational to Joe's safe management and continuing social and emotional development:

- Supervision levels informed by risk assessment

- Consistent and predictable structure, boundaries, and routine so that Joe can experience a sense of safety within his environment

- Availability of an appropriate emotional confidant within Joe's immediate environment to provide emotional support as well as modeling adaptive attachment behaviors

- Access to activities that promote emotional well-being

- Access to age-appropriate social activities that facilitate peer interaction

- Restructuring of family contact so that Joe has continuing opportunities to see his parents while his expectations of visits/calls are managed and disappointment is minimized

- Potential to explore the viability of restorative justice with Joe and his sibling, taking into account his brother's wishes and feelings

It is our opinion that to effectively reduce the risk of Joe's displaying further harmful sexual behaviors he requires a placement that will commit to a supervision program to manage risk and ensure that appropriate conditions are in place to support therapeutic intervention, as outlined above. Consideration should be given to the potential conflicts between Joe's needs for *having people in his life* and *emotional health*. For example, his poor capacity to emotionally self-regulate could result in behaviors that increase his vulnerability to peer rejection, and vice versa. These circumstances could be ameliorated through steps such as assessing Joe's mood states prior to his participation in peer activities and the appropriate provision of external support until he has developed the necessary internal capacities to address this conflict. In view of Joe's learning needs it would be important that key messages from the work are continually reinforced within his care environment in order that learning can be translated into his day-to-day life. It is our view that Joe's current placement will be able to meet his needs and supervision requirements. Should an alternative placement be sourced for Joe, it is important to note that transition has the potential to act as a trigger, in that it could result in increased isolation, and more problematic mood states, linked with his previous display of harmful sexual behavior and self-harm.

Case B: Wayne

Background

Age: 14 years

Ethnic origin: White British

Cognitive functioning: High average

Brief details of harmful sexual behavior: Wayne began accessing pornographic websites both at school and at home undetected. He then began to masturbating by a window overlooking a street, and eventually began exposing himself to females in his local park The fourth time he exposed himself he was recognized and caught by poilice. While he received no criminal sanction he was referred for assessment while remaining at home.

Brief summary of background information: Wayne lived with his parents and was an only child. His father was a teacher and his mother worked part-time as a cleaner in the same school. Both parents provided Wayne with a stable, secure, and nurturing home environment and invested in his development. Wayne's parents had a tendency to dote on him, as their only child, and to respond to his needs and demands with immediacy. Wayne exhibited stubbornness and an egocentric outlook that was more pronounced than what might have been expected for his developmental stage. Moreover, he had a low tolerance for boredom and in such circumstances would sometimes push boundaries or attempt to annoy others.

Wayne had experienced difficulties in school due to his tendency toward disruptive and challenging behavior. Because he was of above-average intelligence, the mainstream curriculum sometimes failed to stimulate and engage him. At these times he would play pranks on his peers and teachers, from which he derived a sense of thrill and excitement. Outside of school, when he joined his friends at the local shops, Wayne began to steal small items and became increasingly daring over time. He ignored the disapproval of his friends, asserting that he enjoyed the "buzz" he got from such risk-taking behavior.

Coinciding with the onset of puberty, Wayne was exposed to pornographic images that were shared among his peer group in school. While his peers tended to respond to the material with humor, Wayne became fascinated by it and sought to access it independently including using both school and home computers to visit pornographic websites, which he would do without detection. Over time he increasingly engaged in this activity and broadened his search to include more atypical sites specializing in various adult paraphilias. During this period, while masturbating in his bedroom, Wayne decided to stand at his window, which overlooked the street. He experienced a high level of arousal as a result of the possibility of being observed and repeated the behavior. Wayne escalated this behavior by exposing his penis to adult and peer-aged females while walking through his local park. While he evaded being identified on the first three occasions, the police apprehended him after he exposed himself to a female who recognized him. Wayne did not receive any criminal sanction but was referred for assessment regarding his harmful sexual behavior while continuing to reside at home.

Good Lives Assessment and Formulation

This section details a Good Lives formulation for Wayne based on brief interviews and the available background information.

Wayne's primary needs appeared to be *having fun, sexual health,* and *emotional health.* During his early years, while able to regulate emotions such as anger, sadness, and anxiety, he failed to develop the capacity to tolerate boredom, being highly reliant on his parents to provide stimulation. With increasing age he sought to regulate boredom via activities that offered a sense of thrill and excitement, consistent with the need of *having fun.* This heightened sense of excitement became so compulsive for Wayne that he began to seek it for its intrinsic value and therefore at times when he did not necessarily feel bored. He increasingly resorted to inappropriate and even illegal behaviors such as shoplifting to gain a sense thrill and excitement. With the onset of puberty Wayne introduced sexual behaviors as a means of meeting his need for thrill and excitement. These behaviors additionally enabled him to obtain sexual gratification, consistent with the need for *sexual health.* As a result of his low threshold for boredom, Wayne escalated his behavior (e.g., moving from publicly masturbating in his bedroom to exposing himself in a park).

Wayne's emphasis on the need of *having fun* meant that he often neglected his need to achieve; it also placed him on the periphery of his peer relationships, in that they did not approve of his anti-social behavior. Additionally, he ignored the need of *having a purpose and making a difference.* Furthermore his tendency to annoy others when he was bored sometimes led to his rejection and therefore resulted in a conflict between the needs of *emotional health* and *having people in his life.*

At the time of assessment Wayne's situation was similar to the time of his sexually harmful behaviors, with the exception that he did not go out alone during evenings or weekends.

Overall Clinical Formulation and Recommendations

This section provides a synopsis of the overall clinical formulation and recommendations for Wayne. The intervention plan will be more fully elucidated in chapter 6 within his Good Lives plan.

A risk assessment indicated that without intervention, there was a high risk of Wayne's harmful sexual behavior recurring. However, the likelihood of harm as a consequence of his sexual behavior was assessed as low to medium. Wayne and his family were assessed as having high strengths that could be used to help manage and reduce risk. These included Wayne's intelligence, high self-esteem, positive future goals, skills and talents, and his parents' willingness to support therapeutic interventions, supervise Wayne in the community, and facilitate positive opportunities for Wayne to meet his needs through alternative prosocial means. Risk was assessed as being most salient at times when Wayne experienced boredom in that he was likely to escalate his harmful behaviors to attain feelings of excitement. However, boredom was not a necessary condition for the behavior to occur since he could also act inappropriately in the context of seeking fun in and of itself. Sexual preoccupation was also identified as a factor likely to precipitate and increase Wayne's risk. To prevent further harmful sexual behaviors from occurring and until a more comprehensive assessment was undertaken, it was indicated that Wayne required full supervision when in the wider community, with the exception of exclusively male activities/groups.

The provisional recommendations included that Wayne undertake a time-limited program of therapeutic work to address his harmful sexual behavior, to include work focused on the needs for thrill and excitement, sexual satisfaction, and emotional regulation in relation to boredom. It was recommended that family work be undertaken alongside Wayne's individual program of work, to include helping Wayne's parents to understand issues of risk and expectations regarding their supervision of him.

Case C: Leanne

Background

Age: 12 years

Ethnic origin: Mixed race (white British/black Caribbean)

Cognitive functioning: Average

Brief details of harmful sexual behavior: At 10 years old Leanne began to sexually harm her younger brothers. The harm involved touching her brothers' genitals and coercing them into touching and licking her vagina. Leanne also penetrated her younger brother's anus using a small toy. When Leanne felt left out on family holiday she sexually harmed a four-year-old boy who was a stranger. The boys' parents prompted the investigation that revealed all of Leanne's harmful behavior and Leanne was placed into foster care during the assessment period.

Brief summary of background information: Leanne was born into a chaotic home environment in which her mother, a regular heroin user, was engaged in a fractious and volatile relationship with her father. Leanne's father was a jealous and controlling man, who was prone to violent outbursts that were often directed at Leanne's mother. Their relationship ended before Leanne was one year old, and her father's whereabouts have since been unknown. Leanne is of dual heritage, with a white British mother and Jamaican father, but in the absence of her father or contact with any member of his extended family, she has no understanding of her ethnicity or cultural heritage.

As a result of her mother's drug misuse, Leanne sporadically spent periods of her early childhood in the care of her maternal aunt, and resultingly has a poor attachment to her mother. This is compounded by her mother's overt hostility toward her as a consequence of Leanne's resemblance to her birth father. For the duration of residing with her aunt, Leanne was subject to sexual assault by her aunt's partner (presently her ex-partner). Despite her displaying sexualized behavior in the nursery, including exposing her genitals to other children and touching their private parts, her victimization went undetected. Leanne returned to live permanently with her mother when she was five, following her mother's drug rehabilitation. However, she enjoyed only a limited period of individual attention prior to the arrival of her brother, now aged seven. At this time Leanne's mother was in a stable cohabiting relationship, and she had a second son, who is now aged six, to this man. The male siblings, by virtue of being a similar age, regularly played together and had a positive relationship. Leanne felt she was on the periphery of the family and was resentful of her siblings' strong bond to each other and to their father. When she had asked her mother for information about her biological father she had consistently been met with an angry response. While the family home was somewhat more stable than it was during Leanne's early years, her mother's enmeshment with her new partner meant that she was often neglectful of the children's emotional needs, and supervision was poor. There was an expectation placed on Leanne, by her parents, that as the eldest she should adopt a caretaking role in relation to her brothers. As Leanne got older she resented the role, since it prevented her from spending time with her friends. She also felt that she was scapegoated by her parents and saw her brothers as both favored and wanted in comparison with her.

Leanne sometimes physically chastised her brothers, and at times when she felt angry and aggrieved would hit them. At the age of 10 years Leanne began to use sexually harmful behavior as a means of expressing her anger and resentment toward her brothers; this continued for a period of two years. She recognized that the behavior enabled her to hurt her siblings in a more covert way than physically harming them and was therefore less likely to result in her being caught and punished. The harm involved touching her brothers' genitals and coercing them into touching and licking her vagina. Leanne also penetrated her younger brother's anus using a small toy. She used threats of physical harm to inhibit her brothers from making disclosures.

More recently, during the course of a family holiday, Leanne sexually harmed a seven-year-old male who was a stranger. The abuse occurred in the context of Leanne feeling aggrieved when her parents took her two siblings to a children's fun park, leaving her alone in the caravan. When walking around the campsite Leanne saw a four-year-old boy playing alone outside a caravan. She led the boy by the hand into nearby public toilets, where she touched his genitals and forced him to touch her. The boys' parents raised the alarm, prompting an investigation. As a consequence, the extent of Leanne's sexual behavior emerged. She was moved to a temporary foster care placement while assessments were undertaken.

Good Lives Assessment and Formulation

Leanne's primary needs appeared to be *emotional health* and *having people in her life*. The obstacles and lack of resources associated with these needs constituted a direct route to Leanne's sexually harmful behaviors. She felt isolated and dismissed within her nuclear family and had limited alternative opportunities to meet her belonging needs. Her emerging sense of difference, linked to confusion about her ethnicity, not knowing her birth father, and the age disparity between her and her siblings gave rise to feelings of alienation and loneliness. These feelings combined with her perception that she was scapegoated by her parents and the responsibilities she was given for the care of her siblings, the latter of which restricted her leisure time and peer relationships, created feelings of anger and resentment. Powerless to alter her position, achieve acceptance, or adaptively regulate her emotions, Leanne firstly used physical aggression, and later harmful sexual acts to meet needs of *emotional health* and *having people in her life*.

At the time of assessment, Leanne had little opportunity within her placement to forge a relationship with her temporary caregivers, and her sense of rejection and resentment had been augmented as a consequence of her brothers' disclosure and her prompt removal from the family home. In this respect she had limited ability or opportunities to meet needs of *emotional health* or *belonging*. Concurrently, Leanne's parents were very rejecting of her and refusing contact, although she continued to have some contact with her maternal aunt. Leanne had restricted scope in that her focus on emotional health was disproportionate to her other needs. Her needs for *emotional health* and *having people in her life* were in conflict in that she was rejecting of her new caregivers as a result of her lack of emotional safety.

Overall Clinical Formulation and Recommendations

Leanne's Good Lives plan is more fully elucidated in chapter 6.

Leanne was assessed as being at high risk of sexual recidivism. Her sexual behavior history indicated that she posed a risk to young males and that she could be sexually coercive and aggressive. Feelings of anger and grievance appeared to be significant triggers to her harmful behavior. Leanne had the potential to perpetrate a serious degree of harm, with her history indicating a range of sexual behaviors, including penetration, as well as the abduction of a child.

Additionally, it was assessed that Leanne had low strengths and although she had some independence skills and a keen interest in art, she had no real sense of future or self-belief. Moreover, she lacked social support from both adults and peers, and had a poor ability to communicate her needs.

The provisional recommendations included that Leanne undertake a program of therapeutic work to address her harmful sexual behavior. This would incorporate work focused on emotional regulation and relationships. Furthermore, it was proposed that Leanne needed to reside in a specialist foster care placement, where her caregivers received therapeutic consultation and support from the practitioners working with her.

REFERENCES

Andrews, D. A. 1996. Recidivism is predictable and can be influenced: An update. *Forum on Corrections Research* 8(3):42–44.

Andrews, D. A., and J. Bonta. 2010. *The psychology of criminal conduct*, 5th ed. New Providence, NJ: Lexis Matthew Bender.

Andrews, D. A., J. Bonta, and R. D. Hoge. 1990. Classification for effective rehabilitation: Rediscovering psychology. *Criminal Justice and Behaviour* 17(1):19–52.

Andrews, D. A., and C. Dowden. 2006. Risk principle of case classification in correctional treatment. *International Journal of Offender Therapy and Comparative Criminology* 50(1):88–100.

Beckett, R. 1994. Assessment of sex offenders. In T. Morrison, M. Erooga, and R. Beckett (eds.), *Sexual offending against children*, 55–79. London: Routledge.

Beech, A. R., and T. Ward, 2004. The integration of etiology and risk in sex offenders: A theoretical model. *Aggression and Violent Behavior* 10:31–63.

Bickley, J. A. 2008. Outline of comprehensive assessment and intervention with young people who sexually abuse. Unpublished personal communication, October 5, 2012.

Bickley, J. A. 2012. Comprehensive assessment framework for young people who sexually abuse. Unpublished personal communication, October 5, 2012.

Bonta, J., and D. A. Andrews. 2007. *Risk–Need–Responsivity model for offender assessment and treatment.* User Report No. 2007-06. Ottawa, Ontario: Public Safety Canada.

Bourgon, G., K. E. Morton-Bourgon, and G. Madrigrano. 2005. Multisite investigation of treatment for sexually abusive juveniles. In B. K. Schwartz (ed.), *The sex offender: Issues in assessment, treatment, and supervision of adult and juvenile populations,* vol. 5, 15-1 to 15-17. Kingston, NJ: Civic Research Institute.

Bremer, J. 2006. Building resilience: An ally in assessment and treatment. In D. Prescott (ed.), *Risk assessment of youth who have sexually abused: Theory, controversy and strategies.* Oklahoma City: Wood 'N' Barnes Publishing.

Calder, M. 2001. *Juveniles and children who sexually abuse: Frameworks for assessment,* 2nd ed. Dorset, UK: Russell House Publishing.

Cann, J., C. Friendship, and L. Gozna. 2007. Assessing crossover in a sample of sexual offenders with multiple victims. *Legal and Criminological Psychology* 12(1):149–163.

Clare, I. C. H. 1993. Issues in the assessment and treatment of male sex offenders with mild learning disabilities. *Sexual and Marital Therapy* 8:167–80.

Clare, I. C., and G. H. Gudjonsson. 1993. Interrogative suggestibility, confabulation, and acquiescence in people with mild learning disabilities: Implications for reliability during police interrogation. *British Journal of Clinical Psychology* 32(3):295–301.

Cockburn, T. 2000. Case studying organisations: The use of quantitative approaches. In B. Humphries (ed.), *Research in social care and social work,* 59–68. London: Jessica Kingsley Publishers.

Craig, L. A., K. D. Browne, and I. Stringer. 2004. Comparing sex offender risk assessment measures on a UK sample. *International Journal of Offender Therapy and Comparative Criminology* 48(1):7–27.

Eells, T. D., and K. G. Lombart. 2011. Theoretical and evidence-based approaches to case formulation, in forensic case formulation. In P. Sturmey and M. McMurran (eds.), *Forensic case formulation,* 1–32. Chichester, UK: John Wiley and Sons.

Finkelhor, D. 1984. *Child sexual abuse: New theory and research.* New York: Free Press.

Flitcroft, A., I. James, M. Freeston, and A. Wood-Mitchell. 2007. Determining what is good in a good formulation. *Behavioural and Cognitive Psychotherapy* 35(3):352–64.

Gilby, R., L. Wolf, and B. Goldberg. 1989. Mentally retarded adolescent sex offenders: A survey and pilot study. *Canadian Journal of Psychiatry* 34(6):542–48.

Grant, H. 2006. Assessment issues in relation to young people who have sexually abusive behaviour. In M. Erooga and H. Masson (eds.), *Children and young people who sexually abuse others: Current developments and practice responses,* 2nd ed., 67–76. New York: Routledge.

Griffin, H. L., A. R. Beech, B. Print, H. Bradshaw, and J. Quayle. 2008. The development and initial testing of the AIM2 framework to assess risk and strengths in young people who sexually offend. *Journal of Sexual Aggression* 14(3):211–25.

Griffin, H. L., and L. Harkin. 2012. *Youth offending: Resilience and protective factors.* Birmingham, UK: University of Birmingham.

Griffin, H. L., and S. A. Price. 2009. *Evaluation of the Good Lives approach: Additional considerations for scoring.* Sale, UK: G-map Services.

Griffin, H. L., and S. Vettor. 2012. Predicting sexual re-offending in a UK sample of learning disabled adolescents. *Journal of Sexual Aggression* 18:64–80.

Haaven, J. L., R. Little, and D. Petre-Miller. 1990. *Treating intellectually disabled sex offenders: A model residential program.* Orwell, VT: Safer Society.

Hackett, S. 2006. Towards a resilience-based intervention model for young people with harmful sexual behaviours. In M. Erooga and H. Masson (eds.), *Children and young people who sexually abuse others: Current developments and practical responses*, 2nd ed., 103–14. London: Routledge.

Hammond, S. 2006. Using psychometric tests. In G. M. Breakwell, S. Hammond, C. Fife–Schaw, and J. A. Smith (eds.), *Research methods in psychology*, 3rd ed., 182–209. London: Sage Publications.

Hayes, D., and J. Devaney 2004. Accessing social work case files for research purposes: Some issues and problems. *Qualitative Social Work* 3:313–33.

Keeling, J. A., A. R. Beech, and J. L. Rose. 2007. Assessment of intellectually disabled sexual offenders: The current position. *Journal of Aggression and Violent Behavior* 12(2):229–41.

Laws, D. R., and T. Ward. 2011. *Desistance and sexual offending: Alternatives to throwing away the keys*. New York: Guilford Press.

Mann, R., S. Webster, C. Schofield, and W. Mashall. 2004. Approach versus avoidance goals in relapse prevention with sexual offenders. *Sexual Abuse: A Journal of Research and Treatment* 16:65–76.

Medoff, D. 2003. The scientific basis of psychological testing: Considerations following Daubert, Kumho, and Joiner. *Family Court Review* 41(2):199–213.

Miner, M. H. 2002. Factors associated with recidivism in juveniles: An analysis of serious juvenile sex offenders. *Journal of Research in Crime and Delinquency* 39:421–36.

O'Callaghan, D. 2004. Adolescents with intellectual disabilities who sexually harm: Intervention design and implementation. In G. O'Reilly, W. L. Marshall, A. Carr, and R. C. Beckett (eds.), *The handbook of clinical intervention with young people who sexualy abuse*, 345–68. Hove, East Sussex, UK: Brunner-Routledge.

Paulhus, D. L. 1999. *Paulhus Deception Scales*. New York: Multi-Health Systems.

Prentky, R., B. Harris, K. Frizzell, and S. Righthand. 2000. An actuarial procedure for assessing risk in juvenile sex offenders. *Sexual Abuse: A Journal of Research and Treatment* 12:71–93.

Prentky, R., and S. Righthand 2003. *The Juvenile Sex Offender Protocol-II (J-SOAP-II)*. Retrieved from http://www.csom.org/pubs/JSOAP.pdf.

Print, B., H. Bradshaw, J. Bickley, and M. Erooga. 2010. Assessing the needs and risk of re-offending of young people who sexually abuse. In J. Horwath (ed.), *The child's world: The comprehensive guide to assessing children in need*, 2nd ed., 260–79. London: Jessica Kingsley Publishers.

Print, B., H. Griffin, A. R. Beech, J. Quayle, H. Bradshaw, J. Henniker, and T. Morrison. 2007. *AIM2: An initial assessment model for young people who display sexually harmful behaviour*. Manchester, UK: AIM Project.

Purvis, M. 2010. *Seeking a good life: Human goods and sexual offending*. Germany: Lambert Academic Press. Published doctoral dissertation.

Purvis, M., T. Ward, and G. M. Willis. 2011. The Good Lives model in practice: Offence pathways and case management. *European Journal of Probation* 3(2):4–28.

Rasmussen, L. A. 2004. Assessing sexually abusive youth. In R. Geffner, K. Crumpton Franey, T. Geffner Arnold, and R. Faconer (eds.), *Identifying and treating youth who sexually offend: Current approaches, techniques and research*, 57–82. New York: Haworth Maltreatment and Trauma Press.

Rich, P. 2003. *Understanding juvenile sexual offenders: Assessment, treatment, and rehabilitation.* New York: John Wiley and Sons.

Rich, P. 2009. *Juvenile Sexual Offenders: A Comprehensive Guide to Risk Evaluation.* Hoboken, NJ: John Wiley and Sons.

Rich, P. 2011. *Understanding, assessing, and rehabilitating juvenile sexual offenders,* 2nd ed. Hoboken, NJ: John Wiley and Sons.

Seto, M. C., M. L. Lalumière, and R. Blanchard. 2000. The discriminative validity of a phallometric test for pedophilic interests among adolescent sex offenders against children. *Psychological Assessment* 12:319–27.

Seto, M. C., W. D. Murphy, J. Page, and L. Ennis. 2003. Detecting anomalous sexual interests among juvenile sex offenders. *Annals of the New York Academemy of Sciences* 989:118–30.

Sturmey, P. 2010. Case formulation in forensic psychology. In M. Daffern, L. Jones, and J. Shine (eds.), *Offence paralleling behaviour: A case formulation approach to offender assessment and intervention,* 25–51. Chichester, UK: John Wiley and Sons.

Taylor, S. E. 1998. The social being in social psychology. In D. T. Gilbert, S. T. Fiske, and G. Lindzey (eds.), *The handbook of social psychology, vol. 1,* 4th ed., 56–96. Boston: McGraw-Hill.

Vizard, E. 2002. The assessment of young sexual abusers. In M. C. Calder (ed.), *Young people who sexually abuse: Building the evidence base for your practice,* 176–95. Lyme Regis, UK: Russell House Publishing.

Ward, T. 2003. The explanation, assessment, and treatment of child sexual abuse. *International Journal of Forensic Psychology* 1(1):10–25.

Ward, T., and C. A. Stewart. 2003. Criminogenic needs and human needs: A theoretical model. *Psychology, Crime, and Law* 9:125–43.

Will, D. 1999. Assessment issues. In M. Erooga and H. Masson (eds.), *Children and young people who sexually abuse others: Challenges and responses,* 86–103. London: Routledge.

Willis, G. W., P. M. Yates, T. A. Gannon, and T. Ward. 2013. How to integrate the Good Lives model into treatment programs for sexual offending: An introduction and overview. *Sexual Abuse: A Journal of Research and Treatment* 25(2):123–42.

Wilson, R. J., and P. M. Yates. 2009. Effective interventions and the Good Lives model. *Aggression and Violent Behavior* 14(3):157–61.

Worling, J. R. 2012. The assessment and treatment of deviant sexual arousal with adolescents who have offended sexually. *Journal of Sexual Aggression* 18(1):36–63.

Worling, J. R., and T. Curwen. 2001. Estimate of Risk of Adolescent Sexual Offense Recidivism (the ERASOR, Version 2.0). In M. Calder (ed.), *Juveniles and children who sexually abuse: Frameworks for assessment,* 372–97. Lyme Regis, UK: Russell House Publishing.

Yates, P. M., D. A. Kingston, and T. Ward. 2009. *The Self-Regulation model of the offence and re-offence process, vol. 3: A guide to assessment and treatment planning using the integrated Good Lives/Self-Regulation model of sexual offending.* Victoria, BC: Pacific Psychological Assessment Corporation.

CHAPTER 6

Good Lives Plans

LAURA WYLIE AND HELEN GRIFFIN

An important element of the Good Lives model is the use of Good Lives plans (GLP) as a "blueprint that includes those goals and activities that are important in achieving the type of life the individual would like to attain and reflect the kind of person they wish to become" (Langlands, Ward, and Gilchrist 2009, 119). At G-map GLPs are additionally used as a working tool to reduce risk and are individualized to the young person. For example, different young people will prioritize different needs; they may have attempted to meet different needs through their harmful sexual behavior; they will have diverse interests, strengths, resources, and aspirations; and they may face dissimilar obstacles and difficulties. Yates, Prescott, and Ward (2010, 248) assert that it is "essential that the plan be personal to each client."

GOOD LIVES TEAM

The GLM specifies that it is important for individuals to meet a range of primary needs; otherwise it may result in "stunted lives, psychological problems and social maladjustment" (Ward and Stewart 2003a, 33). Developing a young person's resources to meet a range of needs is consistent with a holistic approach and ensures that the young person has capacity and opportunity to obtain a "good life." Thus, in an ideal world, practitioners working with young people with harmful sexual behavior would promote the enhancement of needs that are both directly related to and independent of their harmful sexual behavior. In multi-agency teams, this might be achieved by a range of professionals drawing on their diverse experience and expertise to develop the young person's internal competency, augmented by external support structures, in more comprehensively meeting Good Lives needs. Many individuals and groups could have a role in this process, including family; positive peer networks; youth workers; and mental health, social care, education, and youth justice professionals. For example, a mental health worker may have a pivotal role in supporting the young person's *emotional health* needs, while the social care professional could work alongside the family to help them respond to health needs as well as promoting a positive sense of belonging. The young person's sense of relatedness could be further enhanced via a positive peer network, which could bolster his or her self-identity. The needs for achievement and fun could be fostered within education, as well as through activities promoted within a youth work setting. Youth justice professionals, through reparation and/or restorative justice processes, could support the young person in attaining a sense of purpose and in making a social contribution. Collectively such efforts to support the individual's ability to meet a broader range of needs are likely to positively affect self-esteem, as well as his or her investment in both micro and macro systems.

In order to construct the GLP, a meeting takes place following the completion of assessment, involving the young person, his or her caregivers, therapeutic staff, and other relevant individuals who are likely to be directly involved in working with the young person during the intervention process. This group is termed the young person's Good Lives team, and while the individuals that constitute the team may change over time, according to who is required to help, the purpose of the group is to support the young person to successfully meet identified needs in positive, socially appropriate ways. The involvement of a team means that there is a network of people who are knowledgeable of the change process and can actively support the work undertaken, and the inclusion of the young person and his or her family as members of the team promotes their engagement and participation in the process.

While it is desirable that the young people are able to meet a range of needs effectively, not just those relevant to their harmful sexual behavior, this will evidently have resource implications for a single agency. For example, despite being a specialist organization, G-map does not always have the resources to directly address all of a young person's primary needs, but the involvement of a multi-disciplinary team means that other needs can be promoted and addressed by other members of the Good Lives team, which could include family, caregivers, social workers, health workers, and youth justice workers. To ensure that non-criminogenic needs remain on the agenda for the young person, a section at the end of the GLP records the needs not directly linked to the harmful sexual behavior the young person and his or her network should work on or seek to enhance. This is consistent with Willis and colleagues' (2013) recommendation to include non-criminogenic needs in intervention plans in order to highlight to service users how different aspects of rehabilitation can fit together and encourage others to help them to achieve a good life. While it would be hoped that a young person at least attempts to attain most, if not all, primary needs to some degree, there is limited value in designing plans to include needs that he or she attaches little importance to and thus would significantly lack motivation to work toward (Yates, Prescott, and Ward 2010).

It is important to maximize the young people's contributions and foster an atmosphere in meetings where they feel able to actively engage in the planning process and do not feel overwhelmed by the extent of professional input. Therefore, attendance at Good Lives team meetings should be limited to those who have an active role in undertaking or supporting the planned work. Information regarding the GLP can be shared with other relevant professionals and individuals via meeting minutes, telephone conversations, or alternative meetings. Prior to the team initially meeting, the young people and their caregivers are introduced to the adapted Good Lives model (GLM-A), including the theoretical underpinning of the model and what each of the needs comprises, so that they feel competent to engage in the planning process. Encouraging autonomy and empowerment of service users—for example, through collaborative working and being involved in goal setting—is consistent with the focus of the GLM (Willis et al. 2013) and the likely long-term success of interventions (Walters et al. 2007).

CONTENT OF A GOOD LIVES PLAN

In the initial stages, GLPs are likely to be sparse but will become more comprehensive as the young people further engage in the therapeutic work and in the course of Good Lives team reviews. A core part of the GLP is the development of an action plan that incorporates the focus of therapeutic work, including the tasks to be undertaken by young people, their families, caregivers, and professional network. As a dynamic tool, the GLP is revised and refined at three-month intervals throughout intervention.

The GLM identifies that assessment and rehabilitative plans should take account of capacity, obstacles, means, conflict, and scope (Ward and Stewart 2003b). This requires that the GLP, in detailing the ways in which needs can be attained, is tailored to the young people's strengths, resources, and difficulties, and is realistic and achievable. Plans must also be sensitive to any potential flaws: obstacles to needs being met, needs that are neglected or overly focused on by the young people, and conflicting needs that may be difficult to attend to simultaneously. An example of conflict provided by Ward, Mann, and Gannon (2007) might be when individuals experience greater difficulty in meeting their intimacy needs if they meet their autonomy needs by exerting control over their partner. It is also important that means are appropriate, as the use of inappropriate or harmful means to obtain needs is regarded as another potential flaw within the GLM (Willis et al. 2013), as is the potential to use strengths for either positive or negative outcomes (Linley and Harrington 2006). Therefore clinicians must be alert to encouraging individuals to use their internal resources in order to attain positive goals.

Simplistic language should be used in the plans to ensure that they are understood by the young person. Headings within a plan can include, for instance:

- What strengths do I have to help myself? (internal capacity/resources)
- What things/people are around to help me? (external capacity/resources)
- What do I have to change about me to help me manage my harmful sexual behavior? (internal obstacles)
- What do I have to change around me to manage my harmful sexual behavior? (external obstacles)
- How do I meet my most important needs now? How else can I meet these needs? (means)
- Which of my needs fight against each other? (conflict)
- Which of my needs do I neglect? (scope)

By using language that the young people can understand, the GLP provides a vehicle to actively involve them in the planning and intervention process. G-map's GLPs provide a foundation for the young people and their Good Lives team to work collaboratively on understanding risk, reducing risk, increasing internal and external resources, decreasing obstacles, and helping young people to get their needs met and live more fulfilling lives. As such, the plans additionally contain sections where:

- Problem formulations are summarized (Heading: "What do we know about Old Life that might be relevant to my harmful sexual behavior?")
- Harmful-sexual-behavior-related primary needs are listed (Heading: "What needs did my harmful sexual behavior meet?")
- Overarching needs are recognized (Heading: "Which of my needs seems most important?")
- Information specific to the outcomes of risk assessments is provided (Heading: "Keeping myself and others safe")

- Therapeutic plans are summarized (Heading: "The things I need to do in therapeutic work")
- Short-term action plans are detailed (Heading: "What I and others need to do before my next planning meeting")

It is important that the means by which different needs can be achieved are not too limited or narrow—for example, if the GLP focuses exclusively on the young people meeting their needs through a specific relationship with a girlfriend/boyfriend or through them obtaining a qualification, the young people can become vulnerable if the girlfriend/boyfriend relationship ends or if they fail to get their qualification. This risk could be offset by ensuring that the GLP promotes a range of means in order to meet each identified primary need. A consequence of restricted scope and means could result in happiness and the fulfillment of needs being short-lived. Additionally in the long term, it could result in a return to increased risk due to the emergence of factors such as emotional loneliness and poor emotional regulation. Dynamic risk factors should also be addressed within the plan, as they constitute obstacles to getting harm-related needs met and are amenable to change.

When drafting a GLP the Good Lives team should guide and support the young people to reflect on how realistic and achievable the plans is. Consideration should be given to an individual's environment, development, capacity, and support network when goal setting. For example, there are likely to be a greater number of environmental barriers facing a young person in custody than a young person in the community, and the Good Lives team may need to be much more creative and broaden their thinking when considering achievable goals in a secure or custodial setting. It is important that young people are encouraged to develop an awareness of possible obstacles they might encounter when attempting to meet their needs; by highlighting such considerations professionals can help the young people to understand what and how potential flaws could affect them and how to circumvent them. Such a process can, in effect, begin to assist young people to identify risks and employ problem-solving techniques to address them.

REVISING GLPS

GLPs should be revised as a continuous and dynamic process, and as new information becomes available. Amendments should also be made in accordance with how successful the young people and their network have been at putting the plan into action.

Action points are predominantly concerned with enhancing the young people's skills and capacities, providing them with opportunities to overcome obstacles and attain both personally important and harmful-behavior-related needs. Therefore the revisions to GLP become indicators of change, in that they provide a way of tracking progress in how successfully young people can meet their needs at particular points in time. When considering progress and change, it is important to take into account observations by parents and/or caregivers—those involved in therapeutic work and other significant caregivers—alongside a young person's self-report.

In addition to tracking change, revisions to plans should incorporate alternative routes to attaining needs when particular obstacles have been encountered. For example, a plan may include that the young people could gain an increased sense of belonging by improvement in their relationship with parents—but if parents are unwilling or unable to engage in such work, it should be highlighted on the plan as a current obstacle and alternative means to gain the sense of belonging identified, such as by focusing instead on relationships with other family members, caregivers, or peers.

GOAL SETTING

Long-term goals can provide a focus for where young people want to be in the future and as such can help to engage them in the process of change. While the identification of long-term goals is important, young people tend to need goal setting to be incremental, achievable, and to provide more immediate gratification. If goals are out of reach for extensive periods it may interfere with young people's perception of progress and change, resulting in a decline in their motivation. Long-term goals should therefore be constructed from a series of short-term goals in order to allow a sense of impetus and achievement. For example, a long-term goal might be to join a sports club, and the constituent short-term goals could include maintaining a program of physical fitness, improving social skills so as to be able to mix with others successfully, identifying suitable clubs and their membership requirements, etc. Furthermore, long-term goals should anticipate the future environment that the young people are likely to move to, and plans should include preparing and equipping them for their future transition into new environments in a way that promotes their well-being and encourages desistance.

CASE EXAMPLES

In this section of the chapter we provide examples of a GLP for each of the case illustrations provided in chapter 5.

Case A: Joe

Background

Age: 16 years

Ethnic origin: White British

Cognitive functioning: Intellectual disability

Brief details of harmful sexual behavior: At the age of 15 Joe anally raped his 11-year-old brother in the family home. The behavior occurred on several occasions over a seven-month period. The behavior ended after Joe's brother confided in a friend's parent, who subsequently told Joe's parents. The police were informed and Joe received a two-year supervision order. At the point of investigation Joe was removed from the family home and placed in a local authority children's home.

Table 6.1 Case A—Joe's Good Life Plan

YOUNG PERSON: Joe	**Date:** October 2010 (Assessment Period)	**Present:** Joe, residential unit care provider, social worker, therapeutic work staff, Joe's mother

What do we know about my Old Life that might be relevant to my harmful sexual behavior?	
About Me	**Around Me**
My mom has not always been there for me. *(Insecure attachment style (ambivalent))*	My mom showed me how to care by being there sometimes. *(Modeled ambivalent attachment style)*
<ul><li>I used to rely too much on my brother for support and comfort.</li><li>I have been told I have a mild intellectual disability by a doctor.</li><li>I used to feel bad about myself.</li><li>I found it difficult to see the bigger picture.</li><li>I struggled to make and keep friends.</li><li>I found it hard to deal with my feelings.</li><li>Sometimes when I've felt really bad it's helped if I cut myself.</li><li>I found out the person I thought was my dad wasn't really.</li><li>I sexually hurt my brother.</li></ul>	<ul><li>My mom was often sad and down.</li><li>The rules in my house were confusing.</li><li>My mom and dad gave me different messages about how I should behave.</li><li>My best friend sexually hurt me.</li><li>Mom and Dad would often argue, sometimes they would shout and hit each other.</li><li>My parents split up.</li><li>Mom kept secrets from me about who my dad was.</li><li>I didn't get to go out much.</li><li>I did not have many friends.</li><li>School did not help me learn well.</li><li>I was bullied in school.</li></ul>

continues on the next page

Table 6.1, continued

What needs did my harmful sexual behavior meet?
• Emotional health • Having people in my life • Achievement (maintenance)

Which of my needs seems most important? (Overarching need)
• Having people in my life

How do I currently meet the needs that connect to my sexually harmful behaviors? (Means)	
Appropriate	**Inappropriate**
• Talk to my care provider about some of my problems and worries • Play my keyboard • Write songs • Go to the gym • Take part in activities with friends in my residential unit • Do well in education • Some contact with parents	• I sometimes do and say things to my peers and care providers that are not helpful, in order to get attention. • I made small cuts on my arms, but not recently.
Which of my needs do I neglect now, if any? (Scope)	**Which of my needs fight against each other now, if any? (Conflict)**
My wish to have people in my life takes up a lot of my energy. In the past I have ignored the needs of *physical health, being my own person,* and *having a purpose and making a difference.* I am now getting better at meeting my *physical health* needs and doing things for myself.	*Emotional health* and *having people in my life.* For example, when I feel anxious, rejected, or lonely, I sometimes do things that are not helpful and say things that are not true in order to get attention. However, this might make people pull away from me.

How else can I meet my needs?

In the short term

- Use music and song writing to make myself feel better and achieve
- Make new friends
- Join a young person's relaxation/music group near to where I live
- Use the time I'm given to talk more openly to my care provider/other staff about my worries and problems
- Have more contact with my family
- Go to the gym and take part in activities that help me to relax and feel good about myself
- Continue to work hard in education and tell my teachers if I'm struggling
- Start to get to know my therapeutic workers

In the long term

- Have a girlfriend
- Get my relationship with my brother back
- Return to live with my family
- Go to college and learn new things
- Be part of a band and play the keyboard/sing
- Go out in the community without staff

What Do I Need to Change?

What do I need to change about myself to help me stop sexually harming others? (Internal obstacles)

- My need for others to tell me I am doing okay all the time
- My confidence and skills to make decisions
- How I feel about myself
- My ability to make friends and talk to other people
- Become more street-wise or good at reading situations
- Making up stories to get attention
- The feelings I sometimes get because of the bad things that happened in my past
- The way I manage my feelings
- How I cope with difficult situations without getting anxious/scared/wanting to hurt myself
- The amount I rely on my brother

What do we want to change around me to help me stop sexually harming others? (External obstacles)

- The strict rules so when I go out someone doesn't always have to be with me
- How often I see my parents
- Opportunities to make friends
- Being bullied in my placement

continues on the next page

Table 6.1, continued

What strengths do I have to help myself? (Internal resources)	What things/people are around to help me? (External resources)
• My behavior is generally positive • I have a number of interests (e.g., football, music, computer games) • I am really good at keyboard and song writing • I am good looking • I am friendly • I can take responsibility for my actions • I have good personal hygiene • I am quite healthy, physically • I am helpful • I have some ways that I can use to help me cope with my emotions in response to more minor difficulties • I want to achieve and am willing to attempt new things	• I get support and praise from care providers • In education there are lots of opportunities in which I can achieve • In my residential placement I am encouraged to keep up my self-care and independence skills • I have other young people around me to talk to in my residential placement • I have developed a positive relationship with my care provider • Activities are available in my placement (e.g., the gym)
What strengths do I have to help myself? (Internal resources)	What things/people are around to help me? (External resources)
• I can approach others to get help • My sexual knowledge is okay for my age and ability • I masturbate in a private place (my bedroom) • I had a good experience while going through puberty	

Keeping myself and others safe

- My risk assessment shows I have medium concerns/low strengths
- My risk assessment says that I need a medium level of supervision in the short-to-medium term
- I am thought to be a higher risk to male children
- My risk may be increased when I feel rejected and/or upset
- My risk may be lower when I feel accepted and wanted by others and am feeling good about my life, my achievements, and am managing my feelings well
- I am not thought to be a risk to strangers, people my own age, or adults
- The sexually harmful behavior I committed took place in a private place
- My assessment says I could be at risk of serious sexual assault/rape
- It is important that further risk assessments take place as people get to know me better and I do well in my work to meet my needs

The things I need to do in therapy

- Build a sense of safety
- Understand more about my early relationships (attachment) and how this affects my current relationships
- Learn more about how to make better relationships (secure attachment)
- Help my care providers understand more about how I struggle in relationships (attachment style) and how they can help me
- Learn better ways to cope with bad feelings (emotional regulation and distress tolerance)
- Learn to feel good about myself and increase my confidence
- Help me understand why I sexually hurt my brother and the effect it can have
- Learn how to manage my harmful sexual behavior
- Do work on some of the unhelpful sexual thoughts I have
- Help me to deal with being a victim of sexual abuse
- Learn about relationships and communication skills
- Gain skills to help me make and keep friends
- Improve the ways I solve problems especially for social situations
- Work on my family problems

continues on the next page

Table 6.1, continued

What I and others need to do before my next planning meeting (achievable and measurable steps)	
Me	**Therapeutic workers**
• Use music and song writing to help me deal with my emotions • Start to work with my therapists • Allow my care provider/other staff to help me manage my disappointment about my contact with my family • Join the local music or relaxation group • Do five minutes of attunement exercises with care providers everyday • Work on my social skills with my teachers • Work hard in education	• Build a sense of safety within the therapeutic environment (e.g., regular session times, consistency with therapeutic environment and therapeutic workers). • Risk assess community resources so that Joe can safely participate in some local activities to gain a sense of belonging and fun. • Support Joe's care providers and network with issues of risk. • Work with Joe's care providers to help them understand and respond to his attachment difficulties. • Introduce Joe to attachment and attunement. • Do a chronology with Joe to highlight his successes and achievements. • Help Joe to develop a song about his strengths. • Start to learn grounding strategies to help deal with and tolerate distress. • Explore the function of self harm with Joe and develop a safety plan. • Help Joe to apply his existing emotional regulation strategies to more challenging circumstances. • Meet with Joe's parents to explain what work Joe is doing and how they can help.

Care providers	Education
• Continue to provide a consistent and predictable structure, boundaries, and routine so that Joe can experience a sense of safety within his environment. • Undertake five minutes of attunement exercises with Joe everyday. • Investigate what activities/opportunities are available locally that will enable Joe to belong, emotionally regulate, achieve, and have fun (e.g., music groups). • Provide opportunities for Joe to safely access community resources, in consultation with his therapists. • Assess Joe's mood states prior to his participation in peer activities and provide appropriate external support to help Joe manage the conflict between *emotional health* and *having people in my life.* • Monitor Joe for indications of self-harming behavior. • Make sure key messages from the therapeutic work are repeated within his care environment in order that learning can be translated into his day-to-day life. • Continue to encourage Joe to be physically active and to eat healthy foods. • Support Joe in developing a better bedtime routine to aid sleep. • Support a range of staff to get to know Joe to reduce his exclusive reliance on his caseworker as an emotional confidant. • Schedule a contained and structured opportunity for Joe to meet with his caseworker each week to debrief and gain emotional support. • Support Joe's social worker to re-structure family contact.	• Set up a project relevant to Joe's interest (e.g., music). • Continue to focus on making education achievable and fun for Joe. • Do some work on Joe's social skills.

continues on the next page

Table 6.1, continued

Family	Other: Social worker
• Advise Joe's social worker of what is realistic regarding phone and face-to-face contact with Joe. • Apply to social services to reimburse travel costs. • Use social services for child care, or take turns to enable visits to occur with more regularity. • Where possible, provide advance notice of intention to cancel a contact visit. • Meet with Joe's therapeutic workers.	• The social worker will provide feedback to Youth Justice Team workers regarding Joe's Good Lives plan. • Re-structure family contact so that Joe has continued opportunities to see parents while his expectations of visits/calls are managed. • Do a preliminary exploration of the viability of restorative justice with Joe and his sibling, taking into account his brother's wishes and feelings.

I need to maintain and work on the Good Lives needs that are not directly linked to my harmful sexual behavior. These are:

- Having fun
- Being my own person
- Having a purpose and making a difference
- Sexual health
- Physical health

Case B: Wayne

Background

Age: 14 years

Ethnic origin: White British

Cognitive functioning: High average

Brief details of harmful sexual behavior: Wayne began accessing pornographic websites both at school and at home undetected. He then began to masturbating by a window overlooking a street, and eventually began exposing himself to females in his local park The fourth time he exposed himself he was recognized and caught by poilice. While he received no criminal sanction he was referred for assessment while remaining at home.

Table 6.2 Case B—Wayne's Good Life Plan

YOUNG PERSON: Wayne	Date: October 2010 (Assessment Period)	Present: Wayne, parents, therapeutic workers
What do we know about my old life that might be relevant to my harmful sexual behavior?		
About Me	**Around Me**	
<ul><li>I wanted to be the center of attention</li><li>I couldn't stand being bored</li><li>I thought it was fun to wind others up</li><li>I used to get bored a lot in school and so would kick off, disrupt lessons, annoy teachers/other pupils</li><li>I would do dangerous and illegal things for a buzz</li><li>I love excitement</li><li>I used pornography</li><li>I spent most of my time thinking about sex, especially since starting puberty</li><li>My bad behavior was getting worse</li></ul>	<ul><li>Mom and Dad spoiled me</li><li>When I was bored my parents helped keep me occupied so I didn't have to do this myself</li><li>School found it difficult to manage my behavior</li></ul>	
What needs did my harmful sexual behavior meet? <ul><li>Having fun (thrill and excitement)</li><li>Sexual health (sexual satisfaction)</li><li>Emotional health (emotional regulation of boredom)</li></ul>		

continues on the next page

Table 6.2, continued

Which of my needs seems most important? (Overarching need)	
• Having fun (thrill and excitement)	

How do I meet my offense related needs now? (Means)	
Appropriate	**Inappropriate**
• Listen to dance music (linked to emotional regulation) • Play sport and computer games (linked to having fun and emotional regulation)	• Accessing pornographic websites

Which of my needs do I neglect now, if any? (Scope)	Which of my needs fight against each other now, if any? (Conflict)
• My focus on thrill and excitement means that I have sometimes neglected my need to *achieve* and *belong*. I have never really cared about my need of *having a purpose and making a difference*.	• My habit of annoying others when bored and my stealing and antisocial behavior (which my friends don't like) has got in the way of my need to belong.

How else can I meet my needs?	
In the short term	**In the long term**
• Go on a visit with my parents to theme parks (on roller coasters) • Join a rock climbing group (supervised) • When I feel bored, use my coping techniques (e.g., play sports and/or chat to my friends, listen to dance tunes on my iPod, play computer games) • Talk to my parents more about what is going on for me • Have appropriate materials that I use for masturbation	• Do adventure sports • Have a girlfriend • Get good qualifications so that I can get a job in finance (e.g., on the stock market) • Have a fast car • Get married • Maybe have a family (not sure)

What Do I Need to Change?	
What do I want to change about myself to help me to stop my harmful sexual behavior? (Internal obstacles)	**What do we want to change around me to help me stop my harmful sexual behavior? (External obstacles)**
• My use of bad and illegal behavior to get a "buzz" • The way I manage boredom • My use of inappropriate sexual images • The amount of time I spend thinking about sex • My sexual knowledge (I mainly learned about sex from the pornographic websites I visited)	• To be supervised to stop me from risky behavior (for the time being) • More appropriate opportunities to gain thrill/excitement • Having clearer consequences when I behave in unhelpful or harmful ways • Monitoring my computer and internet access • My parents availability to me, so I can talk to them about my successes and problems • Change my bedroom to the spare room which does not overlook a public area
What strengths do I have to help myself? (Internal resources)	**What things/people are around to help me? (External resources)**
• I am intelligent. • I usually get along with people. • People like me. • I have positive interests (e.g., sports, music, computer games). • I have positive talents (e.g., maths, science and sports). • I think I'm good at lots of things (high self esteem). • I have good physical health, appearance, and self care. • I have some ways of coping when I feel bored, angry, or upset. • I get along with my parents. • I am willing to attempt new things. • I can problem solve (although I don't always use this positively).	• My parents want to help me. • My parents are physically, emotionally, and financially available. • My parents are willing to provide supervision and monitoring. • My parents are going to work with my therapeutic workers and have family sessions. • My parents will continue to take me to activities (e.g., sporting events and new activities we identify). • My friends do not usually behave badly or get into trouble. • My school is willing to help me.

continues on the next page

Table 6.2, continued

Keeping myself and others safe

- High risk of exposing myself in public again
- Higher risk to female peers and adults
- No known risk to males or younger children
- High level of supervision required when in the wider community (with the exception of male only activities/groups, e.g., sports) in the short-to-medium term
- My risk assessment shows that I have lots of strengths that can help me to reduce my risk.
- My risk may be increased when I am feeling bored, seeking fun, and/or feeling sexually aroused.
- My risk may be lower when I am meeting my need for excitement, can positively manage my boredom, and am not focusing too much on sex.
- Continuous risk assessment is required.

The things I need to do in therapeutic work

- Build a positive relationship with my therapeutic workers
- Work on how I manage my feelings
- Increase my understanding of why I exposed myself and the possible consequences for my victims
- Work to help me manage my boredom
- Sex education
- Untangle the unhelpful messages and thoughts I have about sex
- Learn how to manage my sexual arousal in positive ways
- Increase my problem solving skills, especially regarding positive things I can do to achieve fun and excitement
- Work with my family so they can better understand my harmful sexual behavior and how they can help me to manage and change it.

What I and others need to do before my next planning meeting (achievable and measurable steps)

Me	Therapist(s)
• Start my therapeutic work • Move to another bedroom so that I don't overlook the street • Adhere to rules about privacy (e.g., closing my curtains and shutting my door before I masturbate) • Adhere to the rules set about my computer use	• Continue to build a positive relationship with Wayne • Meet with Wayne's parents to help them understand his harmful sexual behavior and how they can help him to manage and change it • Joint work with Wayne and his parents about supervision and rules for safe sexual behavior

Me (continued)	**Therapist(s)** (continued)
• Look into what activities there are in my local community to have fun and help me get a buzz • Work on my managing my feelings, especially at times when I am bored	• Meet with Wayne's school to discuss supervision • Work with Wayne to help him understand his harmful sexual behavior and the process of change • Work on emotional regulation strategies and distress tolerance with Wayne
Family (parents)	**Education**
• Meet and work with Wayne's therapeutic workers • Supervise Wayne when he is in the community • Monitor Wayne's computer and internet access • Support Wayne to identify local activities in which he could achieve a sense of fun • Provide clearer consequences for Wayne when his behavior is inappropriate or problematic • Provide encouragement for Wayne to self-manage his boredom in more constructive ways	• Supervise Wayne when he is at school, especially during unstructured time • Monitor Wayne's computer and internet access • Seek to provide Wayne with work that is better suited to his academic level

I need to maintain and work on my Good Lives needs that are not directly linked to my harmful sexual behavior. These are:

- Achieving
- Being my own person
- Having people in my life
- Having a purpose and making a difference
- Physical health

Case C: Leanne

Background

Age: 12 years

Ethnic origin: Mixed race (white British/black Caribbean)

Cognitive functioning: Average

Brief details of harmful sexual behavior: At 10 years old, Leanne began to sexually harm her younger brothers. The harm involved touching her brothers' genitals and coercing them into touching and licking her vagina. Leanne also penetrated her younger brother's anus using a small toy. When Leanne felt left out on family holiday she sexually harmed a four-year-old boy who was a stranger. The boys' parents prompted the investigation that revealed all of Leanne's harmful behavior and Leanne was placed into foster care during the assessment period.

Table 6.3 Case C—Leanne's Good Life Plan

YOUNG PERSON: Leanne	**Date:** October 2010 (Assessment Period)	**Present:** Leanne, therapist, foster care provider
What do we know about my Old Life that might be relevant to my harmful sexual behavior?		
About Me	**Around Me**	
<ul><li>I never felt that I was important to Mom.</li><li>My aunt is nice, she'd sometimes take over when Mom could not look after me.</li><li>I've had no contact with my Dad since I was one year old.</li><li>I found it hard to deal with my feelings.</li><li>I didn't understand what being a different color from my friends and brothers meant.</li><li>I didn't feel good about myself or the way I looked.</li><li>I found it difficult to think things through.</li><li>I did not get along with my mom.</li><li>I found it difficult to get along with others my age.</li><li>I used to feel angry a lot.</li><li>My mom would give more time to the younger kids and I was jealous of them.</li><li>I sometimes bullied my brothers.</li><li>I behaved in sexual ways in preschool.</li><li>I sexually hurt my brothers.</li><li>I sexually hurt a boy I did not know.</li></ul>	<ul><li>I never knew what to expect or how my mom might behave toward me at home.</li><li>My mom took drugs.</li><li>My dad used to hit my mom.</li><li>My aunt's boyfriend hurt me sexually when I was little.</li><li>My mom didn't look after me properly when I was growing up.</li><li>My parents didn't keep an eye on me and I could usually do what I wanted to.</li><li>I was bullied in school.</li><li>I didn't get many chances to meet others my age or to make friends.</li><li>I didn't feel there was anyone to talk to about my feelings or worries.</li><li>I was expected to care for my younger brothers even though it wasn't my job.</li><li>My mom and her boyfriend liked my brothers better than me.</li></ul>	

What needs did my harmful sexual behavior meet?

- Emotional health
- Having people in my life

Which of my needs seems most important? (Overarching need)

- Having people in my life

How do I meet my offence related needs now? (Means)

Appropriate	Inappropriate
- Listen to music in my bedroom - Contact with my aunt	- Push my new care providers away - Getting very angry and damaging my care providers property

Which of my needs do I neglect now, if any? (Scope)	Which of my needs fight against each other now, if any? (Conflict)

- I currently focus on *emotional health* and neglect my need for:
  - Having people in my life
  - Having fun
  - Achieving
  - Being my own person
  - Having a purpose and making a difference
  - Sexual health
  - Physical health
	- *Emotional health* and *having people in my life* for example:
	  - I push away my new care providers because I do not feel happy
	  - I damage my care providers' property because it helps me to cope with my feelings. This is causing arguments and problems in our relationship.

How else can I meet my needs?

In the short term	In the long term
- See my aunt more often - Sort out where I am going to live so that I can start to build relationships and feel safe - Get back to school - Use art to help me to show and deal with my feelings - Do things that make me feel good, for example hair styling, nail art, choosing fashionable clothing to my taste - Start to learn about my culture and ethnicity	- Making up with my family and get along better - Make contact with my dad's family - Have more time when I do not have to have adults watching over me when I am out and about - Maybe move in with my aunt - Have friends - Have a boyfriend - Study art at college

continues on the next page

Table 6.3, continued

In the short term (continued)	In the long term (continued)
• Spend the first bit of my therapeutic work building up relationships with my therapeutic workers • Join the local arts and crafts group for kids over 11 years of age	

What Do I Need to change?	
What do we want to change about myself to help me stop my harmful sexual behavior? (Internal obstacles)	**What do we want to change around me to help me stop my harmful sexual behavior? (External obstacles)**
• How I relate to others • My confusion about who I am • The way I deal with my feelings • How I see myself and my lack of confidence • The way I solve problems • The way I let others know about my needs • My ability to make and keep friends • The anger that bubbles inside me all the time	• My long-term living arrangements • The angry way my parents are behaving toward me at the moment and them not wanting to see me • My school not being sorted out yet • The lack of chances I have to make friends • Not feeling that I have anyone who I can go to talk about my feelings and get help
What strengths do I have to help myself? (Internal resources)	**What things/people are around to help me? (External resources)**
• I am good at looking after myself (e.g., keeping clean and getting dressed). • I get okay grades at school. • I am good at art. • I enjoy doing creative things. • I am helpful. • Other people say I'm attractive but I'm not sure yet. • I like fashion. • I am thoughtful.	• My aunt is always in my life. • My aunt wants to help me. • My care providers are trying to make me feel welcome. • My care providers are giving me rules and consequences. • My care providers have expectations of me that are reasonable for my age. • My care providers supervise me. • I can go to therapeutic sessions to help me with my problems. • My social worker is working hard to get me a permanent place to live and school to go to.

Keeping myself and others safe

- My assessment shows that I have high concerns/low strengths.
- I have to have high levels of supervision in the meantime.
- My assessment says that I am a higher risk to young males (regardless of whether I know them or not).
- I am not thought to be a risk to females, adults, or peers.
- My assessment says there are concerns that I could commit further serious sexual harmful behaviors.
- Risk may be increased and when I feel angry, left out, or that things are unfair.
- Risk may be lower when I when I feel accepted and wanted by others and when I feel good about my life, and manage my feelings well.
- My risk needs to keep being assessed.

The things I need to do in therapy

- Build a sense of safety
- Learn good ways to make myself feel better and to be nicer in the way I view myself and others
- Gain more self confidence
- Understand more about the way I respond to others and how this affects my relationships
- Learn better ways to relate to others and to feel safe
- Learn good ways to deal with my emotions, including anger
- Help me to deal with being a victim of sexual abuse
- Help me to deal with some of my bad experiences as I was growing up and the effect these have had on me
- Learn to better deal with situations that I see as being unfair such as others having favorites
- Learn about relationships and how to talk to and get on with others
- Gain skills to help me make and keep friends
- Learn more about my ethnicity
- Increase my understanding of why I sexually hurt others and the consequences of my behavior
- Learn how to manage my harmful sexual behavior
- Increase my sexual knowledge
- Improve the way I solve problems
- Work on my family problems

continues on the next page

Table 6.3, continued

What I and others need to do before my next planning meeting (achievable and measurable steps)	
Me	**Therapist(s)**
• See my aunt more often. • Undertake 5 minutes of attunement exercises with care providers everyday. • Use art as a way of helping me to show and deal with my feelings. • Engage in things that make me feel good (for example, hair styling, nail art, choosing fashionable clothing to my taste) • Start to work with my therapeutic workers. • Join the local arts and crafts group for kids over 11 years of age	• Tell Leanne's social worker about the Good Lives plan and discussions. • Risk assess opportunities and activities identified for Leanne. • Support Leanne's care providers and network on issues of risk. • In the event of a new specialist foster care placement being identified for Leanne, provide consultation and support to the new care providers. • Build a sense of safety within the therapeutic environment (e.g., regular session times, consistency of therapeutic environment and therapeutic workers). • Compassion focused work (e.g., design a bracelet consisting of beads that individually represent Leanne's strengths). • Help Leanne and her care providers to understand her attachment and attunement needs. • Help Leanne to start to learn grounding strategies to help deal with and tolerate distress. • Introduce Leanne to some realistic emotional regulation strategies. • Use visual and creative methods. • Meet with Leanne's aunt.
Family	**Other – Social worker**
• Leanne's aunt to visit her more regularly and have phone contact with her. • Meet with therapeutic workers.	• Resolve longer term placement issues. • Liaise with Leanne's family to ascertain what role, if any, they want to have in her future. • Subject to placement decision, arrange for reintegration into mainstream education, making relevant disclosures.

I need to maintain and work on the Good Lives needs that are not directly linked to my harmful sexual behavior. These are:

- Having fun
- Achieving
- Being my own person
- Having a purpose and making a difference
- Sexual health
- Physical health

Each of the plans above was developed, following an initial assessment, with the young people and agreed upon at their first Good Lives team meeting. In order to help prepare the young people, the process of the meetings, how their initial assessment outcomes might influence plans, and what they wanted included in plans were discussed with them beforehand. All three young people actively participated in their meetings and were involved in negotiating the plans made. The result was that they felt ownership of their plans; they were clear what they and others would be doing and what goals they hoped to achieve. All three thus considered the plans achievable, and they were motivated to participate, even in some of the work that might be difficult for them.

The initial plans were reviewed and developed every three months at the Good Lives team meetings; people joined and left the team according to their relevance to action points that were made. The following chapter identifies how each of the young people considered here progressed in their Good Life plans.

REFERENCES

Langlands, R. L., T. Ward, and E. Gilchrist. 2009. Applying the Good Lives model to male perpetrators of domestic violence. *Behaviour Change* 26:13–129.

Linley, P. A., and S. Harrington. 2006. Playing to your strengths. *Psychologist* 19:86–89.

Walters, S. T., M. D. Clark, R. Gingerich, and M. Meltzer. 2007. *Motivating offenders to change: A guide for probation and parole.* Washington, DC: National Institute of Corrections, US Department of Justice.

Ward, T., R. E. Mann, and T. A. Gannon. 2007. The Good Lives model of offender rehabilitation: Clinical implications. *Aggression and Violent Behaviour* 12:87–107.

Ward, T., and C. A. Stewart. 2003a. Good lives and the rehabilitation of sexual offenders. In T. Ward, D. R. Laws, and S. M. Hudson (eds.), *Sexual deviance: Issues and controversies,* 21–44. Thousand Oaks, CA: Sage Publications.

Ward, T., and C. A. Stewart. 2003b. The treatment of sex offenders: Risk management and good lives. Professional Psychology: *Research and Practice* 34:358–60.

Willis, G. W., P. M. Yates, T. A. Gannon, and T. Ward. 2013. How to integrate the Good Lives model into treatment programs for sexual offending: An introduction and overview. *Sexual Abuse: A Journal of Research and Treatment* 25:123–42.

Yates, P. M., D. Prescott, and T. Ward. 2010. *Applying the Good Lives and Self Regulation models to sex offender treatment: A practical guide for clinicians.* Brandon, VT: The Safer Society Press.

CHAPTER 7

Therapeutic Practice

LAURA WYLIE AND HELEN GRIFFIN

This chapter does not provide an exhaustive overview of therapeutic intervention with young people who display harmful sexual behavior, but predominantly looks at how the Good Lives model relates to intervention. However, in order to provide a context it is necessary to highlight key considerations in therapeutic work with young people who display harmful sexual behavior. The case studies in the preceding chapters are revisited to illustrate how Good Lives plans (GLPs) are implemented in the therapeutic context and how they provide for the individual needs of young people to be met alongside addressing their harmful sexual behavior.

GENERAL OVERVIEW

Historically intervention with adolescents who display harmful sexual behavior involved a myriad of methods and modalities, many of which were used independently of any discernible evidence base or demonstrable link with effective outcomes. This somewhat expansive, unfocused, and arguably subjective approach to intervention was described by Lab, Shields, and Schondel (1993, 551) as "shooting in the dark and hoping to hit something." Illustrative of this, a survey in the United States involving 30 specialist facilities working with young people who had harmed sexually found approximately 350 different therapies and techniques being used (Sapp and Vaughn 1990). While there is continued support for a holistic and broad-based approach to intervention with young people who harm sexually, consistent with the diverse presenting needs and developmental flux that characterizes this population, it is also important that the efficacy of each element of the intervention process is rigorously evaluated.

There is increasing emphasis on evidence-based practice across health and social care arenas in several countries (Sheldon and Chilvers 2000). While this shift has many positive implications for developing our understanding and practice with these young people, its full implementation has posed challenges at the organizational level, including the time and resource implications of undertaking research and evaluation (Hackett 2003). Moreover, evidencing the effectiveness of intervention with children and young people who harm sexually continues to present significant challenges. They include wide variation in definitions of what constitutes therapeutic effectiveness in outcome evaluation studies; ethical considerations that preclude the use of research designs that could more readily detect cause–effect relationships, such as randomized control trials; low numbers of robustly designed outcome evaluation studies; small sample sizes; and insufficient follow-up times.

While there remains a tendency to adopt a particularly eclectic approach to intervention with this population, intervention programs are now more consistently underpinned by theory, informed by research, and adhere to principles of effective practice, such as the Risk–Need–Responsivity (RNR) model (Andrews and Bonta 2010; Andrews, Bonta, and Hoge 1990; Bonta and Andrews 2007), as well as seeking to achieve intervention integrity (Briggs and Kennington 2006). It is increasingly accepted that the RNR and the GLM, as frameworks for rehabilitation, can work together in a manner that enhances the usefulness of each. For example, the motivational GLM can enhance client engagement that is consistent with the principle of responsivity and thus may augment overall intervention effectiveness (Willis et al. 2013).

As described in chapter 2, another significant impediment to the development of effective intervention approaches for these young people has been the tendency to view them as "mini adults," ascribing the same characteristics and risk factors as those identified in populations of adults who harm sexually and using them to inform the development of interventions. This practice had inherent flaws—for example, it was sometimes punitive and frequently omitted to take account of the developmental needs of young people or the fluidity and variability of the adolescent period (Longo 2003). The practice has been comprehensively challenged over the last decade and a more child-focused, developmentally sensitive, systemic, and holistic approach now generally prevails.

A wide variety of intervention approaches continues to proliferate in this field, including psycho-educational; family systems; emotion-focused; cycle-based; attachment-focused; behavioral conditioning; and relapse prevention. Despite the diversity of approaches, it is the cognitive behavioral approach that, to date, has been most widely endorsed in UK and North American contexts (Hackett 2004). Cognitive behaviorism represents a synthesis of behaviorism, with its focus on the role of external stimuli in the shaping and maintenance of behavior; cognitive theory, with its emphasis on the importance of thought processes and problem solving; and social learning theory (Vennard, Sugg, and Hedderman 1997). Cognitive behavioral therapy (CBT) views harmful sexual behavior as a product of dysfunctional or distorted beliefs held by the individual. As the most established approach with the broadest usage, CBT has readily lent itself to outcome research and has gained empirical support in its use with both adults (e.g., Hanson et al. 2002) and adolescents (e.g., Worling and Curwen 2000). However, one of the most salient criticisms of the CBT approach has been its failure to take sufficient account of the social or personal contexts of harmful behaviors (Farrell 2002). This criticism may have particular implications for young people who harm sexually, in that their age and developmental stage typically mean that they continue to be influenced by a range of social systems, including family.

Multisystemic therapy (MST) is an ecological approach to intervention that incorporates the young person's family and community systems in the process of change, and has consistently demonstrated positive outcomes with adolescents who display various problematic and anti-social behaviors (Henggeler, Melton, and Smith 1992), including harmful sexual behavior (Borduin et al. 1990). The model is underpinned by a clear theoretical rationale that acknowledges the spheres of influence within a young person's life, as well as the interplays among them, and seeks to enhance the functionality in these relationship systems in accordance with their importance to the young people's lives. The inclusion of family in the intervention process is a departure from traditional CBT approaches, but there is increasing support for the view that a comprehensive program that combines a strong family component alongside harmful behavior-focused work is the approach most likely to effect change with these young people (Worling and Curwen 2000).

It is increasingly apparent that the diversity of approaches and wide variation in the risk and presenting needs of young people who harm sexually means that the practice of reporting the findings of intervention-outcome research generically provides limited insight into the crucial mediators of therapeutic effectiveness, such as recipient, therapist, and setting characteristics (Losel 1995). There is a need for more intervention-outcome studies that clearly differentiate intervention types when reporting recidivism in order to elucidate the types of intervention that are most effective with these young people. Moreover, if individual risk and responsivity factors are taken into account in the reporting of recidivism, it leads practitioners to design and implement interventions on a more prescriptive basis.

USING THE GLM TO INFORM INTERVENTION

The GLM is increasing in popularity as a framework to guide rehabilitation (McGrath et al. 2010). It has a theoretical grounding in positive psychology, consistent with upholding intervention integrity, and growing empirical support for its concepts and applications. Although the effect of Good Lives–informed approaches on intervention outcomes is not yet known, there is already some support for the GLM's potential efficacy in enhancing therapeutic outcomes with CBT approaches (Willis et al. 2013). It is important to appreciate that as a guiding framework, the GLM does not dictate the content of intervention; nor does it inform decisions pertaining to the sequencing or duration of therapeutic input. Therefore practitioners need to make decisions about suitable intervention modalities for this client group. This allows practitioners to incorporate approaches that demonstrate the greatest efficacy and are most responsive to the individual needs of young people who exhibit harmful sexual behavior.

As the language of Good Lives increasingly permeates modern parlance, so there appears to be a corresponding drive to embrace and reflect the GLM within intervention programs. However, this does not appear to have come about with any consistency or uniformity, and as a result the GLM imbues programs to varying degrees, ranging from representing a singular element within or adjunct to therapeutic programs, to full integration within the organizational structure, informing assessment, therapeutic work, transition, and evaluation. As outlined in previous chapters, the G-map program has sought to fully embrace the principles of the GLM, albeit adapting it to enhance its accessibility and resonance with its client population, and to integrate it fully within its practice. In this sense, individual intervention programs are devised and implemented in accordance with the GLM, although in practice therapeutic work is undertaken via a number of modalities that include trauma and attachment-focused work, CBT techniques, and biologically driven approaches.

In the context of the GLM, a key aim of intervention is to help individuals meet primary needs in pro-social ways, while reducing their risk of committing further harmful behaviors. This means presenting intervention as something that offers opportunities for a better life and improved well-being, while promoting a harm-free lifestyle, and all within an approach goal framework. Essentially young people are supported in addressing their criminogenic needs and developing the skills and resources to achieve a "good life," reflecting their particular prioritization of needs and, by extension, their self-identity. It is also likely that the components of RNR-based interventions and GLM-informed interventions overlap, and are likely to include modules such as emotional regulation, risk management, relationships, problem solving, and sex and sexuality. In the context of GLM-informed programs an integral component is the development of a feasible Good Lives plan (GLP) that can guide the young person toward personally-valued future goals that are consistent with a non-harmful lifestyle.

A key consideration is that while "therapy," in the formal sense of the word, takes place within the parameters of the therapeutic setting, change, risk management, skills development, and the enhancement of well-being are significantly augmented within the broader realms of the young person's world, including home, educational, and recreational settings. From this perspective the wider support network, including the young person's family or caregivers, can play a crucial role in the intervention process. Hackett (2004) acknowledged the generally accepted view that family work represents an essential component in interventions with this subgroup, regardless of the diverse therapeutic approaches involved. The GLM lends itself to the inclusion of the wider network and promotes a systemic approach from the point of view that meeting the full range of Good Lives needs necessary for an adaptive and satisfying life requires the mobilization of diverse resources, including human resources.

As discussed in chapter 6, while therapeutic services may primarily target helping young people address harmful sexual-behavior-related needs, they can also be pivotal in assisting them to meet a broader range of personally valued needs. By actively working with the young person's professional and familial systems, they can play a crucial role in driving the mechanisms, acquiring the resources, and overcoming the obstacles to the young person meeting the full range of primary needs. As well as offsetting the possibility of the young person experiencing restricted scope, this process invariably complements the work undertaken in therapeutic sessions, with positive implications for the reduction of risk. For example, in G-map's experience although "making a positive contribution" is unlikely to be an offense-related need for young people who display harmful sexual behavior, promoting opportunities for young people to engage in activities that benefit others can give them a sense of pride, enhance their perspective-taking ability, boost self-confidence, and facilitate the development and practice of vital interpersonal and communication skills. This will assist young people in appropriately meeting harm-related needs as well as experiencing improved well-being.

In G-map's experience, using its adaptation of the GLM (GLM-A), the needs that frequently emerge as most salient in respect to young people's harmful sexual behavior are having people in my life, emotional health, and sexual health. To a large extent the desire to belong and to manage emotional arousal mirrors repeated findings among this population of young people of high rates of disrupted attachments and exposure to trauma (Creeden 2005). In taking an attachment and trauma-related perspective, Creeden (2005) posits that for some young people harmful sexual behavior may be a distorted attempt to meet their needs for nurturance, attention, safety, and acceptance. These largely link with the GLM-A needs of *having people in my life* and *emotional health*. Similarly, Willis and Ward (2011) note that relatedness frequently emerges as a prioritized primary need among those who sexually harm.

Research indicates that attachment difficulties may contribute to the development of harmful sexual behavior (Smallbone and Dadds 1998; 2000; 2001). For example, within an Irish context Marsa and colleagues (2004) found that 93 percent of a sample of adults who sexually harmed children showed indications of having an insecure attachment style. The finding cannot be readily generalized to adolescents due to important differences between the populations, including developmental consider-ations. However, it can be hypothesized that insecure attachment styles may negatively influence the development of interpersonal skills, self-image, and social adequacy (Marshall and Barbaree 1990), undermining individuals' capacity to form intimate, safe, and mutually satisfying relationships and thus increasing the risk of them seek-ing to meet these needs via harmful sexual behaviors (Ward et al. 1995). The link between attachment difficulties and harmful sexual behavior remains a tenuous one (Rich 2006), and there is unlikely to be a direct relationship considering the complex and multi-faceted nature of pathways into harmful sexual behavior (Hudson, Ward, and McCormack 1999). Nevertheless, individuals who have not sexually harmed appear to have experienced more secure attachments than those who exhibit harmful sexual behavior (Smallbone 2005).

Similarly it has been suggested that traumatic experiences are one of many predis-posing factors in the development of harmful sexual behavior (Rasmussen, Burton, and Christopherson 1992; McMackin et al. 2002) and feature significantly in the histories of young people who harm sexually. In the context of therapeutic work with young people with harmful sexual behavior at the Whitney Academy in America, Creeden (2005) asserts that he begins with the assumption that all young people accessing this specialist service will have a history of trauma.

There is increasing recognition that early trauma and insecure attachment experi-ences compromise healthy neurodevelopment in children, resulting in a range of neu-robiological changes in the brain and nervous system that can ultimately limit their capacity to respond adaptively to stress or to self-regulate states of arousal (Schore 2002). One of the key neurodevelopmental changes that occurs is limbic irritability, known as a "kindling effect," whereby the young people develop a propensity toward hyper-vigilance within their environment (Creeden 2005), increasingly reacting to even innocuous stressors with activation of the adrenaline stress response, or "survival-in-the-moment states" (Saxe, Ellis, and Kaplow 2007). This difficulty is compounded by other neurological adversities that affect young people's abilities (Creeden 2005), such as processing, integrating, and accessing information adaptively. These resultant difficulties can have significant implications for individuals' capacity to learn, manage mood states, control impulses, problem-solve effectively, and appropriately interpret and respond to environmental cues. This is consistent with the finding that a high proportion of adolescents who have harmed sexually display some level of neuropsychological deficits (Ferrara and McDonald 1996).

Creeden (2004, 238) suggests that the processing of trauma "is essential in addressing the client's own traumatic experiences and in addressing the client's abusive behavior toward others." However, he highlights that attachment and trauma-based intervention approaches are not yet widely employed within therapeutic programs and points to the role of biologically-based interventions to support young people who have harmed sexually in developing the capacity to self-regulate, and in mitigating the effect of a hyperactivated autonomic arousal system (Creeden 2005). This has significant implications for the sequencing and content of therapeutic programs, since young people who are continuing to experience triggers to trauma in their environment, and who lack the skills to emotionally regulate the resultant distress, are unlikely to be able to use higher brain processes to manage situations or effectively self-manage risk. Thus therapy that relies predominantly on CBT techniques, particularly in the early stages of intervention, may not provide young people with the resources they require to meet harm-related Good Lives needs, or to overcome obstacles and address risk.

Using the GLM-A to guide intervention enables a more holistic view of the young person, and therefore lends itself to approaches that consider attachment style and/or trauma history as a fundamental part of intervention. RNR-based interventions frequently incorporate emotional regulation and relationships modules (Ward, Mann, and Gannon 2007), which appear to be consistent with the GLM-A needs of *emotional health* and *having people in my life*. Saxe, Ellis, and Kaplow (2007) introduced the concept of a Trauma Systems Therapy approach that emphasizes the need for a dual focus on the individual and the environment when addressing traumatic stress in young people. It involves reducing threats in the social environment, ensuring that the system of care can support young people in emotionally regulating, and developing the individual's capacity for emotional self-regulation.

In addition to the needs of *having people in my life* and *emotional health*, the need for *sexual health* also features significantly for young people accessing G-map's services, albeit not necessarily with the frequency that might be expected in view of the nature of their behavior problems. In the context of adults who sexually harm, deviant sexual arousal, which is typically operationalized as arousal toward younger children or sexual violence, consistently emerges as one of the most significant predictors of recidivism (e.g., Hanson and Bussiere 1998). However, the sexual arousal patterns of young people who harm sexually appear to be less connected to their sexually harming behaviors. Nevertheless, while only a small percentage of young people who commit harmful sexual behavior appear to display problematic sexual arousal (Worling 2012), sexual health often remains an important therapeutic consideration. As a consequence of displaying harmful and inappropriate sexual behavior it is possible that young people could have some confusion and distortions about sex, relationships, and their own sexuality that may be counterproductive to their rehabilitation.

THERAPEUTIC PROCESS ISSUES

Intervention Intensity

In 2009 the Safer Society undertook a survey of North America regarding current practices and emerging trends in sexual abuser management (McGrath et al. 2010). It included gathering information on the features that typically characterize programs designed for adolescents who had displayed harmful sexual behaviors. Regarding the modes of therapy, relating to whether they were delivered through individual work, group work, or family work, the majority (from 95 to 100 percent) of adolescent community programs that were surveyed tended to predominantly employ individual work with males and females in both Canada and the United States. Interestingly, group work was used in at least 88 percent of community and residential programs for adult males. This is not to say that group and family work were not employed with adolescents; instead it appears that many programs used a mixture of these modalities to deliver interventions. In this survey, the mean number of individual sessions provided to adolescents per month ranged from 3.11 (SD=1.56) to 3.29 (SD=1.39) for community programs in the United States and 2.80 (SD=1.32) to 3.83 (SD=0.41) for community programs in Canada. The numbers tended to be slightly higher when therapeutic intervention was delivered as part of a residential program. The average length of the sessions for community programs ranged from approximately 54 to 63 minutes (with SDs up to 13.66). The average length of "core intervention" in community programs for adolescents was approximately 15 months in the United States, with an additional 8 months for an "aftercare" program, and 10 to 12 months in Canada, with a further 5 months for aftercare.

At G-map the intensity of intervention is varied by the length of time the young person engages in a program of therapeutic work. The length of the program is informed by the young person's assessed risks, needs, and strengths, which are initially determined in assessment and subsequently reviewed by the Good Lives team (see chapter 5), thus reflecting the principles of the RNR model. A typical program of work may last approximately 18 months, and will include both the core and transitional elements of the program. While young people assessed as presenting the highest recidivism risk will require a longer program of work—that is, higher intervention intensity—the length of therapy will also be influenced by a range of other factors, including the young person's age, cognitive ability, mental health considerations, and trauma history. Moreover, as a therapeutic provider G-map makes recommendations about the intensity of intervention based on the young person's risks and needs, although referral agency funding limits can be an obstacle to therapeutic goals being fully realized.

When the young people's living environment does not offer them the prospect of achieving a sense of emotional safety, contains threats to their safety, or cannot provide the levels of supervision and support necessary to enable them to address their harmful sexual behavior, it may not be appropriate to undertake therapeutic work. Such decisions are difficult for practitioners, given their belief that all young people deserve the opportunity to address their harmful behavior and to live safe and more fulfilling lives, and their commitment to making society safer. In circumstances where intervention cannot commence as a result of such obstacles a more time-limited initial assessment can be useful in highlighting risk in the context of the young person's current environment and by making recommendations regarding his or her needs with suggestions as to how these might be met.

Responsivity

G-map undertakes individual therapeutic sessions with all young people in its service, although this can be supplemented with group work when it has been identified that the young person may benefit from peer support and/or the opportunity to reinforce and practice skills and learning developed in individual sessions. Individual sessions allow practitioners to take account of the young person's age, intellectual functioning, attachment style, social presentation, and any presenting mental health needs. The practice of co-working cases, which is integral to G-map's therapeutic approach, helps to overcome some of the risks and shortcomings of individual working, such as overidentification or collusion with the client. The co-working process similarly supports practitioners in recognizing and addressing issues of counter-transference that can occur with clients. An important consideration when working with children and young people who may have been the victims of adult abuse is to provide a therapeutic environment that is safe, transparent, and accountable, and in our experience this is more readily achieved via the allocation of two workers. The arrangement also provides greater protection to practitioners since the young people with whom we work sometimes have a history of making false allegations, or of being physically or sexually abusive toward adults. Most young people in the program, particularly those who have a history of being harmed by adults, have also said that they feel more comfortable with two people in the room when they are working as it feels less intense than one-to-one working. A further practical advantage of co-working is that it provides greater consistency and stability for the young person, minimizing disruption to sessions through, for example, staff sickness and staff holidays. The entire co-working process is enhanced through the provision of regular co-work supervision, provided by a service manager.

Existing literature consistently reveals an overrepresentation of learning difficulties among young people who sexually harm. For example, Ryan et al. (1996) estimated that between 40 and 80 percent of adolescents with harmful sexual behavior have learning disabilities or school-based behavior problems. While figures have generally been consistent, an important caution is the wide variability in how a learning disability is conceptualized, defined, and measured across intervention settings (O'Callaghan 1999). At G-map the use of multi-modal interventions, individualized therapeutic sessions, and the adoption of visual and participatory methods greatly enhances responsivity when delivering therapeutic work to young people with learning difficulties or disabilities. Therapeutic readiness—that is, the young person's receptiveness to intervention and capacity to benefit from intervention—is a further consideration, although readers are referred to chapter 4 for a fuller discussion in respect to this.

THE CHALLENGES OF WORKING SYSTEMICALLY WITH YOUNG PEOPLE

Undertaking work with young people in the context of the systems and environments they occupy has practical and resource implications. It is typically easier for a specialist residential provider to finance materials and activities that enable young people in their care to meet important and harm-related needs than it may be for them or their family of origin. Where young people live independently or semi-independently, or reside in their family homes while involved in intervention, it can be somewhat more challenging to identify and source the support they need to meet personally valued needs. However, although it may sometimes entail more creative thinking, we would argue that the resources required for meeting the full range of Good Lives needs are widely and freely available. For example, playing football with peers in the local park can be as effective in enabling a young person to meet the need of *physical health* as joining a gym, without the financial implications, although consideration needs to be given to appropriate risk management where activities are less structured. When working in partnership with specialist residential settings, G-map has encouraged all providers to be mindful of the need for skills and resources to be transferable to the environment that the young person will eventually transition to, and thus to encourage means of meeting needs that are practical, affordable, and sustainable. Arguably, a more serious setback to young people finding and implementing appropriate means of meeting their needs is the absence of support from family and other key networks.

Since practitioners need to draw on young people's wider support networks in order to ensure that the skills and knowledge developed in the context of therapeutic work are transferable to real-life settings, the absence of motivation within this network, individually or collectively, can present a significant obstacle to intervention progress. As discussed in chapter 4, the adoption of the GLM and G-map's subsequent development of GLM-A have reduced the frequency with which such obstacles are encountered since the concepts of a good life and good life goals are inherently motivational. The forum of Good Lives team meetings and reviews ensures that tasks and responsibilities are shared between the young person and his or her support network, the latter promoting direct investment in the young person's progress. Notwithstanding this, frustrations can still be experienced when elements of the young person's support network are unmotivated or directly impede or undermine therapeutic progress. These can include external professionals who, as a consequence of competing demands on their time and other resources, do not feel willing or able to advocate appropriately for the young person, but more often family members, who by virtue of their own difficulties or disparate beliefs, struggle to make a valid contribution to the process of change. The GLM approach, however, has proven valuable in engaging families as well as young people. Many parents are initially anxious about their involvement with professionals. They fear that they will be regarded as responsible for their child's harmful behaviors and that their suitability to care for other children in the family may be questioned; they may be in denial that their child would commit such behavior or anxious that their parental role will be undermined by professionals. Most parents have a desire to see their children do well, and many are motivated to participate in Good Lives plans if they feel valued and are helped to recognize the contribution they can make in progressing their child toward a positive future. By focusing on their strengths and identifying and attending to the internal and external resources families require to enable them to positively participate, practitioners can significantly increase parents' confidence, hope for the future, and engagement in the program. Their inclusion as members of the Good Lives team confirms to parents that they are viewed as important contributors to intervention plans and ensures that they understand the young person's needs and their part in helping to meet them.

Some families require support and help in reaching their potential to meet their child's needs. This can include practical help with child care or funding to enable them to travel to meetings to support the young person or receive input regarding how they can contribute to the change process. The Good Lives plan may therefore include a program of parental support sessions, joint sessions with the young person and the family, or in some circumstances, individual work with family members facilitated by the Good Lives team when possible.

With its widening appeal and accessibility as a concept, the GLM can help many families feel empowered to make a contribution to positive change, without feeling blamed or judged.

CASE ILLUSTRATIONS

This section considers some of the therapeutic interventions for the case illustrations described in chapters 5 and 6. The objective of this section is to demonstrate how Good Lives assessments and plans can translate into interventions.

As in previous chapters, the case illustration of Joe will be more comprehensive in order to guide the reader through the therapeutic process. The other two case illustrations share some similarities with Joe so the focus will be on the differences among the intervention approaches. It is hoped that this will assist the reader to appreciate that although some therapeutic resources may be applied across different cases, an individualistic approach is required to fully respond to each young person's differing needs and characteristics. An important commonality in the case illustrations is the requirement of practitioners to work with the young person's parents/caregivers to assist them to make relevant contributions while the young person is in the home and the community. This includes observations of the young person's behavior, supporting his or her ability to appropriately manage emotions in different situations, and monitoring his or her sexual arousal to and interest in others. The level of supervision the young person requires is initially determined as part of early assessment (see chapter 5). As the young person begins to respond to and make progress within the intervention program, it is likely that gradual reductions to supervision levels will be implemented. Decisions about changes to supervision levels should be agreed upon by the Good Lives team based on continuing risk assessment that takes into account parent/caregiver observations of the young person, and therapeutic considerations, such as the young person's motivation and capacity to self-manage potential risk.

As the process of making incremental reductions to supervision has been discussed above, it is not included here; instead consideration is given to examples of specific therapeutic exercises and approaches. The reader should refer to chapter 6 for a more in-depth overview of the work plan for each case. Information regarding each young person's harmful-sexual-behavior-related needs, key areas of therapeutic work, and other important areas for consideration are summarized in tables 7.1, 7.2, and 7.3, respectively.

Case A: Joe

Table 7.1 Summary of factors relevant to Joe's therapeutic work

PRIMARY NEEDS MET BY HARMFUL SEXUAL BEHAVIOR	KEY AREAS OF THERAPEUTIC WORK	OTHERS AREAS OF CONSIDERATION
• Emotional health • Having people in my life • Achievement (maintenance)	• Emotional safety, regulation, and distress tolerance • Attachment and relationships • Trauma focused work • Self-identity and self-compassion work • Understanding and managing harmful sexual behavior • Problem solving • Work with family and systems	• Self harm • Intellectual disability • Conflict between the primary needs of *emotional health* and *having people in my life* • Disproportionate focus on the need of *having people in my life*, and may neglect needs such as *physical health, having a purpose and making a difference,* and *being my own person.*

In consideration of Joe's therapeutic engagement, cognitive abilities, retention of information, risks, and needs, it was assessed that he would require an intervention program of work lasting for approximately 20 months, with weekly therapeutic sessions. Joe's need to gain a sense of *having people in my life* had been assessed as overarching, and therefore the focus of foundational work was to establish a strong therapeutic alliance. As part of that process, Joe made a "strengths key ring" that he then used in everyday life. He selected different beads to signify his personal strengths, which he and his therapists had previously identified, and made them into a key ring. In addition to providing a means to help establish a positive therapeutic rapport, the intervention had potential to promote Joe's positive self-regard, feel compassionate toward himself, and identify strengths that could be referred to throughout therapeutic work to support his progress and change. Moreover, developing the strengths key ring was a practical task and provided a concrete reminder to Joe of his different strengths, therefore being responsive to his learning needs. Some Compassionate Mind Training (Gilbert and Proctor 2006) also helped Joe to develop a greater sense of warmth and understanding toward himself. The technique employed with Joe required him to act out his inner conversations using the Gestalt technique of two chairs (Whelton and Greenberg 2005), with one chair representing his "critical self" and the other signifying his "compassionate self." This was useful in helping Joe to recognize his propensity to think about himself in a negative way and through practicing positive self-talk was able to counteract his tendency to anticipate rejection from others.

In sequencing the intervention, it was assessed that therapeutic work focused on emotional health should be prioritized. Joe had a history of difficulties in meeting his *emotional health* needs, and it had been identified that on occasion these needs conflicted with his overarching need of *having people in my life.* It was anticipated that work on *emotional health* would help Joe to form positive relationships and provide opportunities for him to gain internal skills to help him manage later work that he might find more emotionally challenging—for example, discussing difficult life events, such as his prior traumatic experiences. This was particularly important given his history of self-harming behaviors. Because he had not fully secured a sense of safety, he was very emotionally reactive and had a tendency to live in the moment.

It was considered that "bottom-up" processing, where therapy is biologically informed through focusing on what is going on in the body, would initially be better suited to Joe than "top-down" processing, which relies on cognitive strategies to manage or reduce feelings, thoughts, and behaviors. So to assist Joe in recognizing arousal within his body and identifying his own physiological state, a biofeedback approach was used. This included a pulse monitor biofeedback ring and interactive computer software connected to biofeedback finger sensors. Once Joe was better able to decode what was happening in his body he started to learn how to more effectively regulate his emotions, for example by using simple breathing techniques and "safe place" work. Safe place work can be used when individuals are feeling anxious or threatened, or to help them achieve a sense of emotional equilibrium. It is a visualization technique in which they imagine being somewhere they associate with feelings of safety, protection, and calm. Joe's intellectual disability affected his capacity to visualize and retain information, so the technique involved him physically constructing his safe place by taking photographs to produce posters and picture cards that prompt him to use the safe place imagery. The therapeutic process also used Joe's interests and strengths in songwriting and playing music to help him regulate his emotions. Joe constructed songs that he could play on his audio equipment to help develop his awareness of and ability to manage different emotions. Once he had developed skills to help manage his emotions, he was able to practice distress tolerance in the therapeutic session. This entailed him using some of the techniques described above to help him accept and deal with situations that made him feel uneasy.

Joe's overarching need was *having people in my life,* and this was associated with his potential risk of harming others through his sexual behavior. Therefore it was an important focus of the intervention program that extended beyond the confines of the therapeutic relationship. Imagery and video were used to explore and enhance his understanding of different relationships and his ability to identify social cues. Subsequently, he could practice and further develop his social and interpersonal skills through role-playing and then with his caregivers in the residential unit. Joe also joined G-map's group-work program for young people with intellectual disabilities who have displayed harmful sexual behavior. This enabled him to further mix with peers and attain a sense of achievement from demonstrating skills and knowledge he had gained from individual work. The group-work program helped him through sessions that focused on "making good relationships" and "what information should I share with others?"

At the same time Joe was increasingly involved in opportunities and activities that complemented his therapeutic progress and enabled him to practice and transfer his developing skills in community situations. These were risk-assessed and supervised/observed as required. Any difficulties Joe encountered were discussed, explored, and addressed with his caregivers and within the therapeutic work. Over time the activities he engaged in included clothes shopping, going to the gym, attending music classes, joining a youth club, and ultimately going to college. Participation in these pursuits helped Joe to meet a range of needs—for example, clothes shopping and the gym assisted with his physical presentation and health needs, whereas youth club and college helped to meet his need of *having people in my life* and provided him with a sense of achievement. Similarly, clothes shopping and his general opportunities to make decisions for himself helped to meet his needs for being his own person and music classes and the gym helped him to develop self-soothing skills, thus meeting his *emotional health* needs. Additionally, Joe wrote down his anxieties and concerns over the course of a day and routinely discussed them with one of his caregivers, which provided opportunities for Joe to seek emotional support in a contained way, rather than exhibiting attention-seeking behaviors in order to meet his belonging needs when he felt distressed.

Some areas of the therapeutic work that were considered in greater depth in the latter stages used a more cognitive approach that included exploring the effects of Joe's own victimization and his harmful sexual behavior by considering the "ripple effect" so that he began to recognize the consequences of the behavior on victims, family, and the wider community. The ripple effect is when an object is dropped into a pool of water and creates ripples expanding outward; similarly, Joe's behavior also had consequences and impacted on others to varying degrees. CBT was also used to help him develop problem-solving skills. The work involved him examining how his thoughts, feelings, and behaviors were inextricably linked in different situations. For example, Joe's thoughts and beliefs about being unlovable gave rise to feelings of loneliness, which he attempted to resolve by recourse to unhelpful behaviors such as inventing exaggerated stories that he hoped would make him more interesting to others. As Joe was able to make these links he began to problem-solve by considering other more positive ways he could gain attention from others and by utilizing his compassionate voice when he was having thoughts about being unloved. To assist his learning this work was presented visually through illustrations or role-playing. Joe subsequently identified strategies, including cognitive restructuring and his previously developed regulation techniques, that he could use to help him more effectively solve problems in different situations.

Joe was helped to understand the process of his harmful sexual behavior by using Finklehor's model (1984), commonly known as the "four preconditions model." To make the model more accessible for Joe, the language relating to each precondition was simplified. Moreover, the four stages were represented by four wooden blocks that Joe could stand on to provide a more concrete representation of each precondition. By standing on each block Joe was helped to comprehend the distinct points at which he could have prevented his harmful sexual behavior—for example, by using self-management strategies. Following this, Joe and his therapists developed several strategies he could use to help him manage potential risky sexual thoughts, feelings, and behaviors. The strategies were illustrated by symbols and pictures on a laminated credit-card-sized tag (see figure 7.1 on the next page) with symbols of the goals Joe was hoping to achieve on the reverse (see figure 7.2 on the next page). Joe carried the card in his wallet so that both he and his caregivers could use it as a reminder and prompt if they were concerned about risk.

Figure 7.1 Joe's strategies

Figure 7.2 Joe's goals

Although sexual health was not identified as a need specifically related to the origins of Joe's harmful sexual behavior, his own victimization and his abuse of his brother resulted in him having some confusion and distorted thoughts about sex. It was therefore an integral part of intervention to address these through sex education. Joe's teachers provided him with relevant information and in therapeutic work he used interactive sexual knowledge quizzes, information about consent, picture sort exercises, and discussions about his sexual interests; and guidance regarding the development, maintenance, and progression of non-platonic relationships. During this work, Joe indicated that he did not want to rush into sexual relationships but instead make decisions about sex as part of a well-developed trusting relationship. He also acknowledged that he was homosexual and that his previous assertion about being heterosexual had resulted from both wanting his parents' acceptance and his desire to have children in the future (linked to his need for *having people in his life*).

While the current section regarding Joe's intervention program has concentrated on his individual work, rather than his group work or work with family and caregivers, it is important to highlight that these were all significant components in his therapeutic progress. Group work reinforced key messages from individual therapeutic sessions and so helped Joe retain information and provided a forum where he could interact with and learn from peers. Work with caregivers was instrumental to help them provide relevant and risk-assessed opportunities and support for Joe, while their feedback about Joe's day-to-day behavior would sometimes inform the content of therapeutic sessions. Finally, work with Joe's family was necessary to help them understand the origins of Joe's harmful sexual behavior and move toward a more positive future, as discussed further in chapter 8.

Case B: Wayne

Table 7.2 Summary of factors relevant to Wayne's intervention program

PRIMARY NEEDS MET BY HARMFUL SEXUAL BEHAVIOR	KEY AREAS OF THERAPEUTIC WORK	OTHERS AREAS OF CONSIDERATION
• Having fun • Sexual health • Emotional health	• Emotional regulation and distress tolerance (with a specific focus on managing boredom) • Understanding harmful sexual behavior, including consequences for victims • Sex education • Managing sexual arousal • Problem solving • Work with family	• Good cognitive and intellectual ability • Non-sexual anti-social behaviors • Conflict between the primary needs of *having fun* and *having people in my life* • Disproportionate focus on the need to have fun (thrill and excitement), and may neglect needs such as *achieving, having a purpose and making a difference*

Wayne was assessed as requiring 12-months of therapeutic work, with sessions occurring weekly. While his belonging needs were not assessed as an intervention priority, in recognition that the therapetic relationship is a factor for outcome success (Beech and Hamilton-Giachritsis 2005; Marshall 2005), the preliminary focus of sessions was to establish a therapeutic rapport, for example through therapists demonstrating respect, empathy, warmth, honesty, openness, and a non-judgmental attitude.

For Wayne, family work had a greater emphasis in intervention plans compared with Joe. This was because Wayne's present and longer-term residence was with his parents, who had been assessed as having the motivation, strengths, skills, and capacities that could help him progress. Therefore, prior to embarking on distress tolerance work, interventions focused on joint work with Wayne and his parents in order to strengthen their relationship and assist Wayne to more readily use his parents as emotional confidants. This included helping all parties recognize one another's viewpoints and identifying the resources his parents had to help Wayne meet his goals. As part of his individual work, Wayne identified alternative means and strategies he could use to help him regulate his boredom in pro-social ways, such as by participating in sports and games. Some of these activities also met his need for thrill and excitement, including a rock climbing group and visits to theme parks. His parents initially facilitated and supervised all the activities that Wayne attended and were advised and supported by his therapists on how to do this. However, many of the identified activities did not address Wayne's need for instant thrill and excitement as he sometimes had to wait for an appropriate time to attend them. It was clear that he needed the skills, motivation, and capacity to defer gratification until he was able to participate in such activities. Therefore, at the same time that Wayne started to engage in these activities, he was helped in his therapeutic work to develop his emotional regulation skills.

In a similar way to Joe, a biofeedback approach was employed with Wayne to increase his awareness and recognition of his emotional reactions. His therapeutic program also included a number of approaches that were better suited to his cognitive functioning and capacity to employ higher brain processes. For example, to help him learn to manage and tolerate distress in the moment, therapeutic techniques drew on some elements of a dialectic behavioral therapy approach (DBT). DBT was originally developed for people with borderline personality disorder and suicidal tendencies by Linehan (1987), but has produced promising results when applied to other populations (Chapman 2006). It is a type of cognitive behavioral therapy that can be used to help individuals manage their emotions, tolerate distress, and develop interpersonal effectiveness skills. For Wayne, this included exposure to emotions he experienced as distressing, such as boredom, while helping him to gain acceptance of them and practice letting go of the emotion without acting on the impulse to act on or change it. The process was further supported by using self-soothing techniques and helping Wayne learn how to weigh up the pros and cons of his decisions. He also elected to use music and electronic games as strategies to help him regulate his boredom in the moment.

Similar approaches were used with Wayne and Joe regarding sex and relationship education, in understanding their harmful sexual behaviors, and the consequences for others. Given Wayne's prior use of pornography, however, there was a greater focus on the risks associated with this behavior, the distortions he had developed as a result of the sexualized imagery he had been exposed to, and the safeguards he and his parents could put in place to prevent him accessing inappropriate and counterproductive sexualized materials and messages. To help Wayne identify the relationship between his sexual preoccupation and feelings of boredom he kept a sexual thoughts diary, although care was taken to prevent the tool from reinforcing his sexual preoccupation. Wayne's sexual preoccupation was largely addressed by working with his environment to broaden his range of interests so that he was more constructively engaged in activities that he enjoyed, thus making him less reliant on sex and pornography to meet his needs. Moreover, his sex education was grounded in the context of healthy relationships, reducing his focus on more objectified and detached concepts of sexual relationships. He was able to meet his needs for sexual satisfaction by masturbating, using appropriate thoughts, in the privacy of his bedroom.

The problem-solving technique employed with Wayne to help him self-manage risk was the ACE (Avoid–Control–Escape) model. The model is described more comprehensively by Print and O'Callaghan (2004) but in brief it helps young people consider their thoughts, feelings, and environment, and on the basis of these to decide whether they should avoid a situation; whether they believe they can remain positively in control of their behavior; or, if this fails, how they can escape a situation. This model helped Wayne identify potentially risky situations regarding both his sexual and general anti-social behavior. The concept of "control" was emphasized and how it involved making a decision based on whether he felt bored, angry, or other negative moods and whether he felt confident in using the strategies he had learned, such as self-soothing techniques and/or distress tolerance. Wayne rehearsed using ACE in role-playing and in daily life with his parents so that he could either recognize and stay away from difficult situations or get out of them if it became necessary.

Extensive work was undertaken with Wayne's parents to help them practice risk management both within their home and in the community. It included Wayne's use of the computer; the layout of his room in relation to where windows were positioned (i.e., in consideration of his prior indecent exposures from windows that overlooked a public footpath); having an understanding of the ACE model; and the more general strategies advocated in the course of Wayne's therapy. Furthermore, work was undertaken with his parents to help them enforce boundaries and consequences. Wayne's parents were instrumental in helping him to meet the primary needs that were both related and unrelated to his harmful sexual behavior, including advocating on his behalf at school to ensure that he was given work that was consistent with his intellectual abilities; and funding and monitoring a range of activities for him to participate in to increase his independence skills, and opportunities to have fun and regulate his emotions.

Case C: Leanne

Table 7.3: Summary of factors relevant to Leanne's intervention program

PRIMARY NEEDS MET BY HARMFUL SEXUAL BEHAVIOR	KEY AREAS OF THERAPEUTIC WORK	OTHERS AREAS OF CONSIDERATION
• Emotional health • Having people in my life	• Emotional safety, regulation, and distress tolerance • Attachment and relationships • Trauma-focused work • Self-identity and ethnicity • Self-compassion work • Understanding and managing harmful sexual behavior • Learning about healthy sexuality • Problem solving • Work with family and systems	• Dual heritage • Young age • Conflict between the primary needs of emotional health and having people in my life • Disproportionate focus on the need of *emotional health,* and may neglect needs such as *having people in my life, having fun, achieving, being my own person, having a purpose and making a difference,* and *sexual health*

Current research and thinking indicates that effective therapeutic programs with younger children should offer time-limited intervention with the child and involve working with the child's parents and/or caregivers (Chaffin et al. 2008). In consideration of Leanne's age and needs, it was assessed that she should undertake a 15-month intervention program, with sessions occurring weekly. Her foster caregiver and aunt separately attended some sessions, and others were attended jointly by Leanne and her foster caregiver or aunt.

Leanne's primary needs associated with her harmful sexual behavior were similar to Joe's, with the exception of "achievement" as a maintenance factor. Additionally, while

Leanne does not have an intellectual disability, her young age meant that she also benefited from more creative and concrete therapeutic techniques and resources. The work on emotional safety, relationships and communication, emotional regulation, trauma-focused work, understanding her harmful sexual behavior and its consequences for others, self-compassion, risk management, and distress tolerance was very similar for Leanne and Joe. Differences included making sex education more developmentally appropriate to Leanne's age, and rather than music being the focus of "feel good" and relaxing activities, Leanne tended to meet this need through art, beauty, and fashion—for example, drawing, painting, bathing, face masks, nail manicures, and touch-sensitive fabrics. Her interest in fashion and creativity also offered a valuable means of helping her explore her self-identity and dual heritage. Moreover, Leanne was paired with a mentor of a similar ethnicity, and they further explored cultural and identity issues, for example, through discussions and visits to relevant museums looking at art, customs, and dress, and cooking culturally diverse foods.

In contrast with Joe, Leanne participated in attunement exercises with her foster caregiver and her aunt both in and outside of sessions. These were not used with Joe as he did not have the same level of stability with his primary caregiver. Attunement exercises may involve the young person and caregiver mirroring each other's actions. According to Creeden (2005), undertaking regular attunement exercises can stimulate the neural pathways involved in the attunement process and help people re-establish a "social connection"—that is, increase their ability to accurately integrate their affective and cognitive experiences of their environment.

Due to her avoidant attachment style, Leanne's emotions were not as easy for others to recognize and observe as Joe's, who had an ambivalent attachment. Hence, Leanne was given several exercises to more fully explore her emotions. In one exercise Leanne created a mask to represent the person that she allows other people to see (for example, a smiley face for happiness, rosy cheeks for embarrassment). Then, using art, she depicted what was really happening under the mask (for example, a red fist for anger, knots for worry). Another exercise used animal characters to further explore the different personas and emotions that Leanne might present in different circumstances, such as a gorilla to represent the anger she demonstrated toward her siblings. Leanne also kept an emotions diary, which she shared with her therapeutic practitioners, to help her and them understand her emotional responses and behaviors. The diary was also used when undertaking work on problem solving to show how her thoughts, feelings, and behaviors were linked (see Joe's intervention details for more on this). In response to Leanne's high levels of anger, the work aimed to help her regulate her emotions included work specifically targeted at anger management such as progressive muscle relaxation and consequential thinking. Leanne also engaged in mindfulness exercises to assist with her general emotional regulation. Mindfulness involves a particular way of paying attention to the self and the moment without judging them. It is thought that mindfulness and meditation can enhance healthy development and emotional well-being (Siegel 2007); recent research indicates that it may also enhance individuals' capacity for empathy (Lutz et al. 2008). While research has indicated that mindfulness may have utility with individuals who have an intellectual disability (Singh et al. 2004; 2006), this therapeutic technique was employed with Leanne rather than Joe because it better suited her learning style. In contrast with Joe, Leanne was encouraged to ask for help more frequently in view of her specific needs and emotional responses. Leanne could often use distraction first to help her manage her emotions more immediately. As part of her therapeutic work, these two different types of coping were assimilated, so that she might initially use distraction to deal with the problem in the moment, although subsequently she would seek help from and/or discuss her difficulties with her network. Joe, however, was encouraged to learn strategies to better contain his emotions rather than an erratic clinging to others in an attempt to get their help and attention.

Individual sessions with Leanne's specialist foster caregiver and aunt predominantly focused on guidance on how to respond to Leanne's emotions and attachment behaviors and on comprehending Leanne's harmful sexual behavior and risk management. "Keep safe" work was undertaken with Leanne's aunt—for example, establishing rules on privacy and helping her to pick up on cues that may have indicated that Leanne was feeling threatened or unsafe. This was done with specific consideration of Leanne's prior victimization when she stayed with her aunt and her aunt's partner as a young child. In joint sessions with Leanne, her foster caregiver and aunt helped her to translate her learning and skills from the therapeutic environment into everyday living experiences. As the therapeutic work progressed Leanne was provided with relevant and appropriately supervised opportunities to further develop her skills and meet a range of needs. These included integration into mainstream education, attending an after-school group that focused on fashion, attending a local arts and crafts group where her painting was entered into a regional competition, developing her cooking skills with her caregiver, and contact with her aunt.

This chapter demonstrates how the GLM can be used in conjunction with other models and theories to attend to an individual's needs. While intervention is aimed at meeting needs and promoting strengths, issues of risk and the development of risk management skills form an integral part of the intervention process. Good Lives plans are individually designed to help the young people work toward engaging in activities (secondary goods/ means) that not only are attractive to them but will contribute to identified significant needs being met in positive ways. Work with the young people aims to help them to utilize their strengths and develop the necessary skills to enable them to participate in these successfully and safely, and will inevitably include attention to risk awareness and management.

The case examples show how intervention is individualized according to need and how priority to specific needs may be required in order to support a young person's subsequent therapeutic progress.

REFERENCES

Andrews, D. A., and J. Bonta. 2010. *The psychology of criminal conduct*, 5th ed. New Providence, NJ: Lexis Matthew Bender.

Andrews, D. A., J. Bonta, and R. D. Hoge. 1990. Classification for effective rehabilitation: Rediscovering psychology. *Criminal Justice and Behaviour* 17:19–52.

Beech, A. R., and C. E. Hamilton-Giachritsis. 2005. Relationship between therapeutic climate and treatment outcome in group-based sexual offender treatment programs. *Sexual Abuse: A Journal of Research and Treatment* 17:127–40.

Bonta, J., and D. A. Andrews. 2007. *Risk–Need–Responsivity model for offender assessment and treatment*. User Report No. 2007-06. Ottawa, Ontario: Public Safety Canada.

Borduin, C., S. Hengeller, D. Blaske, and R. Stein. 1990. Multisystemic treatment of adolescent sexual offenders. *International Journal of Offender Therapy and Comparative Criminology* 34:105–13.

Briggs, D., and R. Kennington. 2006. *Managing men who sexually abuse*. London: Jessica Kingsley Publishers.

Chaffin, M., L. Berliner, R. Block, T. Cavanagh Johnson, W. N. Friedrich, D. G. Louis, D. L. Thomas, I. J. Page, D. S. Prescott, J. F. Silovsky, and C. Madden. 2008. Report of the ATSA task force on children with sexual behaviour problems. *Child Maltreatment* 13:199–218.

Chapman, A. L. 2006. Dialectical behavior therapy: Current indications and unique elements. *Psychiatry* 3:62–68.

Creeden, K. 2004. The neuro-developmental impact of early trauma and insecure attachment: Re-thinking our understanding and treatment of sexual behavior problems. *Sexual Addiction and Compulsivity* 11:223–47.

Creeden, K. 2005. Integrating trauma and attachment research in the treatment of sexually abusive youth. In M. C. Calder (ed.), *Children and young people who sexually abuse: New theory, research, and practice developments*, 202–16. Lyme Regis, UK: Russell House Publishing.

Farrall, S. 2002. *Rethinking what works with offenders: Probation, social context, and desistance from crime*. Devon, UK: Willan Publishing.

Ferrara, M. L., and S. McDonald. 1996. *Treatment of the juvenile sex offender: Neurologic and psychiatric impairments*. Northvale, NJ: Jason Aronson.

Finklehor, D. 1984. *Child sexual abuse: New theory and research.* New York: Free Press.

Gilbert, P., and S. Proctor. 2006. Compassionate mind training for people with high shame and self-criticism: Overview and pilot study of a group therapy approach. *Clinical Psychology and Psychotherapy* 13:353–79.

Hackett, S. 2003. Evidence-based assessment: A critical evaluation. In Calder, M. C., and S. Hackett (eds.), *Assessment in child care: Using and developing frameworks for practice*, 74–85. Lyme Regis, UK: Russell House Publishing.

Hackett, S. 2004. *What works for children and young people with harmful sexual behaviours?* Nottingham, UK: Russell Press.

Hanson, R. K., and M. T. Bussiere. 1998. Predicting relapse: A meta-analysis of sexual offender recidivism studies. *Journal of Consulting and Clinical Psychology* 66:348–62.

Hanson, R. K., A. Gordon, A. J. R. Harris, J. K. Marques, W. Murphey, V. L. Quinsey, and M. C. Seto. 2002. First report of the collaborative outcome data project on the effectiveness of psychological treatment for sex offenders. *Sexual Abuse: A Journal of Research and Treatment* 1:169–94.

Henggeler, S. W., G. B. Melton, and L. A. Smith. 1992. Family preservation using multisystemic therapy: An effective alternative to incarcerating serious juvenile offenders. *Journal of Consulting and Clinical Psychology* 60:953–61.

Hudson, S. M., T. Ward, and J. C. McCormack. 1999. Offense pathways in sexual offenders. *Journal of Interpersonal Violence* 14:779–98.

Lab, S. P., G. Shields, and C. Schondel. 1993. An evaluation of juvenile sexual offender treatment. *Crime and Delinquency* 39:543–53.

Laws, D. R., and T. Ward. 2011. *Desistance and sexual offending: Alternatives to throwing away the keys.* New York: Guilford Press.

Linehan, M. M. 1987. Dialectical behavior therapy: A cognitive behavioral approach to parasuicide. *Journal of Personality Disorders* 1:328–33.

Longo, R. 2003. Emerging issues, policy changes, and the future of treating children with sexual behaviour problems. *Annals of the New York Academy of Sciences* 989:502–14.

Losel, F. 1995. Increasing consensus in the evaluation of offender rehabilitation? Lessons from recent research syntheses. *Psychology, Crime, and Law* 2:19–39.

Lutz, A., J. Brefczynski-Lewis, T. Johnstone, R. J. Davidson. 2008. Regulation of the Neural Circuitry of Emotion by Compassion Meditation: Effects of Meditative Expertise. *PLoS ONE* 3(3):e1897. doi:10.1371/journal.pone.0001897, http://www.plosone.org/article/info%3Adoi%2F10.1371% 2F journal.pone.0001897.

Marsa, F., G. O'Reilly, A. Carr, P. Murphy, M. O'Sullivan, A. Cotter, and D. Hevey. 2004. Attachment styles and psychological profiles of child sex offenders in Ireland. *Journal of Interpersonal Violence* 19:228–51.

Marshall, W. L. 2005. Therapist style in sexual offender treatment: Influence on indices of change. *Sexual Abuse: A Journal of Research and Treatment* 17:109–16.

Marshall, W. L., and H. E. Barbaree. 1990. An integrated theory of the etiology of sexual offending. In W. L. Marshall, D. R. Laws, and H. E. Barbaree (eds.), *Handbook of sexual assault: Issues, theories, and treatment of the offender*, 257–75. New York: Plenum.

McGrath, R. J., G. F. Cumming, B. L. Burchard, S. Zeoli, and L. Ellerby. 2010 *Current practices and emerging trends in sexual abuser management: The Safer Society 2009 North American survey.* Brandon, VT: Safer Society Foundation.

McMackin, R., M. Leisen, J. Cusack, J. LaFratta, and P. Litwin. 2002. The relationship of trauma exposure to sex offending behaviour among male juvenile offenders. *Journal of Child Sexual Abuse* 11:25–39.

O'Callaghan, D. 1999. Young abusers with learning disabilities: Towards better understanding and positive interventions. In M. C. Calder (ed.), *Working with young people who sexually abuse: New pieces of the jigsaw puzzle*, 225–50. Lyme Regis, UK: Russell House Publishing.

Print, B., and D. O'Callaghan. 2004. Essentials of an effective treatment programme for sexually abusive adolescents: Offence specific treatment tasks. In G. O'Reilly, W. Marshall, A. Carr, and R. Beckett (eds.), *Handbook of clinical intervention with juvenile sexual abusers*, 237–74. Hove, UK, and New York: Brunner-Routledge.

Rasmussen, L. A., J. E. Burton, and B. J. Christopherson. 1992. Precursors to offending and the trauma outcome process in sexually reactive children. *Journal of Child Sexual Abuse* 1:33–47.

Rich, P. 2006. *Attachment and sexual offending: Understanding and applying attachment theory to the treatment of juvenile sexual offenders.* Chichester, UK: John Wiley and Sons.

Ryan, G., T. J. Miyoshi, J. L. Metzner, R. D. Krugman, and G. E. Fryer. 1996. Trends in a national sample of sexually abusive youths. *Journal of the American Academy of Child and Adolescent Psychiatry* 35:17–25.

Sapp, A., and M. Vaughn. 1990. Juvenile sex offender treatment at state-operated correctional institutions. *International Journal of Offender Therapy and Comparative Criminology* 34:131–46.

Saxe, G. N., B. H. Ellis, and J. B. Kaplow. 2007. *Collaborative treatment of traumatized children and teens: The Trauma Systems Therapy Approach.* New York: Guilford Press.

Schore, A. N. 2002. Dysregulation of the right brain: A fundamental mechanism of traumatic attachment and the psychopathogenesis of posttraumatic stress disorder. *Australian and New Zealand Journal of Psychiatry* 36:9–30.

Sheldon, B., and R. Chilvers. 2000. *Evidence-based social care: A study of prospects and problems.* Lyme Regis, UK: Russell House Publishing.

Siegel, D. 2007. *The mindful brain: Reflections and attunement in the cultivation of well-being.* London: W. W. Norton.

Singh, N. N., G. E. Lancioni, A. S. W. Winton, W. J. Curtis, R. G. Wahler, M. Sabaawi, J. Singh, and K. McAleavey. 2006. Mindful staff increase learning and reduce aggression in adults with developmental disabilities. *Research in Developmental Disabilities* 27:545–58.

Singh, N. N., G. E. Lancioni, A. S. W. Winton, R. G. Wahler, J. Singh, and M. Sage. 2004. Mindful caregiving increases happiness among individuals with profound multiple disabilities. *Research in Developmental Disabilities* 25:207–18.

Smallbone, S. W. 2005. Attachment insecurity as a predisposing factor for sexually abusive behaviour by young people. In M. C. Calder (ed.), *Children and young people who sexually abuse: New theory, research and practice developments*, 6–18. Lyme Regis, UK: Russell House Publishing.

Smallbone, S. W., and M. Dadds. 1998. Childhood attachment and adult attachment in incarcerated adult male sex offenders. *Journal of Interpersonal Violence* 13:555–73.

Smallbone, S. W., and M. Dadds. 2000. Attachment and coercive sexual behaviour. *Sexual Abuse: Journal of Research and Treatment* 12:3–16.

Smallbone, S. W., and M. Dadds. 2001. Further evidence for a relationship between attachment insecurity and coercive sexual behaviour. *Journal of Interpersonal Violence* 16:22–35.

Vennard, J., D. Sugg, and C. Hedderman. 1997. *Changing offenders' attitudes and behaviours: What works?* Home Office Research Study 171. London: Home Office.

Ward, T., S. M. Hudson, W. L. Marshall, and R. J. Siegert. 1995. Attachment style and intimacy deficits in sexual offenders: A theoretical framework. *Sexual Abuse: Journal of Research and Treatment* 7:317–35.

Ward, T., R. E. Mann, and T. A. Gannon. 2007. The Good Lives model of offender rehabilitation: Clinical implications. *Aggression and Violent Behaviour* 12:87–107.

Whelton, W. J., and L. S. Greenberg. 2005. Emotion in self-criticism. *Personality and Individual Differences* 38:1583–95.

Willis, G., and T. Ward. 2011. Striving for a good life: The Good Lives model applied to released child molesters. *Journal of Sexual Aggression* 17:290–303.

Willis, G. W., P. M. Yates, T. A. Gannon, and T. Ward. 2013. How to integrate the Good Lives model into treatment programs for sexual offending: An introduction and overview. *Sexual Abuse: A Journal of Research and Treatment* 25:123–42.

Worling, J. 2012. The assessment and treatment of deviant sexual arousal with adolescents who have offended sexually. *Journal of Sexual Aggression* 18:36–63.

Worling, J., and T. Curwen. 2000. Adolescent sexual offender recidivism: Success of specialized treatment and implications for risk prediction. *Child Abuse and Neglect* 24:965–82.

CHAPTER 8

Transitions

HELEN GRIFFIN AND LAURA WYLIE

The transitions that young people undergo during and after therapeutic intervention can be a very important part of the rehabilitation process. During the period of intervention young people who have displayed harmful sexual behavior can be living in a range of environments, including the family home, the care system, or a secure setting. The dysfunction and/or trauma that are often present in these youngsters' histories (Creeden 2005; Hunter and Becker 1994; Longo 2001) can result in them being removed from their parental home prior to them displaying harmful sexual behavior. Alternatively, being placed in local authority care might be a consequence of their harmful behavior or parental rejection. Furthermore, the seriousness of some sexual crimes and the harm caused to victims may increase the likelihood of these young people receiving custodial sentences. Young people who have been placed in the care of the local authority or in the penal system will ultimately transition to community living arrangements. It is important in these cases that transitions are planned and that the environments in which young people will eventually live are anticipated in Good Lives plans (Yates, Prescott, and Ward 2010). Plans need to be pragmatic, achievable, and relevant to the young people's future living environment (Willis et al. 2013).

International research has highlighted the increased risk of social exclusion faced by those leaving care (Stein 2006). Studies indicate that young people who live with their families tend to remain at home for longer, whereas those leaving care often move to independent living arrangements at the age of 16 to 18 years and may have to cope with setting up a new home, getting to know a new area, changes in education, or unemployment (Stein 2006). Since stability can help to protect against harmful behaviors, it is important that it is maximized for young people leaving care. Building resilience and improving outcomes for those leaving care includes providing a gradual and flexible transition period that is developmentally appropriate to the young people's level of maturity and skills, and encompasses continuing support, especially for those who have complex needs (Mendes, Johnson, and Moslehuddin 2011; Stein 2005; 2006). Young people who are moving from secure environments into communities face similar difficulties.

According to Pemberton (2010), "young offenders returning to the community are likely to re-offend without resettlement support." In the United States, the importance of reducing barriers and social isolation in the re-integration of adult offenders into communities has been recognized (for example, the report of the Re-Entry Policy Council 2005, which recommended the expansion of projects to assist with re-entry). However, the practical implementation of such initiatives might be more difficult. Laws and Ward (2011) assert that currently the best approach to overcoming the barriers to re-integration is likely to be through the re-entry court (these are courts in the United States designed to assist with and address the unique circumstances of reintegrating prisoners into communities) and its associated partnerships. The effective re-entry of children and young people from custody into communities has similarly been considered and promoted in other countries; for example, in England and Wales the Youth Resettlement Framework for Action (Youth Justice Board 2006) has sought to develop resettlement plans and has recommended a more coordinated approach by the services involved. Unsuccessful transitions into communities continue to be of concern, however, and appear to relate to poor-quality assessments, a lack of resources, and problems with collaborative working between agencies (Callender, as cited in Pemberton 2010).

Keith's case illustrates an ineffective transition from custody. Keith was an 18-year-old man who was at the end of the custodial part of his sentence, which he received for sexually harming females under the age of 16 years and a violent offense when he was under the influence of alcohol. It was assessed that the primary needs related to his sexual and violent behaviors were *emotional health* and *having people in my life*. He had a history of complex trauma and was removed from home when he was 12 years old due to physical and emotional abuse that he had been subjected to by his parents. He lacked stability and consistency in his previous care placements and had been excluded from school on multiple occasions due to behavioral problems. He demonstrated symptoms of post-traumatic stress disorder and had a number of traits that were consistent with an emerging personality disorder. At the time of release from custody, Keith had undergone therapeutic work for seven months and had responded well to interventions, including emotional regulation strategies, and relationship and risk management skills.

Keith's practitioners had recommended that post-release he required consistent boundaries and some levels of containment in order to initially stabilize him, provide support to find employment, and access to peer-related opportunities in his community; any contact with his parents should be carefully managed and initially supervised. These recommendations were informed by the assessment of his primary needs and risk. Keith was subject to a court-ordered Supervision Order and electronic tag following his release from custody. Youth justice professionals had sought to obtain a supported and supervised tenancy for him, with gradual reductions to supervision levels, but his funding local authority subsequently decided that such provision was too expensive and would not be resourced. Alternative plans therefore had to be made at the last minute. Upon his release Keith was placed in hostel accommodations in close proximity to his family home, where he received minimal support from professionals or the community. He was a lonely young man who craved a sense of belonging and, in the absence of alternatives, turned to unsupervised contact with his family. The influence of his family destabilized him, and he started to rely on alcohol to help him regulate his emotions. He subsequently had a number of violent outbursts in his local community and committed further illegal and harmful sexual behaviors.

Intervention might provide young people living away from home with social skills that they have been able to demonstrate within the network local to their placement, emotional regulation strategies they can effectively use in their safe care environment; access to relevant opportunities in the local community; and support from their caseworker as an emotional confidant. However, these may be of limited benefit if the young people are then moved to a different environment where they feel unsafe; that have limited opportunities for support; where resources they have relied on to help reduce risk and enhance well-being are not available; and where they cannot generalize and transfer the skills they have learned. In a British follow-up study, the preliminary analysis of outcomes for 117 young people who had previously been in receipt of professional services between 10 and 20 years for their harmful sexual behaviors showed that 43 percent had unsuccessful outcomes and only 26 percent had positive outcomes (Hackett 2011). Positive outcomes were defined according to Every Child Matters (HM Government 2004) and Farrington, Ttofi, and Coid's (2009) resilient outcome factors. Factors that influenced positive outcomes included professional support available longer-term, success in education and employment, and stable romantic relationships. These findings highlight that therapeutic intervention for harmful sexual behavior needs to give greater consideration to long-term interventions that support young people in their transitions into adulthood.

The Youth Justice Board (YJB) for England and Wales notes that "the effects of interventions with children resonate into young adulthood and beyond . . . Improving transitions will produce better outcomes for young people as they are supported through the transitions process at a fragile time in their lives" (Harrison and Stevens 2012, 5). The successful transition of young people in the criminal justice system often requires collaboration among different agencies, including youth justice services, adult services, health, education/employment organizations, and housing and community organizations (National Collaborative on Workforce and Disability 2010). Literature indicates that factors such as employment, family, education, health, leisure, and relationships act as positive indicators for desistance from crime (Gibbens 1984; Irwin 1970; Laws and Ward 2011; Moffitt et al. 2002; Stouthamer-Loeber et al. 2004; Trasler 1979; Warr 1998). According to Laws and Ward (2011):

> From a desistance perspective, social capital such as education, relationship, and work possibilities are likely to be inherently motivating for offenders and also woven into the fabric of everyday life. This important point reminds practitioners not to look for generic solutions to offenders' arrays of problems but rather to seek to anchor their GLP's (Good Lives plans) within local communities, one's hopefully accepting of them and ideally, that contain allies and friends (244).

Moreover, the transition from youth to adult justice services represents a significant time for young people (Harrison and Stevens 2012, 5) and therefore requires careful planning and consideration. In some countries, including England and Wales, the approach to service users and the extent of available resources differs between youth and adult services; additionally, for some young people the transition will involve a disruption to established supportive relationships.

Ben, in contrast with Keith, is an example of a case where a transition plan was well considered and effective. When Ben was 12 he sexually harmed an adult female with mental health difficulties. Similar to Keith, the Good Lives needs assessed as relevant to his behavior were *emotional health* and *having people in my life.* Following the discovery of his behavior Ben was moved from his father's home to a specialist residential establishment that exclusively provided care for adolescent males with harmful sexual behavior. Ben's care team and therapeutic practitioners worked collaboratively with him, using a Good Lives approach, and soon he was beginning to appropriately meet his needs for *emotional health* and belonging *(having people in my life.)* Careful and continuous assessment of Ben's progress in therapeutic work and observations of him in the community over several months indicated that the risk of further harmful sexual behavior had significantly reduced, and therefore it was viewed as unnecessary for him to continue to live in the very specialist residential setting. As a return to living with his birth family was not a viable option, it was considered that a foster care setting was most likely to provide Ben with the opportunities to meet relevant Good Lives needs. For example, as a temporary environment shared by a number of young people Ben's residential setting gave rise to quite superficial attachment relationships whereas foster care offered the potential for relationships to be more stable and enduring.

A range of services became involved in Ben's transition, led by the children's services department of the local authority, which was actively receptive to recommendations from Ben's Good Lives team. By the age of 14, Ben was matched with foster caregivers, who were identified as being able to promote clear and consistent boundaries and provide him with high levels of nurturance. Ben was introduced to his new foster family before making the transition, and had overnight stays with them so that the transition was graduated and felt safe for him. Additionally, the foster caregivers had been in receipt of extensive training and guidance from Ben's therapeutic workers to facilitate their understanding of harmful sexual behavior and associated needs. Following his move to the foster caregivers, Ben established an increasingly positive and secure relationship with them and started to confide in them about his problems and concerns. Within a few months he obtained a weekend job, attended community resources, including football, and had a number of positive peer relationships. Ben continued to attend weekly for therapeutic work, that gave him some consistency during the period of transition.

During the final period of intervention, the frequency of Ben's therapeutic input was gradually reduced, although his foster caregivers continued to be offered support from his therapeutic workers for a few months following the termination of his program. As Ben matured, his foster caregivers were funded to offer him supported lodgings rather than "foster care," and he flourished in a college placement. When, due to his age, responsibility for Ben moved from children's to adult services, he experienced minimal difficulty as he had already accessed the necessary resources to help him build a "good life." Following a successful transition Ben demonstrated a capacity to meet his emotional and belonging needs not only by developing his internal resources but also through a variety of ways that were embedded within the "family" systems, peer relationships, and community support that accompanied him into adulthood.

In consideration of the difficulties of transition between different care environments, G-map in conjunction with partner agencies is in the process of developing a tiered and integrated system of residential and foster care. It involves matching young people of varying risk and needs to appropriate care provision. For example, for young people assessed as needing the highest level of supervision and who struggle to maintain boundaries or cope within family settings, a specialist residential placement with highly trained staff and on-site education is often considered to be the most suitable accommodation option. However, as the young people begin to respond positively to interventions, develop social skills, access support, and demonstrate a reduction in risk, they can often be transferred to specially trained foster caregivers. For young people whose need for supervision is not so intensive, specialist foster care placements can offer flexibility in meeting individual needs and provide a particularly useful opportunity for young people to experience positive family life and community involvement. The provision available in foster care placements is tiered in order to meet a young person's level of need. For example, a higher-tier placement for young people with complex needs and medium/high level of risk would consist of highly experienced, trained, and supported caregivers together with intensive therapeutic input; while a lower-tier placement for those with less intensive needs and lower risks provides more time-limited or lower-intensity interventions with significant emphasis on the longer-term support of their foster caregivers.

By building strong links between foster care and residential provision, the difficulties often involved in transitions are significantly reduced and arrangements can be more easily tailored to meet individual needs. For example, it is possible for the young people to establish a relationship with their prospective foster caregivers prior to leaving residential unit. Furthermore, following a move, young people and their caregivers can maintain contact with staff from the residential unit and thus benefit from additional support.

The flexibility of adopting a tiered approach via a range of specialist provision allows young people with differing needs not only to be matched with a suitable type of placement but also to more easily move between them. The transition from residential unit to foster care, wherever possible, extends the likelihood that a young person will establish a long-term support network, preserve attachment relationships, and gradually move into independence in a familiar local community.

At the end of therapeutic intervention, alongside consideration of resource requirements and the likely obstacles facing young people following their transition into a new living environment, it is important that a thorough re-evaluation of risk, support, and supervision needs is carried out. According to Yates, Prescott, and Ward (2010) both post-intervention supervision and maintenance are instrumental parts of the intervention process. In a recent inspection of Multi-Agency Public Protection Arrangements (statutory panels involved in the management of individuals who had sexually and violently harmed in England and Wales), it was found that multi-agency management rarely occurred in a comprehensive way and that intervention plans were dominated by restrictive practice—for example, the imposition of curfews and exclusion zones. Little attention was paid to protective factors that could reduce risk, such as engagement in positive activities, and minimal consideration was given to what would happen to an individual once professional supervision was terminated (Smith et al. 2011).

To promote more positive transitional and long-term planning it can be useful for young people's Good Lives teams to consider:

- Early planning for transitions
- Developing the Good Lives plan to extend into the new placement/environment
- Timely inclusion of young people's longer-term support network as team members so that they have sufficient opportunity to understand individuals' needs and their therapeutic journey
- Commencing transition arrangements in time to allow the continuation of therapeutic work throughout the change period. It is often a time of stress and anxiety for young people, and the availability of therapeutic support while adjusting to a new environment can be invaluable.
- Undertaking regular risk assessments to ensure that risk management and supervision plans are appropriate for the new environment. Supervision plans for the young people should initially reflect their experience prior to the move to avoid a dramatic change, such as from having only supervised activities in the community to no supervision in the new setting.
- Planning endings with the young people at an early stage, such as preparing them for the loss they may experience, incrementally reducing the frequency of therapeutic sessions, and providing opportunities for them to exert greater autonomy and self-reliance.
- Helping the young people to consider new experiences they might encounter. This may include work on safe use of technology; on who, when, and how they might need to tell others about their history; and on how they will organize their time.
- Ensuring that relevant and developmentally appropriate community resources are available to the young people so that they can meet significant primary needs as part of their Good Lives plans. Wherever possible activities in the new environment should be commenced prior to placement change so as to minimize disruption in routine.

Therapeutic interventions should hopefully have provided young people with a full understanding of how their Good Lives needs and other factors relate to their harmful sexual behavior. This should all be summarized in a user-friendly way so the young people have reference materials they can take from therapy to help them in their future. This could include a copy of their final Good Lives plan that is specific to their post-intervention environment, or additionally, in collaboration with the young people, the production of "Good Lives Booklets." These booklets can be colorful, illustrated, and individualized for each young person. They should contain brief information relating to the young person's strengths, future goals, pathways, the attainment of primary needs, how to anticipate and deal with potential barriers, triggers, risk management strategies and/or instructions, and summaries or reminders of important pieces of therapeutic work. Such reference materials provide a reminder to young people of what they are hoping to achieve; in the event that transition does not go according to plan or they encounter obstacles or challenges, it can help them recognize signs they should look for and how to respond.

CASE ILLUSTRATIONS

This section describes the transition processes for the case illustrations described in chapters 5, 6, and 7.

Case A: Joe

Details of the implementation of Joe's Good Lives plan are in chapter 7.

Joe's GLP included recognition that he would legally be required to leave his current residential unit by the time he was 18 years of age. Such a transition had the potential to be very distressing for Joe. He had established positive relationships with a peer and several members of staff at his residential placement and felt anxious about change. It was therefore essential that his transition was carefully planned in advance and that early preparation work was undertaken with him, especially as increases in emotional distress and emotional loneliness were linked to risk of sexually harmful behaviors and self-harming.

The transfer of responsibility for Joe from children's services to the local authority services for adults involved him having a new social worker. In response to a request by Joe's Good Lives team the new worker was identified eight months before the case was transferred and became a member of the team so that he could establish a relationship with Joe and others prior to taking over the case. It was agreed that Joe's therapeutic work would continue for three months beyond his 18th birthday with a graduated reduction in the frequency of sessions. Consequently, while Joe experienced changes in social workers and placement he was able to rely on the consistency of the therapeutic relationship until he was settled.

Some months prior to his anticipated move, a specialist college for young people with intellectual disabilities was identified for him in a locality considered by Joe and his professional network as an appropriate and desirable area in which he could live after leaving the residential unit. Once at college, Joe's sociability, his positive interpersonal skills developed during therapeutic work, his attractiveness, and his likable nature helped him to develop a number of appropriate and positive friendships with developmentally similar peers and made him a popular member of the group. Joe experienced a sense of mastery and fun in the college environment. For example, he played the keyboard in the college orchestra, he was accomplished at crafts, and his work was sold at the college festivals to raise money for charity. Joe discovered that he had a natural aptitude for cookery, and he used this as another technique to help him self-soothe. Moreover, spending time in college helped Joe to become familiar with the local area he would be moving to, and college staff assisted him by taking him to local shops and encouraging him to use local transport as part of his "steps to independence." Additionally, a class called "tai chi for teenagers" (for young people aged 16 to 19 years) was found in the local community close to where Joe would be moving; three months prior to his move, care staff facilitated his attendance in the activity.

Joe was involved in selecting a supported tenancy near his college and was involved in deciding on its furnishings and internal decoration. During the two weeks prior to his move he had four overnight stays in the property with his new support workers. The support package in his new environment was initially for 24-hour supervision in view of Joe's potentially increased risk following a change in environment and support, and in view of his vulnerability as a young man with an intellectual disability. However, given the progress he continued to maintain in his Good Life plan, this was reduced within a month to staff shadowing him (i.e., he was in the line of sight of staff rather than needing to be directly next to staff when he was in the community) and then further reduced as he continued to make progress. Although Joe is likely to need some support for the foreseeable future due to his intellectual disability and potential vulnerability, within six months of his move he was travelling on his own and attending activities in the community without supervision.

Prior to Joe's move, therapeutic work and training was undertaken with Joe's future caregivers and college staff with a specific focus on the GLM, risk, and risk management. During his residential placement, Joe's mother and stepfather had been involved in joint sessions with Joe and were aware of his pathway, therapeutic progress and needs, attachment style, and the implications for their parenting of him. While they had gradually increased the consistency of their support to him, at times they were focused and driven more by their own needs and occasionally let him down. By the time of his move, however, Joe was largely able to cope with the disruptions and upset caused by his parents by using the knowledge and skills gained in intervention, such as recognizing his emotional states, asking for help, and regulating his emotions through music, tai chi, and attending the gym. Furthermore, prior to Joe's move his brother (whom Joe had harmed sexually) indicated to his own social worker that he wanted to resume contact with Joe. This initiated a referral for restorative justice, whereby a meeting was set up between Joe and his brother, each receiving support from a member of his own professional network, and led by an independent chair. Before the meeting the independent chair met with each of the boys on a number of occasions to prepare them and set the agenda for the meeting. At the meeting Joe's brother explained his feelings about what had happened and Joe took full responsibility for his behavior and apologized to his brother. He explained to his brother why he had behaved in the way he had and how he had changed. Following the meeting each of the boys debriefed with their support workers and both stated that they wanted further meetings. Regular supervised contact between Joe and his brother was organized and continued throughout Joe's transition and after his move.

Joe moved into his community placement eight months before his 18th birthday. He settled well, helped by the relationship he had already built with his new support staff, the continuity of his college placement and tai chi classes where he had friends, and the continuity of contact with his family and therapeutic workers. Within two months of his move, Joe expressed an interest in and joined a local gym and a five-a-side football team for 17- and 18-year-old males. He also met a peer-aged young man at college and they started to build an appropriate romantic relationship. This young man was of a similar ability level to Joe, and they were both assessed as having capacity to consent. In the main, Joe presented as having few difficulties and made progress at college and in the community, although he continued to have a tendency to be demanding of significant relationships. This could have been the reason for others becoming tired and rejecting of him, which consequently affected his emotional well-being. At these times Joe's attempts to gain a sense of belonging increased and became more extreme. An example was telling friends at college that he had been suffering from a serious illness when it was not true. Joe, therefore, continued to need work and support for some months from his therapists, his social worker, and his family to help him increase his sense of belonging and manage his relationships and emotions.

In summary, several factors helped Joe to positively experience his placement transition, including careful and early planning regarding his residency and integration into the new community; relevant work with caregivers, parents, and his sibling; a package of support that was graduated in respect to the conclusion of therapy, the transition to adult services, and the provision of supervision and monitoring as determined by a risk and needs assessment; anticipation and rehearsal of managing potential difficulties in the future;

and using his Good Lives plan to guide the identification and sourcing of relevant community resources. By the end of therapeutic involvement Joe was meeting all his Good Lives needs to some extent; more specifically, he had established a range of internal and external resources to meet his harmful-behavior-related needs (i.e., *emotional health, having people in his life,* and *achievement*). The need that was most important to Joe, *having people in my life,* was met through a variety of relationships such as friendships at college, a boyfriend, caregivers, family, professionals, and his participation in community activities. As a result, he was not overly reliant on one significant relationship to solely meet the need, and in the event that any particular relationship broke down, he had other people to whom he could turn to meet his belonging needs. Additionally, through therapeutic work Joe acknowledged potential triggers and difficulties that he might encounter—for example, the possibility of the needs of *having people in my life* and *emotional health* being in conflict. While he gained insight into experiences that could trigger a low sense of worth, a sense of powerlessness, and feelings of not being loved—and how such feelings could lead him to manufacture or exaggerate concerns in order to gain affirmation and attention from others—it remained an area that Joe struggled with. The people involved in his long-term support, however, are aware of his difficulties and are monitoring his needs and supporting him to increase his positive coping strategies until such time that he can consistently manage himself.

Case B: Wayne

Wayne lived with his parents throughout the intervention process, and it was planned that he would remain with his parents following this period. Details of the implementation of Wayne's Good Lives plan are in chapter 7.

At the end of his planned work Wayne was generally making more constructive use of his time, helped by his involvement in more pro-social activities that included sports and regular attendance at a retail outlet that provides opportunities for young people to play interactive computer games. While he continued to experience some difficulties with his ability to defer gratification and manage boredom, these had been significantly reduced by having strategies to offset boredom, such as playing games on his phone and console, listening to music, taking part in sports activities, and using the skills developed in the course of therapy to tolerate distress. Consistent with his propensity to prioritize the need for *thrill and excitement,* his participation in challenging activities such as rock climbing suited Wayne well and also enabled him to establish a stable group of peers. In addition to having fun, Wayne enjoyed the competitive element of sports activities. Just prior to his transition from therapeutic work he began a relationship with a peer-aged female who was part of his adventure sports group. The relationship gave Wayne the opportunity to experience emotional intimacy and to attach a relationship context to what had previously been an exclusive focus on sexual images and feelings. He had a clear understanding of issues such as the legal age of consent for sexual relationships, as well as what constituted appropriate sexual conduct, and in his relationship with his girlfriend he demonstrated the capacity to limit activities of a sexual nature to those that were age-appropriate. Wayne continued to use materials to masturbate to in the privacy of his bedroom, although these were mainstream magazines rather than pornographic websites.

As part of the process of ending therapy, Wayne developed a booklet to remind him of the key messages from the work he had undertaken. It incorporated information on strategies to manage boredom and distress, lists of activities that could appropriately meet his needs for thrill and excitement (*having fun*), advice on developing non-platonic relationships including the importance of consent, rules for public and private spaces, and a prompt about the potential consequences if he were to harm others or break the law.

Following an incremental program of reduced supervision, Wayne enjoyed increasing periods of unsupervised community access that gradually included contact with both male and female peers. His parents were instrumental in providing the necessary supervision and monitoring Wayne's developing capacity to self-manage potentially risky situations. However, they were encouraged to be mindful of their prior tendency to indulge Wayne and the risk of undermining the boundaries they had established. As part of the therapeutic ending Wayne's parents were helped to produce a booklet that covered information on behaviors that might signal concern, potential triggers, and guidelines regarding their supervision and monitoring of Wayne.

In order for Wayne to engage in activities that were consistent with his age and interests but that involved periods away from the supervision of his parents, information regarding possible risk was shared with relevant others. For example, before Wayne took part in an overnight expedition as part of a Duke of Edinburgh's Award, a national charity in the United Kingdom that aims to develop young people's life skills, his Good Lives team made the designated safeguarding officer for the award aware of some of the details of Wayne's history and the risk assessment made in regard to this activity. As part of the transition process, Wayne's parents were given advice and guidance on how and when to share this type of information in the future.

Case C: Leanne

Details of the implementation of Leanne's Good Lives plan are in chapter 7.

Therapeutic work involved Leanne's foster caregiver and her aunt, who were identified as significant members of her network. The aunt maintained frequent contact with Leanne throughout her time in foster care, and in view of their positive relationship and its importance in meeting Leanne's need for *having people in her life,* it was agreed that she could have overnight visits to her aunt's house. They commenced partway through the therapeutic process and were supported by "keeping safe" work undertaken with Leanne and her aunt. The visits were successful, and Leanne's aunt demonstrated that she had understood and was able to implement key messages from the therapeutic work and follow guidelines provided by Leanne's therapeutic practitioners.

Given continuing concerns about Leanne's parents' ability to meet her needs, as well as their continued refusal to have contact with her, it was not viable for her to return to the family home despite her achieving an assessed lower level of risk. While her foster care placement had the potential to continue to accommodate Leanne long-term and was providing her with reasonable stability and care, it had become increasingly apparent that Leanne's emotional investment in and sense of belonging with her aunt were most significant. Following consultation with Leanne's aunt, parents, and local authority, it was agreed that she should reside permanently with her aunt. Consequently, as part of the transition arrangements, Leanne moved to live with her aunt six months before the end of planned therapeutic work. Leanne and her aunt received joint sessions every second week, alternating with Leanne's individual sessions, with a key focus on meeting Leanne's needs for *emotional health* and *having people in my life*. Leanne commenced a graduated program of reduced supervision at that point, so that she might benefit from increased independence by the time of transition from therapy. After therapeutic sessions ceased, the local authority's children's services remained involved to support Leanne and her aunt in managing ongoing care and supervision responsibilities.

Intervention provided Leanne with the skills to ask for help and to regulate her emotions through safe place, anger management, and mindfulness work. In time she began to exhibit more adaptive attachment behaviors with her aunt—for example, using her aunt as an emotional confidante when she was having practical difficulties or needing comfort. Prior to Leanne's admission to the local school relevant information was shared with the child protection officer, and a risk assessment resulted in her receiving some supervision from teaching staff to ensure the protection of more vulnerable peers. School also assigned a support worker to Leanne in order to monitor her mood states and support her learning and emotional needs. By her second term Leanne had started to settle in and enjoy going to school, and although she tended to underachieve in more academic subjects due to the previous disruptions in her education, she participated in age-appropriate tasks and activities, and excelled in art and music. School significantly enhanced Leanne's progress in meeting important needs, including developing peer-aged friendships (consistent with the need of *having people in my life*); participating in games (consistent with *having fun*); and gaining a sense of mastery in more practical and creative subjects (consistent with *achieving*).

REFERENCES

Creeden, K. 2005. Integrating trauma and attachment research into the treatment of sexually abusive youth. In M. C. Calder (ed.), *Children and young people who sexually abuse: New theory, research, and practice developments*, 202–16. Lyme Regis, UK: Russell House Publishing.

Farrington, D., M. Ttofi, and J. Coid. 2009. Development of adolescence-limited, late-onset, and persistent offenders from age 8 to age 48. *Aggressive Behavior* 35:150–63.

Gibbens, T. C. N. 1984. Borstal boys after 25 years. *British Journal of Criminology* 24:49–62.

Hackett, S. 2011. *Recidivism, desistance, and life course trajectories of young sexual abusers.* Paper presented at the National Organisation for the Treatment of Abusers (NOTA) Annual Conference, Brighton, UK, September.

Harrison, P., and D. Stevens. 2012. *Youth to adult transitions: Information paper.* London: Youth Justice Board.

HM Government. 2004. *Every Child Matters: Change for children.* London: Department for Education and Skills.

Hunter, J. A., and J. V. Becker. 1994. The role of deviant sexual arousal in juvenile sexual offending: Etiology, evaluation, and treatment. *Criminal Justice and Behaviour* 21:132–49.

Irwin, J. 1970. *The felon.* Englewood Cliffs, NJ: Prentice Hall.

Laws, D. R., and T. Ward. 2011. *Desistance from sex offending: Alternatives to throwing away the keys.* New York: Guilford Press.

Longo, R. E. 2001. *For our children.* Paper presented at the New Hope Treatment Center's Second Annual Conference, Charleston, SC, August.

Mendes, P., G. Johnson, and B. Moslehuddin. 2011. Effectively preparing young people to transition from out-of-home care: An examination of three recent Australian studies. *Family Matters* 89:61–70.

Moffitt, T. E., A. Caspi, H. Harrington, and B. J. Milne. 2002. Males on the life-course-persistent and adolescence-limited antisocial pathways: Follow-up at age 26 years. *Development and Psychopathology* 14: 179–207.

National Collaborative on Workforce and Disability. 2010. *Improving transition outcomes for youth involved in the juvenile justice system: Practical considerations.* InfoBrief 25:1–12.

Pemberton, C. 2010. *Resettlement for young offenders must be planned early.* Community Care. Retrieved December 13, 2012, from http://www.communitycare.co.uk/articles/22/03/2010/114111/resettlement-for-young-offenders-must-be-planned-early.htm.

Re-Entry Policy Council. 2005. *Executive summary: Report of the Re-Entry Policy Council.* New York: Council of State Governments.

Smith, A., M. Bryant, P. Doyle, T. Rolley, S. Hubbard, C. Simpson, F. Shearlaw, D. Thompson, A. Pentecost, C. Reeves, O. Kenton, S. Hunt, and L. Calderbank. 2011. *Thematic inspection report: Putting the pieces together—An inspection of Multi-Agency Public Protection Arrangements.* A Joint Inspection by HMI Probation and HMI Constabulary. Retrieved December 21, 2012, from http://www.justice.gov.uk/downloads/publications/inspectorate-reports/hmiprobation/joint-thematic/mappa-thematic-report.pdf.

Stein, M. 2005. *Resilience and young people leaving care*. York, UK: Joseph Roundtree Foundation.

Stein, M. 2006. Research review: Young people leaving care. *Child and Family Social Work* 11:273–79.

Stouthamer-Loeber, M., E. Wei, R. Loeber, and A. S. Masten. 2004. Desistance from persistent serious delinquency in the transition to adulthood. *Development and Psychopathology* 16:897–918.

Trasler, G. 1979. Delinquency, recidivism, and desistance. *British Journal of Criminology* 19:314–22.

Ward, T., and S. Maruna. 2007. *Rehabilitation: Beyond the risk assessment paradigm*. London: Routledge.

Warr, M. 1998. Life-course transitions and desistance from crime. *Criminology* 36:183–216.

Willis, G. W., P. M. Yates, T. A. Gannon, and T. Ward. 2013. How to integrate the Good Lives model into treatment programs for sexual offending: An introduction and overview. *Sexual Abuse: A Journal of Research and Treatment* 25:123–42.

Yates, P. M., D. Prescott, and T. Ward. 2010. *Applying the Good Lives and Self Regulation models to sex offender treatment: A practical guide for clinicians*. Brandon, VT: The Safer Society Press.

Youth Justice Board. 2006. *Youth resettlement: A framework for action*. London: Youth Justice Board.

CHAPTER 9

The Response of Adolescents and Practitioners to a Good Lives Approach

SHARON LEESON AND MARK ADSHEAD

INTRODUCTION

In order to review the implementation of G-map's adapted version of the Good Lives model (GLM-A) and its value in assessment and intervention work with adolescents who display harmful sexual behavior, G-map conducted semi-structured interviews with practitioners and young people completing their Good Lives programs. This is the first review of this nature that has been conducted at G-map since the implementation of our current Good Lives program, and the small numbers involved are representative of those young people completing therapeutic work at the time of the evaluation. It is planned, however, that the interviews conducted as part of the review will be included as part of exit interviews with all young people in the future.

AIMS OF THE REVIEW

The central purpose of the study was to evaluate whether practitioners, as well as the young people and families they worked with, found the GLM-A to be a constructive, useful, and effective model and whether there were any elements of the adaptation and implementation of the model that required improvement or revision.

Areas of particular importance to explore were:

- Was the GLM-A language was "user-friendly"?
- Was the model easy for users to understand?
- Did the model help to engage and motivate young people and their families?
- Did the model help in understanding why the harmful behavior occurred?
- Was there agreement in the needs to be met?
- Was the model useful in promoting attention to non-criminogenic needs such as attachment difficulties and psychological trauma?
- Was there consensus in formulating Good Lives plans?
- Did use of the model help to achieve positive outcomes?

METHOD

Semi-structured interviews were chosen as the most suitable information-gathering method with both the practitioners and the young people, as they can be used with sensitivity and flexibility to generate a great deal of information. These factors outweighed the possible disadvantages of the process being time consuming and the information gathered being more difficult to analyze and compare.

Seven G-map practitioners involved in using the GLM-A and four young people were interviewed. The G-map practitioners came from a variety of professional backgrounds including health, social care, psychology, and youth justice. The young people involved comprised three males, two of mainstream ability and one with a learning disability (mild), and one female of mainstream ability. The composition of the sample of young people was three white British; and one male was black Jamaican. With regard to young people the interviews were completed as part of their exit interviews on completion of their therapeutic program.

Prior to undertaking interviews with the G-map practitioners, discussions took place within the organization regarding the preferred method of interview: whether to undertake a group interview involving all practitioners, or to interview practitioners individually. The consensus was to conduct individual interviews, as this would enable practitioners to discuss their views in some depth and they would be less likely to be influenced by the opinions of others. Prior to each interview, the interviewers forwarded a copy of the standard questions to be asked to the practitioners involved so as to allow them time to give thoughtful consideration to their answers. All interviews were recorded, with the practitioner's permission, and transcribed by the authors.

Semi-structured interviews were also completed with the young people participating in the study. Interviews were conducted jointly by one of the authors and a practitioner who worked therapeutically with the young person, as it was considered that this would enhance their openness in responses. Each young person was spoken to prior to interview in order to ensure that he or she understood the reason for the interview, how the information would be used, and that confidentiality would be preserved. A written consent form that included permission to audio record the interviews was signed by the young people.

The data gathered from the interviews was subjected to a data reduction process based on themes and subcategories—for example, whether a response was positive or negative—and entered into a spreadsheet. A qualitative analysis was completed by each of the authors and the results were compared and used to identify common, recurrent, or emergent themes.

THE PRACTITIONER RESPONSES

The interviews were designed to cover several aspects of the practitioners' experience while using the GLM-A. Standard questions were:

- Do you find the GLM-A useful, and how did it compare with other models in practice?
- Did other professionals understand the model?
- Did young people understand the model?
- Do you think the model helps to engage and motivate a young person?
- Do you think the model helps to engage a young person's family and/or caregivers?
- In what ways was the model particularly helpful or unhelpful?
- Were any important elements of work not sufficiently included or attended to, e.g., issues pertaining to risk or risk management?

All practitioners responded that they found the GLM-A the most useful model they had used in practice, and they all commented on the benefits of working with a model that gives such a clear focus to identifying and building upon a young person's strengths. They all stated that they found the adaptations made in the GLM-A helped to make the model understandable to others, particularly the young people they worked with. All the practitioners considered the model helpful in both the assessment and intervention stages of work with young people and their families.

There was a strong sense of confidence expressed by all of the practitioners (n=7) when discussing the GLM-A with other professionals in forums such as the Multi-Agency Public Protection Panels (MAPPP), children's services statutory meetings, and Good Lives team meetings. All interviewees stated that the GLM-A provided a clear framework within which to explore with other professionals the needs met by the young person via his or her harmful sexual behavior, the needs to be addressed in intervention, and the progress of a young person's Good Lives plans. Four practitioners spoke about the GLM's compatibility with other models, such as attachment theory and trauma-based theories, and how this eased explanations and discussions in multi-agency forums.

Each of the practitioners (n=7) considered the GLM-A straightforward enough to explain to young people in relatively simple terms and that the understanding they gained not only improved motivation significantly but helped the young people involved to contextualize their behavior, highlight their priorities regarding needs, and better understand risk and how they could learn to self-manage. All four of the young people involved in the review were said by their workers to have understood and accepted that they needed to use some of their strengths and develop new competencies to enable them to achieve goals successfully, and all of them contributed in identifying the skills they required help to improve.

All of the practitioners (n=7) considered that the GLM-A helped young people to understand that, just like everyone else, when they used behavior to meet needs but that when their actions had been harmful their chosen way to meet needs was unacceptable and had severe consequences. The resulting young people's appreciation that they were not so different from others and that they could be helped to meet their needs in positive ways helped to reduce feelings such as shame, hopelessness, and defensiveness. The consequence for all of the young people (n=4) was that their engagement in the therapeutic process markedly improved following these discussions and they were more able to talk about sensitive topics, including their own harmful sexual behaviors.

All the practitioners (n=7) stated that the GLM-A is an "excellent" framework for engaging and motivating a young person in the therapeutic work. The word "motivational" was used on 23 occasions throughout the interviews in relation to how the GLM-A assisted in engaging young people in the therapeutic process. Practitioners (n=7) expressed the view that the model is "non-judgmental," "non-stigmatizing," and maintains the focus of the intervention on the young people, aiding them to take ownership and responsibility for meeting their needs in more appropriate ways.

G-map practitioners (n=7) also reported that the GLM-A was equally easy to convey to families and caregivers. Three interviewees spoke about how initially the parents of two of the young people were somewhat wary and defensive in their dealings with professionals. They appeared to feel responsible for their child's harmful sexual behavior and were anxious that others would do the same. As a result they were reluctant to openly share information about the family and their child's history. Once the GLM-A was introduced to them, however, and they better understood the reasons for the young person's behavior and felt more confident that they could contribute to intervention plans as members of the Good Lives team, their engagement with professionals improved and they were able to discuss not only the young person's strengths and difficulties but their own.

All practitioners (n=7) spoke about how the GLM-A assisted in looking at the young person more holistically and how a shared understanding of the model helped to promote agreement among relevant parties of the Good Lives plan, including the young person, parents/caregivers, and other professionals, and the roles and responsibilities of those involved. The model provided a shared terminology—for example, discussion of goals, needs, and means was equally understood by all—and this helped to create a sense of inclusion, particularly for the young people and their families. Membership of the Good Lives team allowed for all involved to contribute to plans, comment on progress, and agree on tasks. This not only provided a feeling of "ownership" of plans but ensured that all involved were aware of what others were doing to progress the plan and how they could support and enhance this work.

All the responders (n=7) said that the GLM-A helped when considering problem formulation in that they and the young people could identify significant needs that were met by the harmful behavior, although other theoretical models were needed to understand why the young person's experiences and development had not invested them with the internal and external resources to meet those needs more appropriately.

The positive approach of working toward goals and activities that were attractive to the young people (and would help to meet their needs) was seen by all seven practitioners as particularly helpful in terms of motivation. All the practitioners recognized, however, that it was important to include and identify short-term steps toward longer-term goals in order that success could be frequently recognized and motivation maintained. Some (n=2) also talked about the importance of identifying and attending to the scope of needs and overarching needs as without focused care it was sometimes all too easy for needs that did not relate to the harmful sexual behaviors to slip from the intervention agenda.

The importance of regularly reviewing and reassessing the young person's significant needs was discussed by two of the practitioners, who reported that the assessed needs of the individual they worked with changed over time. In particular it became apparent that the needs he was meeting by repeating his harmful sexual behavior were not entirely the same as those that initiated the behavior on the first occasion.

The sense of progress and achievement that was often identified at review meetings stimulated motivation and a sense of achievement that was felt not only by the young people and their families but also by the professionals involved. These positive feelings significantly influenced a sense of determination and "can do" when any problems or difficulties in the plans arose. This included professionals finding ways to gain useful external resources and young people being more willing to tackle sensitive areas of work such as their own victimization.

All four of the young people involved in the review had progressed in their plans to the extent that they were successfully participating in community activities (goals) and had plans to continue with these following program completion. All had a support network they could rely on for the foreseeable future and all were assessed to have significantly reduced the likelihood of committing further harmful behaviors. Additionally, in Good Lives terms, they were all considered by their Good Lives team to have the prospect of leading a satisfying, healthy, and enjoyable lifestyle. When compared with the intervention approach taken prior to the implementation of the GLM-A, all seven of the practitioners felt the optimism they had for the young people's future was more grounded as it was based on not only on improvements in the level of risk but improvements to the young people's opportunities, attitudes, abilities, and support in everyday life.

There was a general acknowledgment from practitioners (n=7) that the GLM-A did not assist in the sequencing of work (i.e., when to undertake specific areas of work, such as sensitive work that focused on harmful behavior exhibited or suffered by the young person; emotional regulation; or self-esteem building). Five of the practitioners were more influenced by other models relating to issues such as shame, attachment, and trauma to guide them in the ordering of therapeutic work. Two responders added that they had experienced pressure from a commissioning authority to attend primarily to the young people's criminogenic needs rather than the planned program that focused initially on their own traumatic experiences and difficulties with emotional regulation. The support of the Good Lives team helped to resolve this problem by meeting with the authority involved and explaining why the plan should not be changed and how the proposed order would help the young person to more effectively engage with subsequent work on risk awareness, risk management, and risk reduction.

None of the respondents thought that significant areas of work had been missed with the young people. They all (n=7) thought that the Good Lives team had, among them, attended to all the young person's identified needs, although it was agreed that not all interventions were entirely successful in every case. For example, it was not possible to get one young person into a local school as they were not prepared to accept that his level of risk was manageable. He, therefore, had to receive tuition at home for some months until another school, some distance away, was prepared to accept him.

All the participants said that work on the young people's understanding of their harmful behavior, risk awareness, and risk management constituted a significant proportion of the work included in their Good Lives plans. The young people understood that in order for them to participate in some of their identified community activities, they needed to demonstrate to others that they could recognize and manage risk. For one young person the work helped improve his own confidence in dealing with potential risk situations.

THE YOUNG PEOPLE'S RESPONSES

The interviews were designed to explore the young people's experience and retention of the GLM-A. The questions asked were as follows:

- What is your understanding of the Good Lives model?
- Do you think the model was helpful? If so, how?
- What do you think your most important needs are?
- Can you say what needs you think you were trying to meet when you were involved in harmful sexual behaviors?
- Do you think that making a Good Lives plan helped you to understand the work you and others needed to do?
- Do you think your behavior has changed since starting work on your Good Lives plan? If so, how?
- What has been the most important piece of work you completed during your therapy?
- Do you think the work you have done has been considerate of your cultural and identity needs?
- Do you have you any other comments would you like to add?

The responses from all of the young people (n=4) indicated that they understood the GLM-A and each was able to provide a reasonable summary of the model and how it applied to them. They all reported that the explanations given to them by practitioners in their therapeutic work had been helpful and used language they understood. When asked if they had found the model useful they all replied positively. Some of their comments were: "It helped to identify the needs I was meeting with my sexual behavior, but also other needs that are important to me"; "It explained to me, in a way that was uncomplicated, about my sexual behavior"; and "It helps people to look forward to the future and how to be independent." Another young person said he particularly liked the way the model helped him to understand how his early life experiences connected with his difficulties managing his emotions. One young person reported that when first introduced to the GLM-A, he struggled to understand the concept, but the use of visual prompts, such as providing pictures of activities and linking them to specific needs, helped him to grasp the meaning. The same young man also said that it was helpful to use his words in the construction of his Good Lives plan, as this helped him to feel confident in Good Lives team meetings.

The young people interviewed (n=4) said the GLM-A had offered them hope that things could get better. One young person said that his mother's involvement in the Good Lives team helped improve their relationship to the extent that she supported and encouraged him whereas before she had "hated, cried, and shouted at me." Another identified that prior to using the GLM-A his self-view was that he was a "bad person," but the model had helped him to understand he has good things he could use to make a better future. All of the young people said that being able to make sense of their harmful sexual behaviors was important and allowed them to discuss their behaviors more openly and honestly. One young person commented that his opinion of himself prior to using the model was, "I've done things in the past that I couldn't talk about . . . because it hurt too much . . . though I really hoped my life could change . . . when I saw how my behavior fit with the Good Lives model I felt relieved that it was understandable . . . and it was easier to talk about it to others who understood."

All of the young people (n=4) were able to name needs that they thought were the most important for them, and these coincided with the overarching needs identified in their Good Lives plans. *Having people in my life* (n=4) was noted as an overarching need by all four; one young person added *being my own person* as particularly important.

All four of the young people were able to recognize the needs they had met by their sexually harmful behavior, which included: *emotional health* (emotional regulation) (n=4); *having people in my life* (belonging) (n=4); *sexual health* (sexual gratification) (n=2); and *achieving* (n=1). When asked if this recognition had helped them one said that he felt his behavior was more understandable; another said that it made him feel more confident that he could change; and each of the four was able to connect risk of harmful behaviors to times in the future when they might once again struggle to meet their particular identified needs. All four were able to offer examples of the strategies and actions they would take if such circumstances were to arise.

Good Lives plans were unanimously viewed as helpful by the young people. They thought that they helped to make clear what they needed to do and how others could help. All four said that their identified goals provided an incentive to complete the work so that they could successfully participate in activities they would enjoy and benefit from, and each indicated that these benefits, together with the support of their Good Lives team, motivated them to tackle even the most difficult parts of their work.

The respondents (n=4) reported that starting work on their GLP had a positive impact on them and that they felt more confident and optimistic about their futures. The majority of young people (n=3) said they thought they had changed a lot in order to reach the goals that were identified in their GLPs. These young people all commented on the value of having both short- and long-term goals as they could achieve some success in a relatively short period of time and still have things to aim for. Two young people said their general behavior had improved during their program of work and that everyone around them had commented on this. The other two considered that while they felt different inside (one said he felt much calmer, and the other said he liked himself a lot more), they did not think other people noticed any significant change in their behaviors.

All the young people (n=4) identified the following areas of work as particularly useful: "Old Life, New Life," (see chapter 5); storyboarding (creating a story using visual illustrations, often used as a tool to gain young people's account of their harmful behaviors); and the "four steps model" (see chapter 7). Two said that the technique of mindfulness (staying in the moment) was useful; one said that the work he did on improving his relationship with his mother was the most important to him; and one said that knowing he could use ACE (see chapter 7) gave him confidence that he would not commit harmful behaviors in the future.

The identification of strengths was seen as an important piece of work by the majority of those interviewed (n=3). Two of these young people said that they had not found this work easy due largely to the shame they felt about their harmful sexual behaviors; they needed input from those caring for them and the therapeutic team to be able to recognize and accept their talents, skills, and positive characteristics. The three young people who said that this work had been important for them also individually said: "it allowed me to feel good about myself," "enabled me to realize I can achieve some good things," and "made me determined to show that I can succeed." All three said that knowing their strengths and building new ones helped them to take part in sports, attend college, and develop friendships and intimate relationships.

In relation to cultural, gender, and identity needs, one of the respondents was an adolescent from a black culture. He commented that he felt it had been helpful having a black worker as part of his therapeutic team, citing that he felt she would "understand where he was coming from" and that he was more confident when she was talking to his parents. One respondent was female, and she stated that having two female co-workers assisted her in engaging in therapeutic work; without them she doubted that she would have been able to manage to work on her own trauma.

All young people (n=4) thought that working with the GLM-A allowed them to have some input into their GLPs, and three thought that it was important that their parents had been involved in their Good Lives team.

Two young people said that the GLM-A was effective for them as they were able to have very helpful trusting relationships with their therapeutic workers and their caregivers.

The common themes emerging from the review process with practitioners pertaining to the GLM-A included the following:

- *Motivational*, both in relation to the young people and others within their network such as family/caregivers and professionals. Motivational was the most common word used by practitioners when describing the GLM-A. Practitioners spoke about how the GLM-A, when explained to young people and their families, greatly assists in promoting engagement and motivation. The emphasis on identifying and attaining goals is a positive ethos to work with and gives the young people a sense that they have a future.

- *User-friendly:* The GLM-A assisted practitioners in putting the young person's harmful sexual behavior into a context that makes sense and was easy to understand for all parties, including families/caregiver and other professionals.

- *Easy to understand:* The language used within the GLM-A has been developed with the help of young people, therefore it lends itself to being easily interpreted and understood by all of those involved in the intervention process. Practitioners had "confidence" in presenting and discussing the model with other professionals.

- *Complements other models and theories:* The GLM-A sits well with other models such as elements of the RNR and theories such as attachment and trauma.

- *Assists in problem formulation:* Practitioners reported that the GLM-A in conjunction with other theories provides a very useful framework for explaining the pathway that led to a young person's harmful sexual behavior. Furthermore, it was easy to share and discuss his or her pathway with a young person and others.

- *Identifies and utilizes a young person's strengths:* The GLM-A emphasizes using and building strengths, not only with the young people but also the environment in which they live or will move to.

- *Rehabilitative:* GLP's and Good Lives teams ensure that the young person is supported in making positive and measurable progress.

The common themes pertaining to the GLM-A that emerged from interviews with the young people included the following:

- Young people were able to understand and retain important elements of the GLM-A at the end of therapeutic work.

- The GLM-A motivated young people to engage in intervention.

- The model helped young people to understand why their harmful behaviors occurred and how things could change to help them improve their lives so they need not resort to harmful behaviors in the future.

- The identification of needs and goals to meet needs, provided tangible targets to work toward. The young people could understand the work they needed to do to be successful.

- Matching workers to the young people is important. Having a Good Lives team and the involvement of parents/caregivers is particularly supportive for young people. Sharing the terminology of the GLM-A within the team empowered young people to feel able to contribute to their GLPs.

In summary, the responses to the review with both practitioners and young people are very promising in that they suggest the GLM-A was clear, helpful, and very useful. Given the small numbers involved, however, this preliminary finding requires further testing with larger samples before any firm conclusions can be drawn.

CHAPTER 10

Evaluation of the Adapted Good Lives Model

HELEN GRIFFIN

BACKGROUND

Historically, attitudes and priorities in relation to offending, including youth offending, have been influenced by the social and political agendas of the time (see Cavadino and Dignan 2006; Stahlkopf 2008). For example, during the 20th century a number of countries saw a shift from a "welfare model," with its focus on the care and safety of young people, to a "justice model," which prioritized young offenders taking responsibility and receiving punishment (Watt 2003). In England and Wales, the well-being of children and young people involved in the criminal justice system was viewed as the central concern of youth justice practitioners prior to the introduction of the Crime and Disorder Act 1998 (Burnett and Roberts 2004). However, following the youth justice reforms brought about by this act, there was a greater emphasis on the prevention of crime and the reduction of re-offending (Crawford 1998). Hence, practitioners are increasingly required to evidence the effectiveness of their interventions (Hackett 2004; Burnett and Roberts 2004).

Evidence-based practice was promoted through the "what works" approach (Andrews and Bonta 2010a), which has also emphasized cost-effectiveness and has contributed toward measuring youth justice outcomes and attempting to quantify risk through assessments and actuarial approaches (Muncie 2006). As part of this movement, the Risk–Need–Responsivity (RNR) model (Andrews and Bonta 2010a; Andrews, Bonta, and Hoge 1990; Bonta and Andrews 2007) gained popularity and empirical support for its role in reducing recidivism (Hanson et al. 2012). The RNR model (explored in more detail in chapters 2 and 5) has commonly been applied to offenders more generally (Wilson and Yates 2009). However, its applicability to those who sexually harm has also been demonstrated (Hanson et al. 2009). Moreover, the inclusion of studies on adolescents in Hanson and colleagues (2009) meta-analysis of the effectiveness of RNR in interventions with those who sexually harm (for example, Borduin et al. 1990; Borduin, Schaeffer, and Heiblum 2009), indicates that it has transferability to this specialist population.

Despite its relevance to different types of offenders and the evidence that programs fully adopting the RNR approach have reduced recidivism by up to 35 percent (Andrews and Bonta 2010b), it would appear that, in practice, many offender intervention programs do not adhere to all the principles of the RNR model (Andrews and Bonta 2010b; Jeglic, Maile, and Mercado 2010). To advance practice further, Wormith, and colleagues (2007) call for greater collaboration between researchers and practitioners, and advocate that when looking at "what works," greater consideration needs to be given to how it works, when it works, and whom it works for, especially in relation to the rehabilitation of those who sexually harm. The prominence of establishing "what works" in offender rehabilitation has increased knowledge, the ability to differentiate offenders on the basis of the risk they pose, and the effectiveness of rehabilitation (Bonta and Andrews 2007). However, Ward and colleagues (Ward, Yates, and Willis 2012; Willis et al. 2013) assert that the RNR approach could be enhanced, with particular regard to theory, client engagement, and intervention gains, through the Good Lives model (GLM) (Laws and Ward 2011; Ward and Gannon 2006; Ward and Maruna 2007; Ward and Stewart 2003), which incorporates RNR principles of risk, need, and responsivity (Ward, Yates, and Willis 2012). It might be useful to add here that Ward and colleagues have conceptualized the GLM as an enhancement to existing models and not necessarily a shift away from these (Ward, Yates, and Willis 2012). Wilson and Yates (2009) call for the integration of the RNR and GLM to offer a more effective framework in which offender management, responsivity, pro-social functioning, engagement, and risk reduction can be encompassed.

Hackett (2004, 13) defines effective interventions as "the best possible way of intervening in a given circumstance" and "the course of action most likely to lead to a successful (or the most successful) outcome." The GLM, as a comprehensive rehabilitation framework that is grounded in theory, strengths-based, emphasizes approach goals, and is motivational (Ward, Yates, and Willis 2012), is likely to conform to the first part of this definition. However, regarding the latter part of this definition, the GLM, as a relatively new theory, does not have the same empirical evidence base as models such as the RNR model (Andrews, Bonta, and Wormith 2011). This being said, the GLM has received some international empirical support (Laws and Ward 2011, Ward and Gannon 2008). Furthermore, it is complemented by Griffin and Harkins's (in preparation a, b) recent findings from a systematic review and empirical research that resilience and protective factors should be considered and maximized to better facilitate the rehabilitation of young offenders, including those with harmful sexual behaviors. As a framework of offender rehabilitation that is growing in influence and usage (McGrath et al. 2010), it is likely that those services using the GLM to inform their interventions will begin to test and/or add to its evidence base as they seek to evaluate their outcomes.

The preceding chapters in this book have demonstrated that G-map's intervention approach is underpinned by the GLM. Eleven items contained within a coding protocol, used to evaluate the extent to which a treatment program adhered to the GLM in Willis, Ward, and Levenson's (2012) research, were applied to a typical G-map treatment program. On the basis of this, G-map's program of work was assessed as having a strong adherence to the GLM. Consequently, it could be argued that outcomes indicative of positive change in a young person following a G-map program of work provide support for the utility of a Good Lives approach.

THE ADAPTED GOOD LIVES MODEL

Ward and Maruna (2007) highlight that evaluation can take place on a number of levels: evaluation of how robust the model is and evaluation of how effective associated interventions are. The assumptions underpinning G-map's adaptation of the Good Lives model (GLM-A) are largely reflective of those underpinning the GLM (for example, that young people strive for a "good life" and that risk factors are linked to internal or external obstacles to attaining needs in pro-social ways), which to date appear to be reasonable, consistent, and therapeutically useful (Ward and Maruna 2007). The usefulness of the GLM-A framework in respect to clinical practice has been explored in chapter 9. However, in consideration of the current emphasis on evidence-based practice, for many practitioners and stakeholders the priority is likely to be whether it produces desired outcomes and reduces risk. Since the GLM-A has undergone a process of development and revisions over the past few years (see chapter 3), there have only recently been attempts to start to evaluate it, and it is too early to draw any clear conclusions about the potential effectiveness of interventions associated with it.

There are several ways that intervention outcomes can be tested (Harkins and Beech 2007), although the use of multiple and diverse methods are advocated (Beech et al. 2007). A method that has commonly been employed to measure the treatment efficacy of programs targeting anti-social behavior is official recidivism data (Lösel 1998; Peters and Myrick 2011). This being said, official recidivism data is likely to underestimate actual re-offending (Barbaree and Marshall 1990; Laub 1997; Lösel 1998) and necessitates long delays (i.e., a lengthy period of follow-up is required to more effectively measure recidivism) before outcomes can be gleaned (Beech et al. 2007). Despite these limitations, it is the intention of G-map to use recidivism data as part of its future evaluation of the GLM-A, as it provides the most accessible measure of future charges/convictions. Inevitably this would rely on capturing data to measure the extent a young person can and does attain a "good life" (which will be discussed in the latter part of this chapter) and allowing a long follow-up period prior to obtaining data about future offending. However, according to Peters and Myrick (2011) an exclusive focus on recidivism reflects a deficit-oriented approach and fails to recognize pro-social behaviors and positive youth outcomes. When evaluating a strengths-based model such as the GLM/GLM-A, it could especially be important for services to attempt to capture positive youth outcomes in addition to using recidivism data.

Psychometric measures are an additional method employed to measure outcomes. For example, the testing of service users before and after intervention can be used to assess the extent of change, and this can usefully be compared with recidivism data to examine the relationship between re-conviction and intervention effectiveness (Harkins and Beech 2007). While a number of deficit-based psychometric tools exist, strengths-based questionnaires have also been published that measure individual features such as social skills and personal resiliency. On the basis that Farmer, Beech, and Ward (2012) in their study of adults who sexually harmed children, found that "desisters" reported a more positive experience of personal agency, relatedness, and locus of control compared with "potentially active offenders," G-map has used similar measures to assess intervention change following a program of work informed by the GLM-A. This involved a small-scale study (Griffin 2013) consisting of nine young people aged between 13 and 17 years who had sexually harmed and whose therapy had been guided by the GLM-A. Each young person completed the Children's Nowicki-Strickland Internal–External Locus of Control (Nowicki and Strickland 1973), and the Resiliency Scale for Children and Adolescents (Prince-Embury 2007), which were administered both prior to any targeted interventions and at the end of intervention. Due to the small sample size, a conservative significance level was used when analyzing the data, but nonetheless the study produced significant results. It was found that in comparison with pre-intervention scores, after undertaking a program of therapeutic work that had utilized this Good Lives approach, young people typically endorsed a greater internal locus of control (i.e., were more likely to believe that they were in control of their life events); reported increased resilience/personal resources (including their degree of optimism, self-efficacy, capacity to learn from mistakes, and overall sense of relatedness to others); and perceived themselves as less vulnerable (encompassing the extent their personal resources corresponded with their reactivity and arousal to stress).

Using the findings from Farmer and colleagues (2012), it could therefore be hypothesized that inventions based on the GLM-A may increase the likelihood of desistance and thus reduce re-offending through improving young people's internal locus of control and enhancing their overall personal resiliency, including their sense of relatedness and mastery. It will, however, be necessary for future research to provide greater evidence of the association between the GLM-A and desistance. Additionally, while these findings are promising in providing potential support for the GLM-A, the limitations of this small-scale research should be emphasized, particularly in relation to the absence of an appropriate control group and the use of a small sample size.

When evaluating intervention effectiveness, the use of control groups (i.e., comparing those who took part in an intervention program with those who did not), preferably using randomized assignment designs, has been advocated (Harkins and Beech 2007; Hanson 2002), although this method has also received some criticism for potentially withholding interventions from people who need them (see Beech et al. 2007; Harkins and Beech 2007). It is due to such ethical concerns that G-map is unlikely to utilize control groups in any evaluation of the GLM-A. However, without a comparison group it is difficult to determine whether the outcomes are related specifically to the intervention or to other confounding factors (Harkins and Beech 2007). For example, it is difficult to attribute change directly to intervention as it is not possible to partial out the variance accounted for by natural maturation (Nisbet, Rombouts, and Smallbone 2005) or by the impact of other unrelated phenomena.

Another way to evaluate program effectiveness could be to consider reduction to dynamic (changeable) risk factors. In a study undertaken by G-map (Griffin 2013) using a sample of 20 young people aged 14 to 18 years, the AIM2 assessment (Print et al. 2007) was used to assess dynamic risk both prior to and following interventions underpinned by the GLM-A framework. When compared with pre-intervention scores, a significant reduction to dynamic risk was found following intervention, indicating that undertaking a program of therapeutic work that utilized the GLM-A may reduce overall risk of future harmful sexual behavior. However, the same caveat as was previously noted would also be relevant to this piece of research, which should therefore be deemed as exploratory and its findings as preliminary. While these findings need to be supported by longer-term evaluations with larger samples and more robust methodologies, they are nevertheless encouraging.

As noted earlier, a longer-term and more thorough evaluation of the GLM-A for the most part relies on information about young people's "good life" (for example, the resources and obstacles that allow them to attain primary needs) being captured in a practical, measurable, and valid way. The next part of this chapter will describe assessment tools that have been developed, piloted, and refined by G-map with the aim of facilitating further evaluation of the GLM-A. It is hoped that this may help to inform others who are seeking to evaluate the GLM-A or similar frameworks.

THE GLM-A ASSESSMENT TOOLS

G-map developed a number of assessment tools with the primary objective of measuring the extent that Good Lives–oriented interventions elicit change. This relied on designing tools that could be completed by different raters (i.e., practitioners, young people, and parents) to assess the extent to which young people who have displayed harmful sexual behavior could meet their primary needs at various points in time and to map their journey in relation to the resources, barriers, and flaws (such as scope and conflict) that impact on their ability to appropriately meet their needs. The assessment tools were developed through consultations with a number of key professionals from academic organizations as well as adult- and adolescent-based services. Furthermore, revisions were made to the tools following a pilot study and intermediate period of evaluation, which included gaining qualitative feedback from young people and practitioners about the tools and the process. The tools, which were developed by Griffin and Price (2009a; b; c; d) and revised by Griffin (2012), are described below and comprise: (1) an assessment tool to be completed by practitioners working with the young person; (2) a questionnaire to be completed by young people; and (3) a questionnaire to be completed by parents/caregivers. The tools were designed for use with young people aged 12 to 18, although they can be adapted for other populations.

The Good Lives Assessment Tool

The Good Lives assessment tool (GLAT) is practitioner-rated, and despite the positive findings from the inter-rater reliability study (discussion beginning on page 202), it should, where possible, be scored jointly by co-workers responsible for assessment and intervention. It is believed that a discussion and consensus-forming process involving both workers should improve the accuracy and quality of ratings. In an attempt to decrease the level of subjectivity among different raters, guidance, definitions, and/or examples are provided for each item contained within the GLAT.

The GLAT is completed for the following time periods:

- *Offense period:* At the time of assessment the practitioner uses the information gathered through file review, professional meetings, and assessment interviews with the young person and parent/caregivers to complete the GLAT retrospectively as if they were completing it at the time the young person committed the sexually harmful act(s).
- *Pre-intervention:* At the end of an initial assessment and prior to the commencement of any targeted interventions the GLAT is completed based on the young person's circumstances at that point in time.
- *End of intervention:* Ideally completed within the final four weeks of intervention and based on the young person's circumstances at that point in time.
- *Follow-up period:* With consent from the young person, the practitioner contacts and interviews him or her six months subsequent to treatment ending and completes the GLAT based on the young person's circumstances at that point in time.

Additionally, where an intervention program lasts longer than 12 months, there are Good Lives review forms that can be completed at 6-month intervals and enable change to be captured in a way that should not be overly onerous for workers. The review form captures the same information as contained within the GLAT but requires only the re-assessment of information relating to those needs that have changed during that time period.

The GLAT is completed in relation to each of the primary needs identified within the GLM-A (i.e., *having fun, achieving, being my own person, having people in my life, having a purpose* and *making a difference, emotional health, sexual health,* and *physical health;* see chapter 3 for further details). Items within the GLAT involve:

1. A rating of the extent to which the young person was appropriately meeting each need (i.e., through pro-social or non-harmful means)
2. A rating of the extent to which the young person was inappropriately meeting each need and evidence to support this (i.e., means that are not pro-social and may be harmful)

3.   A rating of the external resources that helped the young person to meet each need, with supporting evidence

4.   A rating of the external barriers that prevented the young person from meeting each need, with supporting evidence

5.   A rating of the internal resources that helped the young person to meet each need, with supporting evidence

6.   A rating of the internal barriers that prevented the young person from meeting each need, with supporting evidence

7.   A rating of the importance of each need to the young person

8.   An assessment of scope

9.   An assessment of whether a need was in conflict with other needs

10. A formulation of whether each need was previously met through the young person's harmful sexual behavior

11. A rating of the extent to which the need was a treatment priority

The GLAT contains guidance for the interpretation and scoring of items. Responses to items typically include a yes-or-no dichotomy, an ordinal scale of low, moderate, and high, or a four-point Likert scale (ranging from "never/rarely" to "most of the time"). While presently this tool is only available in hardcopy, an electronic version is currently being developed that will visually display the young person's "Good Lives profile" via charts.

In the absence of having questionnaires with good psychometric properties that directly map onto the GLM-A, new assessment tools were devised and customized. It is of note that while unstandardized clinically-rated assessment tools may have benefits, including their potential to cater to a specific purpose and thus have practical utility, they have several limitations due to their psychometric properties (e.g., reliability and validity) being generally untested and unknown.

To date it has only been possible to undertake a small-scale inter-rater reliability study of the GLAT. This study involved seven different practitioners who were trained to complete the GLAT and nine active cases. Every case was co-worked, and therefore it was possible for two practitioners to independently complete the GLAT for each young person. Within the GLAT, the same questions are used to gain information about the young person's attainment of each of the eight needs within the GLM-A. For each need, the GLAT contains a total of 11 pre-defined rating scales and six text boxes where practitioners expand on the information they used to determine how rating scales were scored. For the purposes of the inter-rater reliability study, only those questions that were rated were analyzed. Moreover, where the same question was used to examine different needs these questions were grouped together, regardless of which need they related to. The rationale for this was that questions that were ambiguous would be easily identified. Therefore the inter-rater reliability of each question (n=11) was considered for every participant (n=9) eight times (i.e., the number of primary needs), creating an overall sample of 72 occasions when each question was assessed by two different raters.

The inter-rater reliability of the questions was analyzed using Cohen's kappa (1960). Landis and Koch (1977) have provided the following guidelines for interpreting kappa: Kappas less than .20 demonstrate poor agreement; between .21 and .40 represent fair agreement; between .41 and .60 reveal moderate agreement; between .61 and .80 indicate good/substantial agreement; and above .81 signify very good/almost perfect agreement. Table 10.1 provides information about the inter-rater reliability for each individual question contained within the GLAT. In acknowledgment that kappa calculations adjust for the proportion of agreement that is expected by chance, details of the actual percentage agreement between raters have been included in this table. In the main, questions with fewer points on the rating scale had better inter-rater reliability. Moreover, from analyzing the results it would appear that the most robust questions were associated with the relevance of the need to the young person's harmful sexual behavior and the level of intervention priority. However, when interpreting this result it is important to highlight that practitioners were likely to have discussed these two questions as part of their everyday practice (i.e., for the purposes of assessing, formulating, and arriving at a Good Lives plan for each young person) prior to participating in this study. Overall, the inter-rater reliability study indicated that when used with trained practitioners, the majority of questions included in the GLAT (73%, n=8) demonstrated substantial agreement (kappa = .69 to .78; p < .001) with a minority of questions (27%, n=3) providing almost perfect agreement (kappa = .90 to .94; p < .001).

Table 10.1 Kappa and percentage agreement between raters for GLAT questions (N=72)

NATURE OF QUESTION	NUMBER OF AVAILABLE RATING OPTIONS	KAPPA STATISTIC	P-VALUE	% AGREEMENT BETWEEN RATERS
Extent need was appropriately met	4	.76	<.001	83%
Extent need was inappropriately met	3	.76	<.001	86%
External resources	4	.75	<.001	82%
External barriers	4	.74	<.001	82%
Internal resources	4	.71	<.001	79%
Internal barriers	4	.69	<.001	79%
Importance of the need to young person	3	.77	<.001	85%
Scope	2	.90	<.001	99%
Conflict	2	.78	<.001	92%
Relevance to harmful sexual behavior	2	.94	<.001	97%
Level of treatment priority	3	.91	<.001	94%

Young Person and Parent/Caregiver Questionnaires

Assessment forms completed by the young people and their parent/caregivers involve a two-page questionnaire to determine their perception of the extent to which the young people meet each of the primary needs. The questionnaire provides examples of what each need incorporates and requires the young people and their parents/caregivers to: (1) rate the extent the young people meet the need; (2) give an explanation of the means used to meet the need; (3) rate the importance of the need to the young people; and (4) list any barriers to meeting the need. The questionnaire was confined to these limited sets of questions in order to keep it simple and concise. The questionnaire is administered to the young people and their parents or caregivers at the pre-intervention stage and at the end of intervention. Additionally, where possible, it is completed six months following the end of program and, when intervention lasts for longer than one year, at six-month intervals over the course of the young people's involvement.

Face Validity of the Tools

The face validity of the assessment tools was independently evaluated by Dr. Willis from Deakin University, Australia. She provided feedback stating that the set of tools appeared to have face validity in terms of their assessment of the importance to the client of each GLM-A need, the extent to which each need is met, and related flaws for each of the GLM-A needs. Dr. Willis suggested the tools could be improved by changing the title "Good Lives assessment tools" in order to make it clearer that the GLM-A rather than the GLM was being measured, and to include the identification of specific risk factors in the practitioner-rated tool. These suggestions will be considered in any further revisions to the tools.

PRELIMINARY FINDINGS FROM USING THE GLM-A ASSESSMENT TOOLS

While the use of the GLM-A assessment tools are still at an early stage, there are some preliminary findings that can be drawn from the assessments completed to date. First, it is encouraging that the tools appear to be capturing intervention change. That is, the scoring and rating scales are indicating that for young people undertaking interventions informed by the GLM-A framework, there are often positive shifts following therapeutic work regarding the extent to which they meet their significant primary needs. However, the current sample size of young people who have completed therapeutic work is too small to undertake a specific research study evaluating outcomes.

In respect to how relevant and useful the GLM-A is when working with young people who display harmful sexual behavior, clinical findings to date, based on 15 young people who attended a G-map program of work, indicated that they were predominantly not able to meet their primary needs in appropriate ways at the time of displaying this behavior. Across the eight different primary needs contained within the GLM-A, between 73 and 100 percent of young people met these needs either never/rarely or occasionally, as opposed to often or most of the time. Moreover, workers viewed that at this time, the majority of young people (between 79 and 100 percent) attached moderate or high importance to these needs, with the exception of the need *having a purpose and making a difference,* for which 64 percent attached low importance. The need that appeared to be most important to young people was *having people in their lives.* This would support the theoretical assumption that young people would be motivated to achieve many of the primary needs considered within the GLM-A framework but either did not have the resources and/or opportunities to meet these. The needs that were typically associated with the young person's harmful sexual behavior were: *having people in my life* (93%, n=14); *emotional health* (93%, n=14); and *sexual health*

(66%, n=10). These findings are not surprising given the literature on trauma, attachment, and sexual health, as discussed earlier in chapter 7. It is positive in respect of the applicability and validity of the GLM-A that the needs that appear to be prioritized by young people and those that are related to harmful behaviors can be grounded within the wider literature and research; for example, Willis and Ward (2011) found in their sample that the majority of adults who sexually harm also viewed their belonging needs as having either moderate or high importance.

SUMMARY AND FUTURE AIMS REGARDING EVALUATION

At this early stage of delivering interventions that are underpinned by the GLM to adolescents, and in the absence of any empirically validated and reliable measures to directly map onto the GLM-A/GLM, the provisional findings and non-standardized tools detailed in this chapter may be of value to others and warrant further exploration, despite their limitations. While there are a number of limitations with the outcome study and evaluation tools described in the current chapter, they begin to provide some examples and ideas practitioners could use and expand on to help them evaluate the outcomes of a Good Lives approach.

There have been some initial attempts to consider the psychometric properties of the assessment tools described above, such as their face validity and the inter-rater reliability of the GLAT. However, as these tools were revised as recently as 2012, it has not yet been possible to accomplish a sample size large enough to allow for reliable inferences about intervention change or to allow for their properties to be more fully tested. It is hoped that over time, as larger sample sizes become available, more analysis on this can be undertaken. For example, the concordance among the ratings of practitioners, parents/caregivers, and young people could be examined, and the test–retest reliability of the measures for a subsample of cases could be considered. Analysis of the relationship between the assessment tools and other measures (such as the Resiliency Scale for Children and Adolescents; Prince-Embury 2007) that may indicate "a good life" could be important for convergent validity. Furthermore, comparisons could be made with psychometrics measuring risks and deficits for discriminant validity, and the predictive validity of the tools could be examined through comparing ratings with recidivism data. It is noteworthy that these assessment tools were developed with the intention of recording the young people's Good Lives journey from the time of their harmful sexual behavior to their transition into the community after intervention. Qualitative feedback thus far would indicate that the tools are meeting this aim. For G-map, any further attempts to validate and test the psychometric properties of the assessment tools will likely be in the more distant future, as sample sizes will not permit this to be done in the short term. However, it may be possible to consider some psychometric properties sooner—for example, test–retest reliability and convergent validity.

Ultimately, it is envisaged that through use of the Good Lives assessment tools, alongside psychometric data, a dynamic assessment of risk, and the collation of recidivism data, it should be possible to make inferences and draw conclusions about the extent of short- and long-term change following treatment that is underpinned by the GLM-A. As an adaptation based on the GLM of rehabilitation, any research support for the GLM-A would contribute to the evidence base for the original GLM. Other services using a Good Lives approach are urged to undertake their own evaluation and research to explore the extent of change following interventions that are Good Lives–oriented. These outcomes ideally would be compared with interventions informed by other models of rehabilitation. However, it is likely that within other organizations, as with G-map, other models such as the RNR will be used alongside the GLM, and therefore it may prove difficult to test the GLM as a "pure" model.

REFERENCES

Andrews, D. A., and J. Bonta. 2010a. *The psychology of criminal conduct*, 5th ed. New Providence, NJ: Lexis Matthew Bender.

Andrews, D. A., and J. Bonta. 2010b. Rehabilitating criminal justice policy and practice. *Psychology, Public Policy, and Law* 16:39–55.

Andrews, D. A., J. Bonta, and R. D. Hoge. 1990. Classification for effective rehabilitation: Rediscovering psychology. *Criminal Justice and Behavior* 17:19–52.

Andrews, D. A., J. Bonta, and J. S. Wormith. 2011. The Risk–Need–Responsivity (RNR) model: Does adding the Good Lives model contribute to effective crime prevention? *Criminal Justice and Behavior* 38:735–55.

Barbaree, H. E., and W. L. Marshall. 1990. Outcome of comprehensive cognitive-behavioral treatment programs. In W. L. Marshall, D. R. Laws, and H. E. Barbaree (eds.), *Handbook of sexual assault: Issues, theories, and treatment of the offender*, 363–85. New York: Plenum.

Beech, A., G. Bourgon, K. Hanson, A. J. R. Harris, C. Langton, J. Marques, M. Miner, W. Murphy, V. Quinsey, M. Seto, D. Thornton, and P. M. Yates. 2007. *Sexual offender treatment outcome research: CODC guidelines for evaluation, part one: Introduction and overview*. Ottawa, Canada: Collaborative Outcome Data Committee (CODC).

Bonta, J., and D. A. Andrews. 2007. *Risk–Need–Responsivity model for offender assessment and treatment*. User Report No. 2007–06. Ottawa, Ontario: Public Safety Canada.

Borduin, C. M., C. M. Schaeffer, and N. Heiblum. 2009. A randomized clinical trial of multisystemic therapy with juvenile sexual offenders: Effects on youth social ecology and criminal activity. *Journal of Consulting and Clinical Psychology* 77:26–37.

Borduin, C. M., S. W. Henggeler, D. M. Blaske, and R. Stein. 1990. Multisystemic treatment of adolescent sexual offenders. *International Journal of Offender Therapy and Comparative Criminology* 34:105–13.

Burnett, R., and C. Roberts. 2004. The emergence and importance of evidence-based practice in probation and youth justice. In R. Burnett and C. Roberts (eds.), *What works in probation and youth justice: Developing evidence-based practice*, 1–13. Devon, UK: Willan Publishing.

Cavadino, M., and J. Dignan. 2006. Penal policy and political economy. *Criminology and Criminal Justice* 6:435–56.

Cohen, J. 1960. A coefficient of agreement for nominal scales. *Educational and Psychological Measurement* 20:37–46.

Crawford, A. 1998. Community safety and the quest for security: Holding back the dynamics of social exclusion. *Policy Studies* 19:237–53.

Farmer, M., A. R. Beech, and T. Ward. 2012. Assessing desistance in child molesters: A qualitative analysis. *Journal of Interpersonal Violence* 27:930–50.

Griffin, H. 2012. *Good Lives Assessment Tool and associated questionnaires (GLAT: Revised)*. Sale, UK: G-map Services.

Griffin, H. 2013. Preliminary support that the adapted Good Lives model elicits change. Unpublished.

Griffin, H., and L. Harkins (in preparation, a). *A literature review following a systematic approach: An assessment of the protective factors that help young offenders to desist from crime.*

Griffin, H., and L. Harkins (in preparation, b). *Comparing resilience of young people who have sexually offended with those who have non-sexually offended and with non-offending controls.*

Griffin, H., and S. A. Price. 2009a. *Young person's Good Lives approach questionnaire*. Sale, UK: G-map Services.

Griffin, H., and S. A. Price. 2009b. *Parent/carer Good Lives approach questionnaire*. Sale, UK: G-map Services.

Griffin, H., and S. A. Price. 2009c. *Good Lives approach scoring manual: Pre-treatment*. Sale, UK: G-map Services.

Griffin, H., and S. A. Price. 2009d. *Good Lives approach scoring manual: Post-treatment*. Sale, UK: G-map Services.

Hackett, S. 2004. *What works for children and young people with harmful sexual behaviours?* Essex, UK: Banardo's.

Hanson, R. K. 2002. Introduction to the special section on dynamic risk assessment with sex offenders. *Sexual Abuse: A Journal of Research and Treatment* 14:99–101.

Hanson, R. K., G. Bourgon, L. Helmus, and S. Hodgson. 2009. The principles of effective correctional treatment also apply to sexual offenders: A meta-analysis. *Criminal Justice and Behavior* 36:851–91.

Harkins, L., and A. Beech. 2007. Measurement of the effectiveness of sex offender treatment. *Aggression and Violent Behavior* 12:36–44.

Jeglic, E. L., C. Maile, and C. C. Mercado. 2010. Treatment of offender populations: Implications for risk management and community reintegration. In L. Gideon and H. Sung (eds.),

Rethinking corrections: Rehabilitation, re-entry and reintegration, 37–70. Thousand Oaks, CA: Sage Publications.

Landis, J. R., and G. G. Koch. 1977. The measurement of observer agreement for categorical data. *Biometrics* 33:159–74.

Laub, J. H. 1997. Patterns of criminal victimization in the United States. In R. C. Davis, A. J. Lurigio, and W. G. Skogan (eds.), *Victims of crime*, 9–26. Thousand Oaks, CA: Sage Publications.

Laws, D. R., and T. Ward. 2011. *Desistance and sexual offending: Alternatives to throwing away the keys*. New York: Guilford Press.

Lösel, F. 1998. Treatment and management of psychopaths. In D. J. Cooke, A. E. Forth, and R. D. Hare (eds.), *Psychopathy: Theory, research and implications for society*, 303–54. Dordrecht, Netherlands: Kluwer.

McGrath, R., G. Cumming, B. Burchard, S. Zeoli, and L. Ellerby. 2010. *Current practices and emerging trends in sexual abuser management: The Safer Society 2009 North American Survey*. Brandon, VT: Safer Society Press.

Muncie, J. 2006. Governing young people: Coherence and contradiction in contemporary youth justice. *Critical Social Policy* 26:770–93.

Nisbet, I., S. Rombouts, and S. Smallbone. 2005. *Literature review: Impacts of programs for adolescents who sexually offend*. Ashfield, Australia: NSW Department of Community Services.

Nowicki, S. Jr., and B. R. Strickland. 1973. A locus of control scale for children. *Journal of Consulting and Clinical Psychology* 40:148–54.

Peters, C. S., and S. Myrick. 2011. Juvenile recidivism—Measuring success or failure: Is there a difference? *Corrections Today* 73:32–34.

Polaschek, D. L. L. 2012. An appraisal of the Risk–Need–Responsivity (RNR) model of offender rehabilitation and its application in correctional treatment. *Legal and Criminological Psychology* 17:1–17.

Prince-Embury, S. 2007. *Resiliency scales for children and adolescents: A profile of personal strengths*. San Antonio, TX: Harcourt Assessment.

Print, B., H. Griffin, A. R. Beech, J. Quayle, H. Bradshaw, J. Henniker, and T. Morrison. 2007. *AIM2: An initial assessment model for young people who display sexually harmful behaviour*. Manchester, UK: AIM Project.

Stahlkopf, C. 2008. Political, structural, and cultural influences on England's Youth Offending Team practices. *International Criminal Justice Review* 18:455–72.

Ward, T., and T. A. Gannon. 2006. Rehabilitation, etiology, and self-regulation: The comprehensive Good Lives model of treatment for sexual offenders. *Aggression and Violent Behavior: A Review Journal* 11:77–94.

Ward, T., and T. A. Gannon. 2008. Goods and risks: Misconceptions about the Good Lives model. *Correctional Psychologist* 40:1–7.

Ward, T., and S. Maruna. 2007. *Rehabilitation: Beyond the risk assessment paradigm*. London, UK: Routledge.

Ward, T., and C. A. Stewart. 2003. The treatment of sex offenders: Risk management and good lives. *Professional Psychology: Research and Practice* 34:358–60.

Ward, T., P. M. Yates, and G. M. Willis. 2012. The Good Lives model and the Risk–Need–Responsivity model: A critical response to Andrews, Bonta, and Wormith (2011). *Criminal Justice and Behavior* 39(1):94–110.

Watt, E. 2003. A history of youth justice in New Zealand. *Court in the Act* 6. Wellington: Department of Courts.

Willis, G. M., T. Ward, and J. S. Levenson. 2012. The Good Lives model (GLM): An evaluation of GLM operationalization in North American treatment programmes. Manuscript submitted for publication.

Willis, G. W., P. M. Yates, T. A. Gannon, and T. Ward. 2013. How to integrate the Good Lives model into treatment programs for sexual offending: An introduction and overview. *Sexual Abuse: A Journal of Research and Treatment* 25:123–42.

Willis, G., and T. Ward. 2011. Striving for a good life: The Good Lives model applied to released child molesters. *Journal of Sexual Aggression* 17(3):290–303.

Wilson, R. J., and P. M. Yates. 2009. Effective interventions and the Good Lives model: Maximizing treatment gains for sexual offenders. *Aggression and Violent Behavior* 14:157–61.

Wormith, J. S., R. Althouse, L. R. Reitzel, M. Simpson, R. D. Morgan, and T. J. Fagan. 2007. The rehabilitation and reintegration of offenders: The current landscape and some future directions for correctional psychology. *Criminal Justice and Behavior* 34:879–92.

Index